Belief and Uncertainty in
the Poetry of Robert Frost

Previous Books by Robert Pack

POETRY

The Irony of Joy
A Stranger's Privilege
Guarded by Women
Home from the Cemetery
Nothing but Light
Keeping Watch
Waking to My Name: New and Selected Poems
Faces in a Single Tree: A Cycle of Monologues
Clayfield Rekoices, Clayfield Laments: A Narrative Sequence of Poems
Before It Vanishes: A Packet for Professor Pagels
Inheritance: Reflections on a Gene Pool
Fathering the Map: New and Selected Later Poems
Minding the Sun
Pounding It Out
Elk in Winter

POETRY FOR CHILDREN

The Forgotten Secret
Then What Did You Do?
How to Catch a Crocodile
The Octopus Who Wanted to Juggle

ESSAYS AND CRITICISM

Wallace Stevens: An Approach to His Poetry and Thought
Affirming Limits: Essays on Mortality, Choice and Poetic Form
The Long View: Essays on the Discipline of Hope and Poetic Craft

Belief and Uncertainty in the Poetry
of ROBERT FROST

ROBERT PACK

University Press of New England

Hanover and London

Published by University Press of New England, One Court Street, Lebanon, NH 03766
www.upne.com
© 2003 by Robert Pack
First UPNE paperback edition 2004
Originally published in 2003 by Middlebury College Press/UPNE
Printed in the United States of America 5 4 3 2 1

"Acquainted with the Night," "After Apple Picking," "Bereft," "Design," "The Draft Horse," "Fire and Ice," "Home Burial," "Hyla Brook," "Maple," "The Need of Being Versed in Country Things," "Neither Out Far Nor In Deep," "Never Again Would Bird's Song Be the Same," *A Masque of Reason,* "The Most of It," "Out, Out—" "The Oven Bird," "Provide, Provide!" "The Silken Tent," "Two Look at Two," and "Wild Grapes" from the POETRY OF ROBERT FROST edited by Edward Connery Lathem. Copyright 1923, 1928, 1930, 1939, 1969 by Henry Holt and Company, copyright 1964, 1967, 1970, 1973 by Lesley Frost Ballantine. Copyright 1936, 1942, 1945, 1951, 1956, 1958, 1962, 1964 by Robert Frost. Reprinted by arrangement with Henry Holt and Company, LLC.

Library of Congress Cataloging-in-Publication Data

Pack, Robert, 1929–
  Belief and uncertainty in the poetry of Robert Frost / Robert Pack.—
1st ed.
      p.   cm.
Includes bibliographical references (p.) and index.
    ISBN 1–58465–326–4 (cl.: alk. paper)   ISBN 1–58465–456–2 (pa.: alk. paper)
    1. Frost, Robert, 1874–1963—Criticism and interpretation. 2. Belief and doubt in literature. I. Title.
  PS3511.R94Z865 2003
    811'.52—dc21   2003007721

This book is dedicated to my friend Jay Parini,
with whom I have enjoyed many conversations and shared
enthusiasms about the poetry of Robert Frost.

I would also like to express special gratitude
to Abra Chernik and Ellie Pojarska for much support and
substantial editorial advice in my writing of this book.

With special thanks to the
R & H Rubin/Pearl Robinson Foundation.

Contents

Preface

This book concerns itself with major themes that appear throughout the body of Frost's poetry, such as uncertainty, belief, nature, and loss. I bring different interpretive approaches to bear on these subjects as seems appropriate: psychological, Darwinian, and, above all, close textual reading, since Frost's poems are so marvelously intricate that they reward attention to details of imagery, allusion, and tone. The book, I believe, has its own continuity, yet the chapters are designed to be read, as well, as individual essays. For the reader who would like to choose or skip around, here is a brief description of the content of each chapter.

In chapter 1, the most general and sweeping of the book, I attempt to set Frost in the grand Western tradition of nature writing. I start with a consideration of the ambivalence toward nature as expressed in the Book of Genesis, then I examine Homer's *The Odyssey*, Shakespeare's *The Tempest*, ecological concerns in the American tradition, a group of American poets, then some poems by Robert Frost that depict what I call Frost's "heroic skepticism."

In chapter 2, I examine the deep influence the Book of Job had on Frost's thinking as I analyze Frost's comic version of Job in his poem *The Masque of Reason*. At the same time, I explore the influence of Darwin and evolutionary theory on Frost, which, so I argue, has many parallels to the concept of God as the creator of Nature in the Book of Job. The pervasive Darwinian influence on Frost's poetry is explored throughout this book.

In chapter 3, continuing to consider what I take to be primary poetic influences on Frost's writing, I compare a major poem by Wordsworth, "Michael," concerned with themes of loss and inheritance, with one by Frost, "Wild Grapes." I emphasize the similarities of both structural and philosophical elements, such as the virtue of endurance, in the two poems.

In chapter 4, I examine another major theme—that of grief and grieving ("Grievances are a form of impatience. Griefs are a form of patience.")—

by comparing some of Frost's poems on the subject with poems by other writers such as Blake, Wordsworth, Hopkins, and Thomas, in order to give some sense of Frost's uniqueness and emotional power in this elegiac genre. The psychological phenomenon of repression and denial is observed in detail in the poems analyzed in this chapter.

The theme of the potency of the imagination is then taken up in chapter 5 as I compare Frost's representation of the Muse, for example in "The Silken Tent," with that of his great contemporary Wallace Stevens, who also regards the theme of imagination as essential to his conception of poetic composition. The dialectic of imagination and Reality, of Belief and Skeptical observation, is central, so I propose, to the understanding of both poets.

In chapter 6, Frost's artistic stance as teacher and preacher, and his parabolic style, are examined in a group of Frost's poems. His posture as poet/teacher/preacher is considered as an aspect of typical Frostian irony, innuendo, and allusiveness.

In chapter 7, Frost's conception of the imagination is extended to include his concept of how beliefs are affirmed even against the grain of tough-minded skepticism, particularly in his most speculative mode, which so often is introduced by the inviting phrase, "as if." The imagination at play, for Frost, is invariably counter-balanced by his unwillingness to console himself with unconvincing assertions of faith.

In chapter 8, I further consider Frost's attraction to the idea of belief as a form of knowing against his equally powerful suspicion of false comfort and rationalizing consolation. In doing so, I explore the deep psychology of lying and truth-telling from both a Darwinian and a Freudian point of view, focusing finally on Frost's depiction of unconscious motivation.

In chapter 9, I deal with the underlying duality of place and nothingness, which form the existential background for Frost's "stay against confusion"—his key phrase to describe the affirmative purpose of his poetic art. The crucial concept of "nothingness" is examined as well in other poets, mainly Shakespeare and Stevens, according to current theory in modern physics, in which the universe emerges from nothing "in a random quantum fluctuation." I examine this crucial concept of nothingness in order to provide a larger context for understanding Frost as an existential poet.

Finally, in chapter 10, the double perspective of narration that Frost learned from Wordsworth—in which adult memory and immediate childhood sensation are represented simultaneously—is explored as another fundamental aspect of Frostian technique and as a manifestation of another major Frost theme: leaving an inheritance. Frost's characteristic use of an uncertain and fallible poetic narrator is compared with such narrative usage in other poets notable for the storytelling aspect of their lyric styles.

All poems by Frost quoted here are indicated in the text by page numbers from *The Poetry of Robert Frost,* edited by Edward Connery Lathem (Henry Holt and Company, New York, 1969).

Some of the material published here is revised and augmented from analysis that appeared in earlier books of mine: *Affirming Limits* and *The Long View.*

Thanks to the *Colorado Review* for first publishing "Frost's 'As If' Belief." Thanks to the University Press of New England for first publishing "Taking Dominion over the Wilderness" in *Poem for a Small Planet.*

R.P.

✍ Jay Parini

Introduction

Robert Pack is mainly a poet, known for over a dozen finely crafted collections of verse that have been widely admired over the past five decades. But he is also a critic of considerable elegance and power, as demonstrated by his early book on the poetry of Wallace Stevens—the first full-length consideration of that major poet's work. In that seminal book, Pack demonstrated gifts for close reading and clarity of expression that have sustained him over the decades in which he has written about a wide range of poets from Shakespeare through Wordsworth and the moderns.

He has consistently brought a poet's sensibility and sensitivity to his critical writing, regarding a poet's accomplishment from the inside, paying attention to the language and its music, explaining the intimate relationship between a poem's meaning and its form. Memorably, he has written about the "affirming limits" that a poet discovers within the formal boundaries of verse, and he has explored the complementary forces of rule and energy in the work of many of our greatest American and British poets over a lifetime of critical reading and critical writing.

This book of intimately linked essays on Robert Frost is an important addition to both the critical body of Pack's writing and to the criticism of Frost in general. Pack confronts the major themes in the poetry, including the delicate nature of belief, which in Frost often seems hesitant and tentative. Frost, of course, was a close reader himself of the major philosophers and poets of the past, and what is especially remarkable in Pack's book is the way he reads Frost against the traditions of Darwinian thinking. Frost certainly thought long and hard about the consequences of natural selection and evolution, and his poetry grew out of intimacy with the issues raised by Darwin. While other critics, such as Robert Faggen, Peter J. Stanlis, and Richard Poirier have profitably studied Frost in relation to Darwin and American pragmatism, few have written so intimately about the consequences (or refractions) of this manner of thinking for the poetry itself, as reflected in the peculiar tonalities we associate with Frost, who tacitly and explicitly understood the very human desire "to save ourselves unaided."

Pack—who taught for decades at Middlebury College and directed the Bread Loaf Writers' Conference for many years—spent most of his life in rural Vermont, which is Frost country. He has studied nature closely himself and has read widely in the tradition of American nature writing. Not surprisingly, he pays particular attention in these essays to Frost as a nature poet. Frost was not, of course, a purely Emersonian student of nature; his skepticism ran deep, and he shaded every observation with a rueful undertone of doubt. In "Birches," for example, Frost appreciates the boy's unwillingness to spring heavenward in Transcendental fashion, since "earth's the right place for love." That earthly love is celebrated in many of Pack's essays, as in chapter 3, where he considers the intimate relationship between Wordsworth and Frost, seeing differences in Frost's vision of nature that can be traced back to his reading of the Old Testament. Frost—especially in the late masques—considered the challenging questions raised by the Book of Job, and Pack examines these connections in a moving fashion.

"All modern thinking is about loss," writes the contemporary poet Robert Hass, whose work has been strongly influenced by Frost. It might be argued that all poets, like Job, must confront (among other losses) the loss of vision that seems to come with the gift of vision itself. With considerable skill, Pack treats this complex theme—the relationship between vision and loss—in a range of poets from Blake and Wordsworth to Hopkins and Thomas. He studies these poets in order to better understand Frost's own peculiar relationship with this major theme, and his canny way of revisiting an earlier poet's vision and making it firmly into his own.

Pack has always been interested in the traditions of psychoanalysis, especially Freudian analysis, and the impact of his long reading of Freud and Freudian criticism is subtly on display in these essays, which often consider the psychological dimensions of a poem. The theme of repression and recovered vision permeates his critical writing, here as elsewhere. Frost's evasions and silences in his poems are often a key to their full meaning, which are rarely as easily apprehended as one initially imagines. Pack is wisely suspicious of easy explanations, and he reads Frost by not taking him at his word, and by looking beneath the word and through the word to a deeper level of apprehension.

Like his great contemporary Wallace Stevens, Frost endlessly pondered the relationship between reality and the imagination, and like Stevens he believed that the function of the poet was involved in the re-imagination of reality: a theme that can be traced profitably back to the

Romantic tradition. Again, this avenue of inquiry brings Pack to reconsider the relationship between poetry and belief, which Stevens also pondered deeply, as when he suggested that, in an age of disbelief, it was the poet's job to create belief and to feed the reader on "the bread of faithful speech." Frost's own method for creating and sustaining a sense of belief, as Pack explains, involved the making of parables and the use of myths. Like so many poets of the modern era, Frost relied on the systems of myth and symbol generated by the poets and philosophers of the past, though he was not often explicit in his use of these associations, unlike Eliot, for example, who wore his learning on his sleeve. Pack's work is useful here in helping readers to make connections between the poet's reading and writing.

As a poet, Pack has mined the vein of narrative poetry with considerable success, so it comes as no surprise that he should study the narrative dimension of Frost with particular enthusiasm. His reading of Frost in relation to the Job narrative leads, in the last chapter of this collection, to his reading of Frost's justly famous narrative poem through the prism of Wordsworth's own complex narrative techniques—the use of what Pack calls "double perspective." He examines the skillfulness of Frost as a storyteller who could simultaneously work evocations of past and present into a poem, generating various levels of consciousness in the frame of a single narrative.

In all, Pack's essays on Frost and the traditions that played a role in the making of his poetry constitute a significant addition to modern poetry studies and to Frost criticism. Perhaps even more important, these essays, which consistently reinforce, amplify, and reflect each other, offer a guide to poetry itself and the conventions of modern poetic thought. Pack, writing as a poet, knows how a poem is made, where it comes from, and where it can go. His mind is plentifully stocked, rich in associations, and the satisfactions of this work are both complex and bountiful.

Belief and Uncertainty in
the Poetry of Robert Frost

Chapter 1

Taking Dominion over the Wilderness

I

The origin of humankind's ambivalence toward nature can be located metaphorically in the Book of Genesis. The language that describes the six days of divine creation is filled with wonder and awe, and God's assertion of the goodness of His creation anticipates the praise and celebration offered by his creatures. In the first account of God's creation of human beings, both male and female are created in God's image; in the second account, Eve is created from Adam's rib. The initial account is followed by God's first commandment—"Be fruitful and multiply"—but this imperative is succeeded by a second one—"subdue [the earth], and have dominion over the fish of the sea, and over the fowl of the air, and over every living thing that moveth upon the earth"—which will prove antithetical to the first. This second commandment to subdue and have dominion is a projection of the human wish to possess and master, as we see, for example, in its fullest implications in the figure of Shakespeare's Prospero. Beyond a certain limit—a limit that our species confronts today—this commandment and the wishes it embodies are not in harmony with the spirit of celebration and appreciation for the diversity and beauty of the physical world. Adam's taking dominion over nature will be followed, after the Fall, with his taking dominion over Eve, and that will be followed by Cain's taking dominion over Abel through murder. This split in human desire between seeking to give praise and seeking to take dominion has accelerated vastly in the age of industrialization and technology and has led inescapably to the current ecological crisis.

The morality inherent in the commandment to be fruitful and to multiply, which accords with the innate evolutionary imperative to promote survival and has served that purpose well, has brought about a paradoxical fate. We have reached the point at which to succeed is to fail, for if we continue to multiply as a species at the current staggering rate, we will defile our space and exhaust our resources in a short time. The rampant in-crease in population, which leads inevitably to widespread famine, is likely, sooner or later, to prove irreversible for a long time into the future. Our only hope is to reinvent ourselves in light of a psychology that under-stands that a fruitful world is not one in which the multiplication of one species, our own, causes the annihilation of other species. What this prognostication means, then, is that we must devise a new morality of re-straint, a curtailment of the wish encoded in our genes to replicate—a morality not of domination, but of sharing; not of acquisition, but of aes-thetic appreciation; and not of species self-idolatry but of reverence for a world of diverse forms of life. A renewed sense of the marvelous com-plexity of natural systems will have to replace the longing for power as the heart of human motivation, but such a morality in which the self is not central is the fundamental opposite of what we have taken to be our species' biblical and genetic injunction to procreate.

It is my purpose here to consider our predicament today, both through the eyes of poetic metaphor and in its evolutionary context. I will regard Shakespeare's Prospero as an example to be emulated of someone who willingly chooses to relinquish his power over nature and his fellow human beings, and I will examine some poems by Robert Frost as repre-sentative of our ongoing ambivalence toward nature. I will put forth the thesis that the immemorial idea of the vastness and inexhaustibility of na-ture needs to be replaced with the idea of the finiteness and vulnerability of nature, for the commandment to subdue nature never assumed that nature could indeed be subdued and replaced by human creation and human culture on this delicate planet. If nature's evolutionary plenitude is superseded by human creation, then there will be nothing outside of ourselves worthy of reverence and awe. Taking dominion over nature fi-nally must come to mean that we will have nothing left but our species-centered self-idolatry to be inspired by and worship. The ultimate irony of our assuming the role of "God" is that it already appears that we may replace ourselves with our own super-intelligent machines. Perhaps that is a consummation devoutly to be wished, for, surely, it would be folly to assume that evolution stops with us. Even if we assume that the desire to preserve human nature reveals the nostalgia of human beings for their own kind, this allegiance represents our deepest feelings about what is valuable and thus gives meaning to our lives. When the primary models for beauty and creativity no longer are grounded in nature, we will al-ready have evolved into another kind of species. Though we can predict and imagine where new technologies might take us, we have not begun to conceive the new values that would replace our capacity to recognize and love beauty and our gift for empathy.

In appreciating nature, in giving thanks in the spirit of awe for its diversity of forms and its evolutionary history, however, we need to beware of sentimentality and keep prominently in mind nature's wanton profligacy, indifference to suffering, and general destructiveness, as so succinctly described by Darwin:

We behold the face of nature bright with gladness, we often see superabundance of food; we do not see or we forget, that the birds which are idly singing round us mostly live on insects or seeds, and are thus constantly destroying life; or we forget how largely these songsters, or their eggs, or their nestlings, are destroyed by birds and beasts of prey.[1]

To the extent that taking dominion over nature has meant that wilderness has been tamed and cultivated into orchards, farms, and gardens, where fruitfulness continues to be honored, subduing natural forces still can be seen as a good. But the full appreciation of the images of the farm and the garden depends on the awareness that we have made something from materials that have preceded us, whose divine or evolutionary creation is wondrously beyond us, and on whose substance we necessarily depend.

The awareness of the need for balance between the wildness of untamed nature and the human cultivation of nature is exemplified for the modern American imagination in the writing of Henry Thoreau who, in his influential essay "Walking," argues for the essential human need for wilderness and claims that "The most alive is the wildest," but also acknowledges the need for human cultivation: "I would not have every man nor every part of a man cultivated, any more than I would have every acre of earth cultivated: part will be tillage, but the greater part will be meadow and forest."[2] At Walden Pond Thoreau maintained a connection both with town and with society (though he pretended this was not the case) since he well understood that the mind also requires cultivation. Roderick Nash, in his comprehensive *Wilderness and the American Mind,* summarizes that for Thoreau "wildness and refinement were not fatal extremes but equally beneficent influences Americans would do well to blend."[3] Such blending, however, never envisaged the fundamental diminishment of nature's power over humankind; it never foresaw the pollution of rivers and the sea; it never foresaw the sky besmirched with smog and ripped by a cancer-inducing hole in the ozone. Not only is physical health associated with the need for natural wilderness, however; so, too, is the human spirit refreshed by this sense of otherness, this plenitude, this power beyond human contrivance: "Give me the ocean, the desert, or wilderness!" cried Thoreau.

II

When the Lord answered Job out of the whirlwind, He presented Himself in the language of inscrutable and infinite power: "Where wast thou when I laid the foundations of the earth?" The unmistakable implication of that question is that nature is too vast to be subdued by humankind. Although this view of nature, proposed by the Lord, is both humbling and frightening to Job—since divine creation and destruction are inextricably bound—the poem's implicit optimism is that, despite the failure of human longing to find meaning and justice in the design of physical reality, nature nevertheless is of infinite beauty and value. Job's morality and smallness in relation to a universe indifferent to his personal anguish takes on meaning because Job sees himself as part of an unfathomable design, and therein lies Job's affirmation of his creaturehood, his resignation to his role in nature—nature which has dominion over him and against which he meaningfully struggles. As Frost in "A Masque of Reason"[4] had God say to Job: "Look how far we've left the current science / of Genesis behind. The wisdom there though, / Is just as good as when I uttered it." Although the version of nature with God as its creator has been replaced in most scientific circles by Darwin's theory of evolution, as Frost correctly asserts, the attempt to honor nature, even as we also seek to take dominion over it, has not diminished.

Job's wish never to have lived—"Let the day perish wherein I was born"—is a perverted version of the desire to be immortal, of the wish not to be bound by the basic law of nature: that nothing survives, that all matter, organic or inorganic, undergoes change. The rejection of that hopeless wish to achieve godhead, which results finally in Job's acceptance of his own mortality, is synonymous with Job's affirmation of nature's having dominion over him. In this sense Job, as Adam's inheritor, has reconciled himself to Adam's and Eve's punishment for desiring forbidden knowledge and power. Adam and Eve were banished from the garden, the emblem of natural bounty, because their wish for immortality was antithetical to natural limits even though these limits were not experienced as such in prelapsarian Eden. The limits we must contend with here in the fallen world are the result of our attitude toward them. The Fall occurs as a state of mind in which Adam and Eve rebel against limits, against the perception of their finitude The Lord sends them into exile, both physical and psychological, when He casts Adam out, "lest he put forth his hand, and take also of the tree of life, and eat, and live forever." Adam's bloated desire to seize dominion proves to be fatal. In contrast, Job's reconciliation to his mortal condition, his acceptance of human limits, becomes a model for us to emulate as our numbers, like a spreading cancer, continue to abuse the exhausted earth that has mothered us, now that we have reached the critical limit that the earth can sustain, a limit that historically we could not believe existed.

Nature in the Book of Job is represented by God's voice in the whirlwind, as His extended descriptions of the weather indicate:

> Who cuts a path for the thunderstorm
> and carves a road for the rain—
> to water the desolate wasteland,
> the land where no man lives;
> to make the wilderness blossom
> and cover the desert with grass[5]

and His detailed portrayal of the animals He has created:

> Do you deck the ostrich with wings,
> with elegant plumes and feathers?
> She lays her eggs in the dirt
> and lets them hatch on the ground
> (Job 83)

As in the Book of Job, the power of nature in Homer's *Odyssey* is represented by uncontrollable forces, particularly the storms at sea, which will destroy all of Odysseus's fellow sailors. Odysseus is introduced to the reader as a man who has "weathered many bitter nights and days / in his deep heart at sea," a man singled out for enmity by the sea-god, Poseidon:

> Yet all the gods had pitied Lord Odysseus,
> all but Poseidon, raging cold and rough
> against the brave king until he came ashore
> at last on his own land.[6]

The angry forces of nature are not the only cause of Odysseus's prolonged suffering and his men's destruction; rather, as Homer makes clear, it is the men's own "recklessness destroyed them all—/ children and fools, they killed and feasted on / the cattle of Lord Helios, the Sun." Their disregard for nature, their violation of nature's sanctity finally brings about their ruin. Much later, in book 12, after Odysseus's men have committed the crime of killing the Sun god's "peaceful kine," Lord Helios asks Zeus for retribution, threatening to withdraw his nurturing light from the living world and "go down forever / to light the dead men in the underworld." Zeus placates Helios and, like Poseidon, turns against Odysseus's men:

> Peace, Helios: shine on among the gods,
> shine over mortals and the fields of grain.

> Let me throw down one white-hot bolt, and make
> splinters of their ship in the winedark sea.
> (Homer 222)

Thus, Zeus's will is enacted, and Homer, in his typical fatalistic tone, concludes:

> No more seafaring
> homeward for these, no sweet day of return;
> the god had turned his face from them.
> (Homer 223)

In opposition to the imagery of nature as flux, of nature as a destructive and adversary force, Homer poses the enduring power of art and the symbol of solidity and longevity, the marriage bed, which Odysseus had carved out of the trunk of an olive tree. The carved marriage bed, wrought with the care given to a work of art, is an emblem of Odysseus's finally taking control over his own instinct for wandering. The description of the bed, given in loving detail, is the culmination of the numerous instances in which art is extolled by Homer. For example, when the minstrel at the palace of Alkinoos in book 8 sings the story of the fall of Troy, the usually poised and canny Odysseus is so moved that he

> let the bright molten tears run down his cheeks,
> weeping the way a wife mourns for her lord
> on the lost field where he has gone down fighting.
> (Homer 140)

Although Alkinoos empathizes with Odysseus's emotion, he says:

> Tell me why you should grieve so terribly
> over the Argives and the fall of Troy.
> That was all gods' work, weaving ruin there
> so it should make a song for men to come.
> (Homer 142)

This extreme claim that life and suffering should become subject matter for song and story asserts that the flux and brevity of nature can be redeemed through the power of memory as preserved through art. So, too, when Odysseus in revenge is about to slaughter the suitors in book 22, the court minstrel, Phemois, thinks first to protect his precious harp.

> But first to save
> his murmuring instrument he laid it down
> carefully between the winebowl and the chair,
> then he betook himself to Lord Odysseus,
> clung hard to his knees, and said "Mercy,

mercy on a suppliant, Odysseus!
My gift is song for men and for the gods undying.

(Homer 420)

Odysseus, accepting Alkinoos's claim, spares Phemois for the sake of his art. The order of art is seen by Homer as antithetical to the destructiveness of nature, yet the source of art is to be found in nature itself, as Odysseus's bed, made of a great olive tree, makes manifest. Thus, nature is seen as providing the substance for art out of its own mothering material as the etymology of the word *mater* (meaning material) itself suggests. Odysseus's description of the bed confirms his identity, and through Odysseus's meticulous and loving description, Penelope knows for certain that Odysseus has returned to her:

> There is our pact and pledge, our secret sign,
> built into that bed—my handiwork
> and no one else's! An old trunk of olive
> grew like a pillar on the building plot,
> and I laid out our bedroom round that tree,
> lined up stone walls, built walls and roof,
> gave it a doorway and smooth-fitting doors.
> Then I lopped off the silvery leaves and branches,
> hewed and shaped that stump from the roots up
> into a bedpost, drilled it, let it serve
> as model for the rest. I planned them all,
> inlaid them all with silver, gold and ivory,
> and stretched a bed between—a pliant web
> of oxhide thongs dyed crimson. There's our sign!

(Homer 435)

The transformed trunk of the olive tree, made of what endures in nature, becomes the sign of marriage—the art of human constancy—and this constancy in love is the essence of Odysseus's choice of mortality as the proper state for humankind. This is Odysseus' remarkable heroism. Unlike Adam, he rejects the temptation of immortality, as offered to him by the goddess Calypso, in fidelity to his mortal wife.

But it is not Odysseus's fate to die at home in the bed of his own design; his destiny before being allowed a peaceful death by land is to return to the sea, to the nature against which he had pitted himself. When Odysseus had descended to the underworld in book 11 to receive a prophecy from Teiresias, he was told what trials and sorrows awaited him if Helios's kine were violated, and he was instructed to make a sacrifice to Lord Poseidon. He was assured then that his death, though on land, would partake also of the element of the sea and that this "seaborne death," at last free of the enmity of Poseidon, would symbolize Odysseus's final acceptance of nature as a force to which human control and human art must give way:

> Then a seaborne death
> soft as this hand of mist will come upon you
> when you are wearied out with rich old age,
> your country folk in blessed peace around you.
> And all this shall be just as I foretell.
>
> (Homer 189)

And so, in acceptance of nature's domination and the death that nature exacts, Odysseus, like Job, will die a peaceful death, honored and reconciled to the fate that he shares with all other natural creatures.

III

Perhaps the most comprehensive work of the human imagination to depict the rival claims of responding to nature's power and beauty in the spirit of dread and awe, on the one hand, and of taking dominion over nature, cultivating and controlling it, on the other, is Shakespeare's late play *The Tempest,* which Leo Marx claims "may be read as a prologue to American literature."[7] The storm in *The Tempest,* like the sea in Homer's *Odyssey* or the whirlwind in the Book of Job, is an agent of both destruction and renewal, and Prospero's power for good derives from his ability to simulate a storm, temporarily take dominion over the island and its inhabitants, and finally relinquish that dominion. Like Job, Prospero's humility (meaning "of the earth") comes from the acknowledgment that he is dust and must accept this fact as the basis for his shared bond with all other creatures. Miranda, at the beginning of the play, does not understand Prospero's uses of nature. In saying, "Had I been any god of power, I would / Have sunk the sea within the earth," she reveals her wish to eliminate the destructive element of nature, which is an element Prospero himself can transform only by employing nature's own power.

To comprehend Shakespeare's balanced attitude toward nature in this play, we must consider, in addition to the imagery of the storm, the relationship between Ariel and Caliban, both inhabitants of the island before Prospero's arrival. Both can be seen as symbolizing primal forces in human as well as in external nature, but it should be noted that Caliban's witchlike mother, Sycorax, when pregnant with Caliban, was banished from "Argier" (Algiers) and deposited on the island by sailors. Unlike Ariel, Sycorax is not original to the island, and Shakespeare's implication may well be that natural beauty and creativity are forces older than greed and murderousness. At the turning point of the play in Act V, Prospero chooses to forgive his treacherous brother, Antonio, rather than indulge himself in the dark pleasure of revenge; he does this, however, at the hint and gentle prodding of Ariel:

> ARIEL: Your charm so strongly works them,
> That if you now beheld them, your affections
> Would become tender.
> PROSPERO: Dost thou think so, spirit?
> ARIEL: Mine would, sir, were I human.
> PROSPERO: And mine shall.
> Hast thou, which art but air, a touch, a feeling
> Of their afflictions, and shall not myself,
> One of their kind, that relish all as sharply,
> Passion as they, be kindlier mov'd than thou art?
> Though with their high wrongs I am struck to the quick,
> Yet with my nobler reason 'gainst my fury
> Do I take part: the rarer action is
> In virtue than in vengeance.[8]
> (*Tempest* V, i, 17–25)

Although Ariel can be thought of as a projection of Prospero's conscience or superego, in contrast to Caliban, who represents murderous and sexually rapacious instinct, or id, I believe that Shakespeare's metaphorical structure presents both Caliban and Ariel as aspects of primal as opposed to socially conditioned human nature. Their significant linkage is to be found in Caliban's main virtue, which he comes by not through reason—since he considers language to be a curse—but instinctually: his appreciation of the island's natural beauty and music.

> CALIBAN: The isle is full of noises,
> Sounds and sweet airs, that give delight, and hurt not,
> Sometimes a thousand twanging instruments
> Will hum about my ears; and sometimes voices,
> That, if I then had wak'd after long sleep,
> Will make me sleep again: and then, in dreaming,
> The clouds methought would open and show riches
> Ready to drop upon me; that, when I wak'd,
> I cried to dream again.
> (*Tempest* III, ii, 146–54)

Caliban is not capable of moral understanding or empathy; for him Miranda—even though he can appreciate her beauty—is merely a vehicle for multiplying, for populating the island with more Calibans. Still, Caliban does have an innate capacity for taking delight in the sensuous beauty of the island. The music that moves him so deeply, of course, is Ariel's music, which Prospero, in freeing Ariel, has put to his own moral, as well as aesthetic, uses. Ariel thus represents a beauty and harmony inherent in nature, even more fundamental than Caliban's lust and hostility. The power of art—as Shakespeare represents it in *The Tempest* through Prospero's book and Ariel's music—is not merely the human imposition of order upon chaotic force, but the human ability (as if by magic) to exploit and redirect a natural force for human purposes. Shakespeare's central paradox is that human beings cannot transcend nature without the aid of nature, whereby what may begin as a curse, nature's violence, ends as a blessing, nature's transfiguration of itself through human art. Despite Prospero's power over the elements and over his own innate drives, as represented by both Ariel and Caliban, Prospero's ultimate and consummating magic—which he achieves only through an extreme effort of will—lies in his ability to forgive his treasonous brother. Forgiveness, as in many of Shakespeare's plays, is represented as the transforming power of moral goodness, which is made to seem as if possessed of a kind of magic of its own. The full realization of this paradox can be seen in Ferdinand's response to Ariel / Prospero's music:

> FERDINAND: Where should this music be? i' th' air, or th' earth?
> It sounds no more;—and sure, it waits upon
> Some gods o' th' island. Sitting on a bank,
> Weeping again the king my father's wrack,
> This music crept by me upon the waters,
> Allaying both their fury, and my passion,
> With its sweet air.
>
> *(Tempest* I, ii, 385–91)

Just as Ferdinand is able to recognize the redemptive power of the music, so, too, at the play's end, he can express wonder at the potency of stormy nature to bring about reconciliation and opportunity: "Though the seas threaten, they are merciful: / I have cursed them [as Miranda had earlier] without cause." To which the kindly Gonzalo replies, "Now all the blessings / Of a glad father compass thee about!"

Shakespeare's play explores the different meanings of servitude and freedom in bodily, psychological, and political terms, and he makes precise distinctions to show when servitude and when freedom is the appropriate condition for particular characters. For example, Ariel, the spirit of nature and, as I have argued, of creative human instinct, was imprisoned by Sycorax, Caliban's witch mother, before the action of the play begins. Sycorax is not a native of the island, but a cast-off from human civilization; thus, she represents the destructiveness of the fallen world, of nature corrupted, of social and political evil. What can it mean to set Ariel free?

This is one of the great mysteries of the play. In freeing Ariel does Prospero free nature of the human consciousness of nature and thus of human presence?

What Shakespeare does make perfectly clear is that Caliban's good qualities, such as his ability to perform useful work like carrying logs, will only be released when he is under the control of a proper master. (Otherwise, Caliban, as we can readily see in his conspiracy with Stephano and Trinculo to kill Prospero, will give in to his penchant for destructive wildness in the form of rape and murder.) Servitude in the name of love also can be a good thing, and Ferdinand accepts such servitude willingly on behalf of Miranda in obeying Prospero's order to carry logs. Ferdinand must, in a sense, pass through a Caliban-like stage, after which he will be able to recognize the paradox of freedom in accepted servitude:

> Might I but through my prison once a day
> Behold this maid: all corners else o' th' earth
> Let liberty make use of; space enough
> Have I in such a prison.
> (*Tempest* I, ii, 487–98)

The play ends with both Ariel and Prospero, each according to the needs of his own nature, being set free. Prospero, having taught Caliban language, is now responsible for him. He fully accepts this when he says, "This thing of darkness / I acknowledge mine," and so Prospero will have to take Caliban back to Milan with him, where he can be controlled like the other rebellious and primarily murderous forces that are part of every human psyche. Caliban is in that sense an aspect of Prospero himself, as Prospero well understands. In taking Caliban with him, Prospero will be leaving the island in its natural state—as it was before the interventions of Sycorax and of Prospero himself—to Ariel alone. Inviting the audience to identify with him, Prospero asks for their empathetic forgiveness when he says in conclusion: "As you from crimes would pardon'd be, / Let your indulgence set me free." In acknowledging Caliban as his own, Prospero, in effect, confesses that all the crimes committed or intended during the play are to be found in potential form within himself, including his own proclivity for revenge, which must be controlled and suppressed. Prospero's self-knowledge explains finally his capacity for forgiveness. The crimes for which Prospero needs the audience's "indulgence" are those that he himself might have committed if he had not achieved self-understanding.

Prospero seeks not only moral peace at the play's end but also the rest and repose that follow creation like a sabbath. The model for such needed rest is to be found in the Bible, as suggested by Ariel when he responds to Prospero's question, "How's the day?" with the cryptic remark: "On the

sixth hour; at which time, my lord, / You said our work should cease."
The analogy here is to God's resting after six days of creation, nature hav-
ing been completed. When Prospero decides it is time to abjure his
"rough magic," which he describes as "heavenly music," he withdraws his
controlling hand and returns nature to itself, to its original condition of
wilderness.

> I'll break my staff,
> Bury it certain fathoms in the earth,
> And, deeper than did ever plummet sound,
> I'll drown my book.
>
> (*Tempest* II, i, 54–57)

While Prospero's magic prevailed, no one in the play drowned, but now
that he must "drown" his book, a storm, once again, will be a storm; na-
ture will return to its original condition, independent of the human wish
for revision or rebellion, a condition described in the Bible: "And God
saw that it was good."

Ariel's freedom is closely related to Prospero's acceptance of the fact
that nature both precedes and follows human art. Prospero's final words
to Ariel—"then to the elements / Be free, and fare thou well!"—indicate
that Ariel, as elemental nature, must, in some sense, remain free of
human imposition. It is right for Prospero to control Caliban, but it is not
right for Prospero to exercise ultimate control over Ariel. If Ariel, like
Caliban, represents not only some aspect of original nature, but also
some aspect of Prospero's human nature, of human nature, then Ariel's
freedom must mean some final liberation from the burden of conscious-
ness back into matter, back into the cosmic materials out of which
human life emerged. Language in this play is seen both as a curse and as
a blessing, but like Prospero's visionary pageant, his story and his art,
words must "dissolve" back into nature, Ariel's element, out of which
they came, "into air, into thin air."

The quintessential argument for the human need for wilderness may
be seen as expressed in Shakespeare's dramatic vision of our little lives
being "rounded with a sleep." One only can make sense of human life and
human values when one perceives them as a vanishing temporary efful-
gence of nature. Thus, it is to nature that we must give our deepest alle-
giance, rather than to what we, in passing, make of nature through
human contrivance or even art. Without wilderness, our humanity is di-
minished because we fail to perceive the beauty inherent in our ephemer-
ality; we fail to acknowledge ourselves as creatures among other crea-
tures, among other evolving and vanishing forms. When Prospero abjures
his "rough magic" at the play's end, declaring "I'll drown my book," he

makes his most heroic and most significant choice—the choice to accept the limits of nature, including his own mortality, and to relinquish the attempt to take dominion over nature. Prospero's final freedom, then, in giving up "Spirits to enforce," is the freedom from human arrogance and pride which seek the overthrow of nature in order to replace natural fecundity with human contrivance. And so Prospero's final words to the audience, which express his sense of their mutual bond and interdependence—"As you from crimes would pardon'd be / Let your indulgence set me free"—acknowledge the play's ultimate paradox: human power must be used to limit the use of human power. The mastery of nature must find its culmination in our mastery of ourselves.

IV

The great rebellious reader of the *Book of Job,* William Blake, who claimed that "Where man is not, nature is barren," sought to give equal status to human creation, to the artful power of the human imagination to take dominion over what it beholds. In his visionary definition, Blake sees nature as being dependent on human perception: "The fool sees not the same tree the wise man sees." God's "fearful symmetry" in creating a tiger, for example, is balanced by Blake's creation of a tiger in which the first stanza returns almost exactly as the last. Thus Blake imposes the symmetry of his own poem upon the symmetry of the physical tiger as created by God. An unimaginatively perceived world, thus a fallen world according to Blakean theory, has met a potent adversary or complement in the visionary artist. Blake thus identifies the human imagination and artistic creativity not with what he conceives as the limiting laws of nature but with God when, for example, he claims that "All deities reside in the human breast." Yet Blake is equally aware that the imposition of human organizations, such as religion or social custom, on nature (including human instinct) can destroy the very nature that the artistic imagination has the power to reinforce and celebrate.

In his poem "The Garden of Love,"[9] Blake envisions the destruction of fruitful nature, symbolized by the garden, as the result of the moralizing priests who have lost the sense of natural beauty and thus have turned the garden into a cemetery "filled with graves, / And tombstones where flowers should be." And in "The Human Abstract," Blake attempts to disassociate the image of the tree as a symbol of guilt, which corrupts the mind, from the innocent tree as it exists simply in nature: "The Gods of the earth and sea, / Sought thro' Nature to find this Tree / But their search was all in vain: / There grows one in the Human Brain." In other words, the perversion of the human desire to appropriate nature, made manifest in the mind as guilt, leads to deceit and hostility, exacerbating the split in human beings between their sense of themselves as creatures of nature and their wish to take dominion over nature. Thus Blake, though champion of the artistic imagination, maintains original awe in the face of nature's plenitude.

Original awe in response to the inexhaustible vastness of nature pervades Wordsworth's poetry even though he has begun to worry about the encroachment of the city, "greetings where no kindness is," on human psychology. In Wordsworth, the fear of subduing and taking dominion over nature, symbolized by the city as the exemplary human structure, becomes a central theme and a deep source of anxiety and possible despair. In the climactic scene in *The Prelude*[10] in which Wordsworth crosses the Alps, he has a vision of nature's infinite and eternal capacity both to create and to destroy: "The immeasurable height / Of woods decaying, never to be decayed." This vision is sublime because it is frightening and consoling at the same time: frightening in that it places all creation, including human life, under the sway of change, and thus makes everything temporal and finite, and consoling because it implies that the source of endless change leads continually into further creation and new life. Ultimately, then, nature is seen as the capacity for multiplying without limit, and this consoling belief enables Wordsworth to affirm the personal limit of his own mortality. Although all living things are mortal, nature's mutability makes manifest the power of divinity to bring forth life out of death. Beauty for Wordsworth, therefore, is the experience of nature that enables us to find ecstatic happiness even in the awareness of our own extinction, precisely because we can connect mortality with a creative force of continuity. Blake and Wordsworth, like Job, contemplated the inevitability and necessity of destruction, and they found ways to make peace with both the indifference and transience of nature, but they did not have to face the destruction of nature through human domination, a dilemma that is new to human awareness. Although poetry for them is the proper vehicle for lamentation, for personal sorrow, the burden was not forced upon them, as it is on us today through science and technology, to consider the replacement of natural power by human power as the primary determinant of evolutionary change. We have unlocked the secrets of the genome as well as the atom. Blake and Wordsworth are fully aware of how deeply destructive human behavior can be in their analyses, for example, of city life, but neither of these visionaries can foresee that nature itself can be destroyed and superseded. Their faith is securely based on the assumption of humankind's limited power—the assumption that humankind is safe precisely because we do not have the ultimate power to take dominion over nature.

Wordsworth's great inheritor, Gerard Manley Hopkins, portrays our modern predicament in "God's Grandeur,"[11] a poem about the besmirching of nature through industrialization, when he says that "all is seared with trade; bleared, smeared with toil." Human desecration, however, has only minimal power compared to nature's power of renewal, for "nature is never spent; / There lives the dearest freshness deep down things." Yet Hopkins does provide us with the glimmering of a nightmare vision of what the world would be if nature were to be entirely subdued, if human domination became a final reality:

> What would the world be, once bereft
> Of wet and wildness? Let them be left,
> O let them be left, wildness and wet;
> Long live the weeds and the wilderness yet.
> (Hopkins 13)

Hopkins's cry for the preservation of nature is raised to a high pitch of urgency, one that even Wordsworth's most passionate successors have difficulty in sustaining. Even modern war, as we see in Dylan Thomas's "Ceremony After a Fire Raid,"[12] cannot prevent nature from continuing its process of renewal. Although a bombing raid on London causes Thomas to envision "Beginning crumbled back to darkness / Bare as the nurseries / Of the garden of wilderness." Thomas's faith—the stubborn and traditional faith in an indomitable nature—leads him to proclaim nature's triumphant power of revival and renewal:

> The masses of the infant-bearing sea
> Erupt, fountain, and enter to utter for ever
> Glory glory glory
> The sundering ultimate kingdom of genesis' thunder.
> (Thomas 146)

For Thomas, nature never loses the power of domination in its own kingdom; it can forever recreate itself.

v

The fundamental optimism, though deeply tinged with prophetic anxiety, of the English Romantics' and post-Romantics' belief in the sovereign power of nature is carried over into the American wilderness movement and into the substantial body of nature writing in American poetry. Two central concepts that mark this transition are the idea of "correspondences," the links between nature and the human spirit, and the idea that nature is the means by which human beings maintain their connections with their origins. At the beginning of *The Prelude,* for example, Wordsworth declares that "While the sweet breath of heaven / Was blowing on my body, I felt within / A correspondent breeze." Here, the influence of God's creative force is experienced in nature as a breeze, as if the gentle wind were the same breath that God originally breathed into Adam to give him life; this breath of nature, then, becomes the source of human inspiration.

So, too, does Emerson, in his essay "Nature,"[13] argue that "Every natural fact is a symbol of some spiritual fact: Every appearance in nature corresponds to some state of the mind." Emerson develops this idea— "this radical correspondence between visible things and human thoughts"—culminating in his assertion that "the whole of nature is a metaphor of the human mind." The unmistakable implication of such reasoning is that the body of nature and the human body are indivisible; any violation of nature is equally a violation of the human mind, the human spirit.

In Wordsworth, Emerson's most influential predecessor, the quest for self-identity and self-knowledge necessarily involves the search for human origins. "How shall I seek the origin?" Wordsworth asks, and, typical of the way he seeks to answer his own question is his representation of moments of looking and listening, attending to the world of natural images:

> and I would stand,
> If the night blackened with a coming storm,
> Beneath some rock, listening to the notes that are
> The ghostly language of the ancient earth,
> Or make their dim abode in distant winds.
> (*Prelude* II, 306–10)

Again, listening to the winds, now their grimmer and less gentle aspect, Wordsworth senses a connection between mere physical sounds, perceived nevertheless as "notes," and human language which has emerged from matter itself. To understand our humanity, we must, according to Wordsworth, understand the medium of nature out of which language, our distinguishing human characteristic, has been born.

In America, the equally worshipful language of John Muir constantly reminds us of the need to understand the mystery of human identity as growing out of, and being dependent upon, what is beyond us and what has preceded us in evolutionary time. When describing the High Sierras, Muir says: "In so wild and so beautiful a region, every sight and sound [was] inspiring, leading one far out of himself, yet feeding a building up of his individuality."[14] So, too, is humankind's deepest spiritual resource, the sense of beauty (Wordsworth claims that we are "fostered alike by beauty and by fear"), dependent upon the imagination's response to physical imagery: "We felt our faith in Nature's beauty strengthened, and saw more clearly that beauty is universal and immortal, above, beneath, on land and sea, mountain and plain, in heat and cold, light and darkness." Roderick Nash, reflecting on the tradition of American nature writing, considering how it has led to the "new ecology-oriented environmentalism," emphasizes the human need for connection with both the planet's and our human evolutionary past when he speaks of our need to remember "man's biological origins, his kinship with all life, and his continued membership in and dependence on the biotic community." Man, as Darwin claimed,

is descended from some less highly organized form. . . . [T]he close similarity between man and the lower animals in embryonic development, as well as in innumerable points of structure and constitution, both of high and of the most trifling importance,—the rudiments which he retains, . . . are facts which cannot be disputed. . . . Man is the co-descendent with other mammals or a common progenitor.[15]

VI

In addressing the issue of the need for a new philosophy of nature that could support the new environmentalism, founded on a renewed sense of the "biotic community," Nash argues for a fundamental shift from human arrogance, based on the assumption that the earth was created for human exploitation, to an attitude of humility, respect for the earth and other creatures as valuable in their own right: "The lesson most frequently drawn from both ecology and wilderness was the need for humility on the part of man." This humility would allow humankind to adopt a philosophy of restraint, of the acceptance of limits: "Preserving wilderness means establishing limits. We say, in effect, we will go this far, and no farther, for development. We agree to do without the material resources the wilderness might contain." The word *humility,* as in the Book of Job, is again well chosen, for it derives from the Latin "humilis," literally meaning of the ground or, by practice, to cover oneself with dirt, a gesture that reminds us both of our origins and the fate we share with all other creatures on planet Earth.

To the ecological writers selected here for their passion and persuasiveness as exemplifying this new morality of setting limits must be Rachel Carson and Bill McKibben. The approach these writers adopt is to reinforce their philosophical positions with scientific evidence that demonstrates what the catastrophic effects will be to the planet and to our health, both physical and spiritual, should our species not radically alter its self-indulgent ways that are grounded in an attitude of domination.

In 1962, with the publication of *Silent Spring*,[16] Rachel Carson sounded her heroic cry in defense of protecting the American landscape from the chemical assault directed against it. She begins by arguing that an unprecedented and unforeseen danger to the earth has appeared on the evolutionary scene: "Only within the moment of time represented by the present century has one species—man—acquired significant power to alter the nature of the world." This means that the earliest human wish to take dominion now can be realized through human technology. In evolutionary terms, human technological power belongs in the same category as other catastrophes (what David M. Raup, in *Extinction*,[17] calls "first-strike scenarios," p. 29), like the demise of the dinosaurs as a result of the crashing of a comet into the earth. What the devastating comet or asteroid was to the dinosaurs, who had insufficient time to adapt to the suddenly changed atmosphere, we human beings are to mammalian and forest life today. But with this difference: the dinosaurs were not the agents of their own destruction, as we are likely to be of ours. Shakespeare succinctly expresses his insight into the consequences of human greed for possession and exploitation when he describes human rapaciousness: "And appetite, an universal wolf, at last eats up itself."

Carson emphasizes the evolutionary origin of both the planet and our species, one among many: "It took hundreds of millions of years to produce the life that now inhabits the earth—eons of time in which that developing and evolving and diversifying life reached a state of adjustment and balance with its surroundings." And she points out that what is new in environmental terms is the RATE OF CHANGE brought about by technological intervention. This difference in degree in the speed of environmental change completely alters the capacity of the whole ecological system to keep itself in balance: "The rapidity of change and the speed with which new situations are created follow the impetuous and heedless pace of man rather than the deliberate pace of nature."

Human beings, themselves the products of gradual evolutionary changes, are not designed to comprehend the consequences human culture and human reproduction have wrought upon the earth. Increasing population has become a threat to survival of humankind. Given our biological inheritance, we have great difficulty in addressing ourselves to any long-range vision of the future. Carson argues that "we have allowed these chemicals, as with other human indulgences, to be used with little or no advance investigation of their effect on soil, water, wildlife, and man himself."

Just as Carson offers numerous examples and details about the chemical pollution of our environment and ourselves, so, too, does Bill McKibben offer statistics to prove that "we have substantially altered the earth's atmosphere." He details the various possible consequences of the "greenhouse effect" and points out that just "an increase of one degree in average temperature moves the climatic zones thirty-five to fifty miles north." The next round of consequences that will follow is that trees will die, releasing further "staggering amounts of carbon into the atmosphere." In an inevitable future we refuse to foresee, McKibben tell us that "reproductive failure and forest die-back is estimated to begin between 2000 and 2050." McKibben's analytic prose rises to passionate imploring when he exclaims: "The trees will die. Consider nothing more than that—just that the trees will die."[18]

At the heart of McKibben's analytical approach to environmental dangers lies an aesthetic and philosophical appeal to what he believes constitutes our essential humanity. To destroy nature, for McKibben, is to remove the primary model—a model of structural coherence that encompasses diversity—upon which our cultural sense of beauty is founded. McKibben perceives a profound sadness lurking beneath the noise and rush of modern society. He sees this sadness as "an aesthetic response—appropriate because we have marred a great, mad, profligate work of art, taken a hammer to the most perfectly proportioned of sculptures." He envisions that the loss of nature will result also in the loss of beauty and of meaning.

McKibben's judicious pessimism, however, leaves him room to say that "I hope against hope," and this hope is based on an appeal to reason, which he considers also to be natural to our species. "As birds have flight, our special gift is reason," McKibben declares, yet he reminds us that our reason is antithetical to the "biological imperatives toward endless growth in numbers and territory," the unconscious forces beneath the biblical morality of taking dominion, the imperative to "Be fruitful and multiply." With visionary (but perhaps desperate) hopefulness, McKibben says: "We could exercise our reason to do what no other animal can do: we could limit ourselves voluntarily, choose to remain God's creatures instead of making ourselves gods."

Whether one believes literally in God or not, McKibben's meaning is clear, and, to my mind, it corresponds to the morality implicit in the biblical account of God's punishment of Adam because he rebelled against his bond with nature by seeking to become immortal. God sends Adam forth from the garden of Eden "lest he put forth his hand, and take also the tree of life and live for ever." In taking dominion over the planet Earth, human beings, of course, have not mastered the universe or taken dominion over the second law of thermodynamics or, most significantly of all, achieved eternal life that would set the human species apart from the fate of all the other creatures that have walked upon the face of the earth. The morality so needed to guide us is again one of humility based on the awareness of our creaturehood, our bond with all other living things.

With the first human awareness of death as an ongoing state of nonbeing, the desperate wish not to die must simultaneously have been born, as is implied, for example, in the earliest burial sites in which possessions are placed in the grave to be taken as if on a journey. But taking dominion cannot mean that we can possess our bodies for long or that the Yeatsian speculation, "Once out of nature I shall never take / My bodily form from any natural thing,"[19] can ever be realized, except as a fantasy of artistic power that enables one to give birth to oneself—the artistic power that Prospero renounces so definitely at the end of *The Tempest*. No, taking dominion over nature can only mean for our species that we will have proven that our particular genius has been the destruction of many wondrous living forms, including ourselves. No doubt, bacteria and cockroaches will survive our folly or some more adaptable life form will emerge in another solar system. To choose to remain creatures, then, as McKibben proposes, is to accept limits—the limits of mortality, the limits of power and possession—and thus to remember and remain true to our evolutionary origins.

The human imagination continues to depend on natural images and natural beauty, on trees and plants and birds and animals, on the seasons and the weather; without them, the human spirit, nurtured by its own poetic expression of a world beyond itself, a world of "wildness and wet," is diminished and impoverished. Without a sense of beauty that derives from otherness, from nature's independent existence, a prior world on which our fabricated cultural world depends—nature as a source of metaphor—the capacity for taking delight in our surroundings must wither away. Even before the planet becomes inhospitable to the human species, we will die in spirit, though perhaps super-intelligent creatures of our own technological creation, not dependent on food or air or space or a moderate climate, will evolve to survive us in a state of happiness that we, still the children of natural laws, who live, as Prospero says, "'twixt the green sea and the azur'd vault," have not evolved to comprehend.

VII

In American poetry, also, we see a major and recurring theme in the attempt to give nature its due, to respect its beauty and its power, even as we make claims for the legitimacy of culture and the goodness of imposing some human order upon the wilderness, since this wilderness corresponds to an animating energy inherent in human instinct. In Emily Dickinson's poem "I started Early—Took my Dog,"[20] for example, a young woman, the poem's speaker, takes a walk with her dog to visit the sea. In her fantasizing mind, the sea becomes her first lover and seduces her:

> But no Man moved Me — till the Tide
> Went past my simple Shoe —
> And past my Apron — and my Belt
> And past my Bodice — too —
> (Dickinson 254)

Although the youthful speaker of the poem experiences an infantile fear of sexual violation when she says of the tide that "He would eat me up," the language of the poem is remarkably delicate; the speaker's anxiety is minimized through an aestheticizing analogy in comparing the masculine tide to "a Dew / Upon a Dandelion's Sleeve."

The speaker turns from the sea to return home, but the tide pursues her:

> And He — He followed — close behind —
> I felt His Silver Heel
> Upon my Ankle — Then my Shoes
> Would overflow with Pearl —
> (Dickinson 254)

This fantasy of impregnation by nature, as personified by the tide, comes to an abrupt conclusion in the last stanza with the confrontation of two forces (both depicted as male): nature, embodied as the tide, and civilization, embodied in the "Solid Town":

> Until We met the Solid Town —
> No One He seemed to know —
> And bowing — with a mighty look —
> At me — the Sea withdrew —
> (Dickinson 254)

The opposition between nature and civilization, between lover/Sea and father /Town appears to pit each against the other as irreconcilable adversaries. The father/Town's failure even to recognize the lover/Sea suggests the immense repression of instinctual nature that Freud described as the super-ego. Dickinson's poem ends with a tactically deferential gesture: nature withdraws. The poem's concluding inference, however, is that the sea, according to the rhythm of the tide, will return, and so, too, will the sexual urges that have been awakened in the initiated speaker.

In Whitman,[21] the sensuous pleasure nature has to offer and natural limitation, which ultimately must require individual death, merge and become one in the figure of a mother, as in "When Lilacs Last at the Dooryard Bloom'd." Whitman chants:

> Come lovely and soothing death.
> Undulate round the world, serenely arriving, arriving,
> In the day, in the night, to all, to each,
> Sooner or later delicate death.
>
> (Whitman 335)

Death is the "Dark mother always gliding near with soft feet" who will be envisioned again as a mother in Stevens's early masterpiece "Sunday Morning": "Death is the mother of beauty, hence from her alone shall come fulfillment to our dreams and our desires." And so, too, it is nature herself, nature as it precedes human invention and contrivance, that remains the source of inspiration for Whitman, so that he says in "When I Heard the Learn'd Astronomer" that he walked out of the lecture room and "Look'd up in perfect silence at the stars." This response implies both revelation and consolation, a far cry from Frost's description in "Desert Places" of the "empty spaces / Between stars," a vision that evokes the deepest loneliness.

If Whitman finds order inherent in the cosmos, and if the individual soul and the cosmos ultimately are one, Stevens, despite his Whitmanian roots and influences, sees the need to impose order on nature. This need is manifest, for example, in his witty and famous little poem "Anecdote of the Jar," in which the speaker, as prototypical poet, places a jar on a hill in the Tennessee landscape in order to give aesthetic cohesion to his perception of the landscape. The effect of this artistic placement of the jar is to make "the slovenly wilderness / Surround the hill." The jar does not partake of the plenitude of the wilderness since it does not "give of bird or bush," though by organizing them pictorially, according to an aesthetic principle, the jar "took dominion everywhere." This playful poem differs, however, from Stevens's fundamentally Heraclitean view of nature as flux—a view quite similar, as we shall observe in detail, to Frost's vision of decay in the "frozen swamp" in his poem "The Wood Pile." The latter was probably written partly in response and as a corrective to Thoreau's ecstatic claim, in his essay "Walking," that "Hope and the future for me are not in lawns and cultivated fields, not in towns and cities, but in the impervious and quaking swamps" (44).

For Stevens, paradoxically, change is the only universal constant. In "The Auroras of Autumn,"[22] the aging speaker is walking along a deserted beach, deeply aware of his own finitude in relation to the stars and the effulgent night sky; he virtually sees himself disappearing when he says: "Here, being visible is being white." When he looks up at the streaming lights, however, he has a vision of the universe as a theater of change. This cosmic spectacle, for which he is the audience, is extremely beautiful, though totally indifferent to him. Yet it is as if the universe enjoys being observed, as if human consciousness were the means by which the universe could contemplate itself:

> It is a theater floating through the clouds,
> Itself a cloud, although of misted rock
> And mountains running like water, wave on wave
>
> Through waves of light. It is of cloud transformed
> To cloud transformed again, idly, the way
> A season changes color to no end,
>
> Except the lavishing of itself in change,
> As light changes yellow into gold and gold
> To its opal elements and fire's delight,
>
> Splashed wide-wise because it likes magnificence
> And the solemn pleasures of magnificent space.
>
> (Stevens 416)

The lavishness and lushness of Stevens's language, built of incremental repetitions and variations of phrases, conveys the speaker's sensuous delight in the act of looking. To be a spectator to this cosmic theater—even though the changes it makes manifest will obliterate the rapt observer, since he, too, is part of the spectacle of change—is to partake of nature's universal beauty. The dread of annihilation, for this moment, is absorbed in the impersonal grandeur of the spectacle, the dominion nature takes over any human being who contemplates its ongoing and endless transformations.

It is not enough for Stevens, however, to lose himself in a sublime instant of aesthetic observation; he must force his vision of change to include the awareness of his own annihilation, and then force this awareness to include the annihilation even of awareness. This is the extreme to which he attempts to extend consciousness when, in response to his vision of the night sky as a "theater" of change, he exclaims:

> This is nothing until in a single man contained,
> Nothing until this named thing nameless is
> And is destroyed.
>
> (Stevens 416)

The naming mind must contain its own destruction, its own unnaming, its own resulting namelessness, and, in doing so, the imagination must experience nature in the aspect of nothingness. There is, of course, an element of what I will call "cosmic dread" in such a vision, and Stevens articulates this basic emotion in comparing the little light of his own life with the vastness of the Northern Lights when he says:

> The scholar of one candle sees
> An Arctic effulgence flaring on the frame
> Of everything he is. And he feels afraid.
>
> (Stevens 417)

This fear, this awareness of nature's dominating power, makes possible the poet's apprehension of beauty in the extreme and gives to the moment of mortal consciousness its precious poignancy. In doing so, the poet becomes a kind of Prospero, a maker of visionary pageants, as Stevens suggests in his line "The father fetches pageants out of air" (415). The same idea recurs in another poem, "The Planet on the Table," where Stevens claims that "Ariel was glad he had written his poems," poems that are perfectly balanced between taking dominion over nature and celebrating nature as it precedes and inspires human imaginings:

> His self and the sun were one
> And his poems, although makings of the self,
> Were no less makings of the sun.
>
> (Stevens 532)

In William Carlos Williams also, the awareness of annihilating change intensifies and gives focus to thought and to poetic art. But nature's destructiveness, for Williams, has been vastly enhanced through human technology. Now that the atomic bomb, in particular, has enlarged our powers of destruction, human consciousness never again can be the same: "the bomb / has entered our lives / to destroy us. Every drill / driven into the earth / for oil enters my side / also," Williams claims in "Asphodel, That Greeny Flower."[23] In "The Orchestra," Williams addresses the issue of the radical change in the history of humankind's relationship to nature. In a prose passage inserted to interrupt Williams's normal poetic stanza, the step-down tercet, he asserts: "Man has survived hitherto because he was too ignorant to know how to realize his wishes. Now that he can realize them, he must either change them or perish." The wishes that Williams alludes to here might be interpreted simply as inherent human destructiveness, which inevitably turns against itself, perhaps out of guilt or the awareness of original sin. Such wishes might well be driven by an instinct for death, the Freudian Thanatos, as Freud hypothesizes at the conclusion of *Civilization and Its Discontents* in a passage that Williams might well have rewritten for his poem:

Men have gained control over the forces of nature to such an extent that with their help they would have no difficulty in exterminating one another to the last man. They know this, and hence comes a large part of their current unrest, their unhappiness and their mood of anxiety.[24]

Or these wishes as alluded to by Williams might be seen as synonymous with the desire for domination, the wish to become like gods, which, when thwarted by nature's demand that we must die, are perverted into the blind wish to destroy or the fatal attempt of civilization to subdue nature. In any case, what Williams asks of our species is no less than a total change of heart, an act of will that would enable us to reinvent human psychology. Williams calls the fatal wish for domination the "wrong note," and the implication of his carefully chosen musical metaphor is that human beings have evolved to threaten nature's fundamental harmony—the harmony that Caliban hears on the island of "a thousand twangling instruments." The opening comparison in Williams's poem between bird calls at dawn and the tuning up of a human orchestra establishes the idea of the interdependence of the fate of human beings and of nature:

> The precise counterpart
> of a cacophony of bird calls
> lifting the sun almighty
> into his sphere: wood-winds
> clarinet and violins
> sound a prolonged A!
> (Williams 80)

Ultimately, the triumph of the human wish for domination—if we are to survive—must assume the form of human beings taking dominion over their own wish to dominate, taking dominion, not over nature, but over themselves as the figure of Prospero exemplifies. Williams continues to develop this theme of self-mastery by expanding the analogy between self-control and musical or poetic artistry: "it is a principle of music / to repeat the theme. / Repeat and repeat again, / as the pace mounts. The / theme is difficult / but no more difficult / than the facts [of human destructiveness] to be / resolved." The final lines of the poem celebrate the human capacity for resolving the danger we have created for ourselves by redesigning our own nature—a nature in which we are linked as fellow creatures to the birds, and yet set apart in having to make the paradoxical choice not to set ourselves apart:

> The birds twitter now anew
> but a design
> surmounts their twittering.
> It is a design of a man
> that makes them twitter.
> It is a design.
>
> (Williams 82)

VIII

In the heroic skepticism of the poetry of Robert Frost—our preeminent modern expositor of man's ambivalence toward nature—we find nature represented both as seducing and threatening, both as glorious spectacle and as the power to destroy and annihilate. In "Out, Out—" for example, Frost depicts the landscape seemingly in the mode of the Wordsworthian sublime: "And from there those that lifted eyes could count / Five mountain ranges one behind the other / Under the sunset far into Vermont." These lines become ironic, however, when lifting eyes becomes the distraction that causes the young boy to lose his hand in the buzz saw and die shortly thereafter with the onlookers unable to rescue him. And this irony deepens when the reader realizes that Frost's lines are a parody of Psalm 121, which reads, "I will lift mine eyes unto the hills, from whence cometh my help." In Frost's depiction of nature here, no help will come from the hills or from the great beyond. The final chilling lines of the poem—"And they, since they / Were not the one dead, turned to their affairs," which appear to suggest a callous or indifferent response from the boy's family—carry within them the sense that these farm people know that life must go on and that the commitment to work is inseparable from the strength of endurance.

In Frost's poem "The Wood-Pile," the speaker chooses to walk out into the swamp with profoundly divided feelings: "I will turn back from here. / No, I will go on further." We can contrast Thoreau's effusive praise of the swamp, of which he says, "if it were proposed to me to dwell in the neighborhood of the most beautiful garden that ever human art contrived, or else in a Dismal Swamp, I should certainly decide for the swamp," with Frost's bleak "frozen swamp." While walking in the swamp "one gray day," Frost's speaker chances upon an abandoned pile of split wood stacked neatly, "four by four by eight," as if its order revealed some kind of reciprocity between natural material and human effort. Significantly, the pile is held up, framed as it were, between a "tree / Still growing" and a humanly fashioned "stake," between what nature provides and what humans make of natural resources. Frost's speaker wonders, "I thought that only / Someone who lived in turning to fresh tasks / Could so forget his handiwork," but such optimism, based on an assumption of indefatigable human energy in the face of a wilderness to be tamed and used, conceals the more likely but repressed (by the poem's speaker) explanation for why the "measured" pile has been left in the woods: the farmer has not turned to fresh tasks because he has died.

The irony of this passage turns grimmer if the reader considers that perhaps the fresh task is for the farmer to die. This, of course, is everyone's final task. Indeed, the ending of the poem offers us increasingly darkening ironies. The speaker is baffled as to why the farmer's effortful work, "the labor of his axe," should be spent in vain to leave the woodpile "far from a useful fireplace / To warm the frozen swamp as best it could / With the slow smokeless burning of decay." The decaying woodpile, to be sure, cannot warm the swamp, and the attentive reader can hear much sardonic bitterness in the phrase, "as best it could." This is a pathetic "best," indicating Frost's belief in nature's dominance over human effort and ambition. From the perspective of Frost's typically human desire for personal survival (as seen in many of his poems), the cycling of nature means destruction and decay for the individual, exactly the opposite of Wordsworth's vision of "the immeasurable height / Of woods decaying, never to be decayed," in which life is seen forever emerging out of death.

To read this poem simply as a typical Frostian vision of "decay" that overrides "useful" human effort, however, would offer an incomplete picture of Frost's view of nature when considering the body of his work. The very fact, grim though it is, that nature's power surpasses human power often is a source of awe and reverence for Frost, evoking a mysterious sense of beauty in such typical lines as "Far in the pillared dark / Thrush music went," as if the dark were some kind of holy cathedral. And on the other side of the visionary spectrum from seeing wilderness as a challenge to human survival, one finds Frost's remarkably optimistic poem "Two Look at Two," in which the lovers can only understand their bond to each other within the context of their bond to nature, as exemplified by the deer across the wall who mirror the lovers' own desires and creaturehood. Frost ends his poem with the lovers looking at the deer and thus seeing a mirrored image of the physical aspect of themselves. This act of looking carries with it a tidal upsurge of feeling, an emotion that it-self becomes an aspect of nature, expressing the unity of the natural world and the human response to it, much as Wordsworth had described nature in "Tintern Abbey": the "mighty world / Of eye, and ear,—both what they half create, / And what perceive."

As with Williams, who sees the final result of the human enterprise to take dominion over nature in the form of the creation of the atomic bomb,

> The bomb speaks.
>   All suppressions,
>   from the witchcraft trials at Salem
> to the latest
>   book burnings
>   are confessions
> that the bomb
>   has entered our lives
>   to destroy us.
> Every drill
>   driven into the earth
>   for oil enters my side
> also.
>   Waste, waste!
>   dominates the world.
> It is the bomb's work
>   (Williams 168)

and with Stevens's apocalyptic vision of cosmic dread such as "I saw how the planets gathered," or "This is nothing until in a single man contained, / Nothing until this named thing nameless is / And is destroyed," so, too, we find moments in Frost in which ultimate destruction seems to be the culminating result of the human wish to dominate and subdue: "There would be more than ocean water broken / Before God's last put out the light was spoken," says Frost in "Once by the Pacific," in which God's in-itial "Let there be light" is countered by His "Put out the light," with the heavy suggestion that God's "rage" is a response to human violation of some kind, even as if God's rage and human rage were indistinguishable from each other. God's destruction of nature in this poem seems to be a metaphor for humankind's destruction of nature, just as in Frost's sar-donic little poem "Fire and Ice" the human emotions of "desire" and "hate" are presented as equivalent to the natural destructive forces of "fire" and "ice."

> Some say the world will end in fire,
> Some say in ice.

> From what I've tasted of desire
> I hold with those who favor fire.
> But if it had to perish twice,
> I think I know enough of hate
> To say that for destruction ice
> Is also great
> And would suffice.
>
> (Frost 220)

Part of the chilling (and burning) effect of this poem is that its sneering delivery seems to express the very hatred of which it speaks, as if the poet's primal appetite for aggression, which "tasted of desire," was projected upon the entire species.

In Frost's great poem "Directive," in which, like Wordsworth, he seeks to discover human prospects, even the possibility of salvation, by journeying "Back out of all this now too much for us" to uncover his origins, everything is cast in an uncertain light by virtue of the poem's tonally shaded ambiguity. The reality of the "playhouse" to which the journeyer returns is contingent upon whether poetic and religious belief is fictional in the sense that it is false, or fictive in the sense that it evokes a mythic truth with its own kind of validity and credibility:

> There is a house that is no more a house
> Upon a farm that is no more farm
> And in a town that is no more a town.
>
> (Frost 377)

The house, the farm, and the town, either exist or do not exist depending on what the reader makes of the paradox of loss according to one's reading of the Bible where Jesus says, in Matthew 10:35, that "He that findeth his life shall lose it: and he that loseth his life for my sake shall find it," and again in Mark 8:35, "For whosoever will save his life shall lose it; but whosoever shall lose his life for my sake and the gospel's, the same shall save it." The speaker of the poem identifies himself with the biblical paradox in assuming the role of guide for the reader: "The road there, if you'll let a guide direct you / Who only has at heart your getting lost." And thus the journey back progresses through further fictionalization, "Make yourself up a cheering song"; and committing yourself as the guide urges even more deeply to the mode of paradoxical belief and its contingency of whether one can believe in belief: "And if you're lost enough to find yourself / By now."

Everything becomes a matter of making or fabricating (which may imply lying or self-deception as well as invention and creation) as in the accretion of phrases such as "make yourself at home" and "make believe."

The culmination of the journey back to the "source," the house with the brook that is associated with it also is presented in antithetical terms. On the one hand the speaker-guide, weeping over the sense of loss, repeats the earlier assertion, "the house that is no more a house," but then goes on to contradict that assertion with: "This was no playhouse but a house in earnest." Frost's parabolic journey is given further Christian reference in its allusion to the quest for the Holy Grail, the cup from which Jesus himself drank, with the line: "A broken drinking goblet like the Grail." But the mystery and uncertainty of salvation is complicated even further by the guide's allusion to Saint Mark's reference to the "wrong ones." Frost's lines about the Grail claim that it is "Under a spell so the wrong ones can't find it, / So can't get saved, as Saint Mark says they mustn't." Frost's reading closely follows the biblical text:

And he [Jesus] said unto them, Unto you it is given to know the mystery of the kingdom of God: but unto them that are without, all *these* things are done in parables: That seeing they may see, and not perceive; and hearing they may hear, and not understand; lest at any time they should be converted, and *their* sins should be forgiven them. (Mark 4:11–12)

Questions abound about who the wrong ones might be when one realizes that Frost's poem as elusive parable might also be read as a Saint Markian parable that is designed to exclude, and so the motivation of the guide then becomes even more deeply suspect. And the reader's suspicion about the validity of the guide is encouraged still further as the guide in the line "I stole the goblet from the children's playhouse" seems to be confessing to his own illegitimacy as the thieving owner of the goblet/Grail.

Where does this leave us as readers of Frost's supremely enigmatic poem? Are we lost enough to find ourselves or are we just plain lost? The poem is certain in its uncertainty, and thus the final "Here" of the poem can be read in opposite ways: either it is actually a source, mythically true in its fictive representation, or it is nowhere, merely an illusion. Likewise, one can read the final lines, "Here are your waters and your watering place. / Drink and be whole again beyond confusion," in a voice of exultation or with total irony, indicating that we can never be whole again beyond confusion or make ourselves at home in the natural world.

What I take to be Frost's heroic skepticism lies precisely in his courage of uncertainty. In his sonnet "For Once, Then, Something," where he taunts his critics back for taunting him as a poet merely of surfaces, the poet looks down to the bottom of a well to try to discern the identity of the "something white" that is down there. He looks hard, but what he sees is "uncertain" (that key Frostian word!), and quickly he then says "I lost it." Just as in "Directive" the reader is unable to distinguish between illusion and revelation, so here, too, the Frostian speaker cannot tell whether he has had a glimpse of something as large and grand as "Truth" or merely something physical, with no symbolic importance, like a "pebble of quartz." The poem ends in uncertainty, yet uncertainty is not dismissed as nothing; uncertainty has its own validity, its own specificity, about which the poet can say in summing up his quotidian (or visionary?) experience: "For once, then, something."

Perhaps Frost's philosophy of uncertainty finds its primary antecedent in Keats's concept of "negative capability," which Keats in a famous letter articulates as follows:

Negative Capability, that is, when a man is capable of being in uncertainties, mysteries, doubts, without any irritable reaching after fact and reason.[25]

But there can be no doubt that adherence to the principle of his certainty about his own uncertainty contains an aspect of both humor and irony that is endemic to Frost's character and personality as manifest in much of his poetry, particularly the poems that attempt to offer a reading of nature.

I have, in effect, argued here that the ambivalent wish to both dominate and celebrate nature, to both transcend nature and live within its limits, is the Bible's main theme, beginning with the disobedience of our first parents. Adam and Eve simultaneously want to live in the garden of Eden and also eat the fruit of immortality; this mixed desire causes them to become rebels against the condition of mortality, the very condition that makes nature what it is and makes human life possible. And, likewise, I have argued that the Romantic poets and their inheritors reenergize this theme of dichotomy as when Wordsworth in *The Prelude* offers two absolutely contradictory statements describing human longing, one longing for infinitude (echoed by Frost in his line in "Directive," "Your destination and your destiny's / a Brook") and one for this world:

> Our destiny, our being's heart and home,
> Is with infinitude, and only there;
> With hope it is, hope that can never die,
> Effort, and expectation, and desire,
> And something evermore about to be.
> (VI, 604–608)

And here is the above passage's antithesis:

> Not in utopia,—subterranean fields,—
> Or some secreted island, Heaven knows where,

But in the very world, which is the world
Of all of us,—the place where, in the end,
We find our happiness, or not at all!

(XI, 140–44)

Other typical examples that express this same dichotomy are when Keats projects himself into the figure of a symbolic nightingale, wishing to transcend the earth—"Thou wast not born for death, immortal bird"— but also hears himself summoned back to earth: "Forlorn, forlorn! The very word is like a bell to call me back from thee to my sole self." Or when, in "Sailing to Byzantium," Yeats immortalizes himself as a work of art: "Once out of nature I shall never take my bodily form from any natural thing," and then, having imagined himself beyond time and nature, he takes time and nature as his subject and theme to sing "Of what is past, or passing, or to come." Or when Stevens, with great succinctness, in "An Ordinary Evening in New Haven" tells us that "The instinct for heaven had its counterpart: / The instinct for earth."

This antithetical view depicts nature both in its destructiveness and its beauty, as is typical of Darwin in such a passage as "each being lives by a struggle at some period in its life; that heavy destruction inevitably falls either on the young or the old during each generation or at recurrent intervals"[26] in which the struggle against death is also described as part of a process leading to "exquisite adaptations" or "beautiful co-adaptations." Such a comprehensive view, which reconciles what Wordsworth calls "discordant opposites," finds no more compelling modern representation than in Frost's poetry: "My long two-pointed ladder's sticking through a tree / Toward heaven still" is the metaphor Frost uses in "After Apple Picking" to evoke his sense of the human longing for some kind of transcendence, either in attitude, like Darwin, or, hopefully, in fact, as in Wordsworth. Despite its upward longing, Frost's poem leads us insistently downward, back to the earth with each apple to be cherished as it is plucked and, in an oxymoronic phrase, to "lift down." In "Birches," too, the wish to fly off and escape and the wish to return are inextricably bound to one another: "I'd like to get away from earth awhile / And then come back to it and begin over." And so the biblical imagining of a deep division with the human soul, between acceptance and rejection, celebration and rebellion, continues to play itself out in the modern literary imagination. It seems that between the affirmation of nature and its laws, "Let there be light" ($E=mc^2$), and the hostility toward nature—as in Frost's "Put out the light"—which we would subdue to remove the limits it places upon us, lies our human destiny awaiting what still appears to be an unattainable resolution beyond any likely certainty.

Darwin, the Book of Job, and Frost's *A Masque of Reason*

I

The most astonishing aspect of Darwin's *On the Origin of Species,* from a psychological perspective, is that it does not culminate in pessimism or despair. What Darwin calls the "struggle for existence" is inevitable and unrelenting, leading inexorably to the replacement of one species by another as conditions change. Unlike a Christian God who loves every hair on each human head, Darwin's nature is not concerned with the failure or suffering of individuals:

As more individuals are produced than can possibly survive, there must in every case be a struggle for existence, either one individual with another of the same species, or with the individuals of distinct species, or with the physical conditions of life.[1]

At no point does Darwin speculate that nature could ever be revealed as sympathetic to human wishes and needs. Darwin nevertheless sees beauty in the process of change and in the absolute interdependence of creation and destruction:

I can see no limit to the amount of change, to the beauty and complexity of the co-adaptations between all organic beings, one with another and with their physical conditions of life, which may have been effected in the long course of time through nature's power of selection, that is by the survival of the fittest. (Darwin 61)

Darwin's description of how evolution works, however, is not simply factual and objective; it is also evaluative. In order to regard nature as "beautiful," Darwin must take what I call "the long view"; he must think of time not on the human scale of generational love extending to children and grandchildren, but on the scale of millions of years in which individual identity and achievement are imperceptible. Darwin expresses this view in his final paragraph:

Thus, from the war of nature, from famine and death, the most exalted object which we are capable of conceiving, namely, the production of the higher animals, directly follows. There is grandeur in this view of life, with its several powers, having been originally breathed by the Creator into a few forms or into one; and that, whilst this planet has gone cycling on according to the fixed law of gravity, from so simple a beginning endless forms most beautiful and most wonderful have been, and are being evolved. (Darwin 123)

In the rapture of his meditation, Darwin moves beyond the themes of the war of nature, famine, and death, as if they should not be dwelt upon for long. He speculates about the endlessness of creation and the emergence of new forms without mourning for what has been superseded. His theory of evolution does not at this point in his writing necessarily negate the idea of God, but it does change the image of God from that of a compassionate intercessor to that of a potent but profligate creator. God might, so Darwin here allows, in the beginning have created life from only a few prototypes, or perhaps from only one: "I believe that animals are descended from at most only four or five progenitors, and plants from an equal or lesser number" (119). Darwin is liberated from thinking about his own particular fate, or the fate of his generation, or even the fate of humankind, and what he contemplates instead fills him with the sense of beauty and wonder. The spectacle of evolution endlessly unfolding its productions, and the manifestations of this whole process are what Darwin means by nature—a view that, essentially, Robert Frost will come to embrace. Darwin's theory focuses on creation itself and on the ongoingness of creation. Creation, Darwin believes, does not culminate in the emergence of human beings and is, indeed, indifferent to human happiness or suffering. The detachment from human involvement that characterizes Darwin's vision is both terrifying and magnificent; it can be the cause of personal despair or, from another point of view, can serve as a corrective for a view of nature that regards the species *Homo sapiens* as nature's teleological goal or crowning achievement.

This detachment, however, carries with it a growing human need to express and offer sympathy precisely because such sympathy cannot be found in nature or in the God who created nature. Darwin's visionary detachment, combined with his emphasis on the development of human sympathy, which suffuses his later writing in *The Descent of Man*,[2] expresses his deep belief in the human capacity to offer comfort and to cooperate even in the face of nature's essential indifference: "The first foundation or origin of the moral sense lies in the social instincts, including sympathy; and these instincts no doubt were primarily gained, as in the case of the lower animals through natural selection" (Darwin 202).

We see the direct influence of Darwin on Frost's thinking about nature as an indifferent backdrop against which human striving is acted out. The Book of Job, as does Darwin, also depicts God as a creator who cannot be comprehended in moral terms, yet who seems to approve of morality—the keeping of laws, telling the truth, being generous to the poor—as appropriate to the human realm.

II

There are two moralities in the Book of Job:[3] God's morality of creation and humankind's morality of justice. God takes pride in power and plenitude, the bounty and energy of living forms, while humans concern themselves with punishment and reward, pain and happiness, demanding from God that there be a connection between personal behavior and fate. These two moralities of God and humans appear to be in fundamental conflict because they seem to be mutually exclusive. The confrontation between God's manifestation of his power and man's cry for justice is the dramatic heart of the Book of Job.

Unpredictability and randomness are represented in the prologue by the casualness with which the discussion between the Lord and the Accusing Angel is introduced. No necessity elicits this encounter; it simply happens:

One year, on the day when the angel came to testify before the Lord, the Accusing Angel came too.
The Lord said to the Accuser, Where have you come from?
The Accuser answered, From walking here and there on the earth, and looking around.
The Lord said, Did you notice my servant Job? There is no one on earth like him: a man of perfect integrity, who fears God and avoids evil.

(Job 6)

The Accuser's reply—"Doesn't Job have a good reason for being so good?"—provides the preliminary insight into the need for humans to imagine God in reference to themselves. We expect to be rewarded for being virtuous; thus, the virtue of loving virtue for itself escapes us. In confronting the Lord with this knowledge, the Accuser, in effect, forces the Lord to reveal a flaw in the Lord's own creation: the Lord has created a creature who is only virtuous for selfish reasons. In attempting to demonstrate to the Accuser that Job will continue to praise the Lord even under adverse conditions, the Lord perversely and unjustly gives the Accuser power to abuse Job without cause. And so, in response to the

Accuser's taunt, the Lord says to the Accuser: "All right: everything he has is in your power," and even knowing that He is abandoning rational morality, the Lord acknowledges petulantly to the Accuser that "you made me torment him for no reason." It is as if the Lord turns Job over to nature in the guise of a whirlwind, an image that depicts nature's indifference to human need and human deserving.

Even after Job's possessions are taken away and his body is afflicted with boils, Job continues to cling to his belief in the Lord's ways, whatever their apparent manifestation: "The Lord gave, and the Lord has taken; may the name of the Lord be blessed," and Job extends this thought even further when he admonishes his disenchanted wife: "We have accepted good fortune from God; surely we can accept bad fortune too." When Job's three friends come to comfort him, assuming that Job's affliction is the result of some unspeakable sin Job has committed, Job's acceptance of the will of the Lord collapses and he accedes to his wife's blunt advice: "Curse God and die." What finally breaks Job's stoicism, what he finds unacceptable and insupportable, is the misjudgment of his friends. Beyond the loss of his wealth and the agony of his body, the failure of human sympathy momentarily defeats Job's spirit and destroys his optimistic faith. He sinks into despair and turns against his creator, cursing him:

> God Damn the day I was born
>   and the night that forced me from the womb.
> On that day—let there be darkness;
>   let it never have been created;
> Let it sink back into the void.
>
> (Job 13)

Job's curse represents the satanic spirit of absolute negativity—*non serviam*—for it is directed against creation itself, including Job's own creation, and thus Job sets himself against the will of God. God's original "Let there be light" is reversed in Job's "let there be darkness," and even the past, time itself, is rejected by Job as if memory, too, can be obliterated. Job wishes for the nothingness, the void, that preceded God's creation. Job must recover from this nihilism in the course of this epic poem; his spiritual journey leads him to confront his friends, himself, and, finally, through revelation, his God.

Caught up in his curse of the creation of his bodily being, and doubly cursed by the burden of consciousness, Job desires to be relieved of his sorrow through death. Every unanswerable question is a form of unjust punishment to him:

> Why is there light for the wretched,
>   life for the bitter-hearted,
> who long for death, who seek it
>   as if it were buried treasure,
> who smile when they reach the graveyard
>   and laugh as their pit is dug?
>
> (Job 14)

Then, at the conclusion of this curse, Job makes a desperate acknowledgment: "My worst fears have happened; / my nightmares have come to life." In other words, he has always known that he would have to confront God's creation, but throughout the days of his well-being, Job had repressed his inner knowledge. It is this newfound ability to express his worst fears that begins the process of his transformation and redemption, and the debate with his friends provides Job with the opportunity to define his newly emerging identity as questioner, as witness to the excruciating truth that nature, and nature's God, do not represent any principle of justice that Job can discern.

It is the intention of Job's friends to give useful advice and true comfort to Job according to the conventional wisdom that can be reduced to a basic premise: a good God would not allow a good man to suffer. From this premise, according to his would-be comforters, Job's suffering and misfortunes are irrefutable evidence of the presence of evil in his deeds or thoughts. Thus Eliphaz, the first of the comforters, rhetorically asks Job:

> Can an innocent man be punished?
>   Can a good man die in distress?
> I have seen the plowers of evil
>   reaping the crimes they sowed.
> One breath from God and they shrivel up;
>   one blast of his rage and they burn.
>
> (Job 17)

In projecting this image of a just God onto the universe—a God who can be comprehended through moral reasoning—Eliphaz in effect represents the human need for consolation in the face of forces that seem cruel and indifferent to human desires and wishes. Indeed, the comforters express the point of view with which Job rationalized his previous wealth and happiness as divinely merited.

Job's complaint continues as he responds to Eliphaz, "God has ringed me with terrors," and he continues to seek death—"If only he made an end to me"—at the same time that a new assertiveness begins to well up in him. He wants his suffering to be recognized for what it is, not reasoned away, and so he resists Eliphaz's implication that he confess to a crime that he has not committed:

> Do you want to disprove my passion
>   or argue away my despair?
> Look me straight in the eye;
>   is this how a liar would face you?
> Can't I tell right from wrong?
>   If I sinned, wouldn't I know it?
> (Job 22)

Job insists on holding to the truth of his own moral intelligence, which conflicts with the belief that God's justice can be found in the world and in human affairs. Job's identity, then, resides in his testimony to the terrible truth that justice cannot be found in the world. Job has become the voice of his suffering: "I refuse to be quiet; / I will cry out my bitter despair."

Job's second comforter, Bildad, is more vociferous in his criticism of Job, as if Job's claim of innocence has somehow threatened him. In defense of his own moral system, Bildad reveals his anger against Job's apparently blasphemous truth, going as far as to attack Job's children for their misfortune as well:

> How long will you go on ranting,
>   filling our ears with trash?
> Does God make straightness crooked
>   or turn truth upside down?
> Your children must have been evil:
>   he punished them for their crimes.
> (Job 25)

Bildad insists on the connection between behavior and reward, for without such a belief God's power would be too mysterious and too terrifying for him to contemplate: "God never betrays the innocent / or takes the hand of the wicked."

In his reply, Job rejects this rational account of God, and although he is dismayed by God's seemingly random exercise of his power, Job, nevertheless, expresses his widening sense of mind-expanding bewilderment and awe:

> His workings are vast and fathomless,
>   his wonders beyond my grasp.
> If he passed me, I would not see him;
>   if he went by, I would not know.
> (Job 27)

Insisting still upon his innocence, Job offers to testify before God in his own behalf. He has not yet relinquished the idea of a just God, though he now denies that God's justice can be seen in the vagaries of human fortune. Still, Job imagines that in God's court—should such a court be provided by God—he would be acquitted:

> If I testify, will he answer?
>   Is he listening to my plea?
> He has punished me for a trifle;
>   for no reason he gashes my flesh.
>   (Job 28)

Then a great change occurs in Job's imagining of his relationship with God. Having been accused by his friends and apparently punished by God, yet having proclaimed himself guiltless, Job reverses his relationship with God by becoming God's accuser, and, in effect, putting God on trial:

> I am guiltless, but his mouth condemns me;
>   blameless, but his words convict me.
> He does not care; so I say
>   he murders both the pure and the wicked.
> When the plague brings sudden death,
>   he laughs at the anguish of the innocent.
> He hands the earth to the wicked
>   and blindfolds its judges eyes.
> Who does it, if not he?
>   (Job 28)

With utter blasphemy, Job holds God accountable for His power to bring about or to prevent death and suffering. From here on, the motif of man in God's court, and God in man's court, informs the poem.

The argument of the third comforter, Zophar, is more subtle than those of Eliphaz and Bildad, though its premise that God can be understood through moral reasoning is the same. Zophar realizes that Job has not committed a crime against God's law, so he assumes that Job has sinned in his heart and has concealed that sin even from himself. Sustaining Job's image of himself as a man on trial, Zophar says:

> But if God were to cross-examine you
>   and turned up your hidden motives
> and presented his case against you
>   and told you why he has punished you—
> you would know that your guilt is great.
>   (Job 31)

Zophar's arrogance is twofold: first, he presumes to understand Job's inner motivation better than Job, and, second, he presumes to understand the ways of God. Thus, it is ironic when Zophar says, "How can you understand God / or fathom his endless wisdom?" since Zophar himself has acted as if his understanding of God were accurate and complete.

This irony deepens as we remember that the comforters are Job's friends who want to help him through his ordeal, but who are repressing their motives of self-justification out of a desperate need to protect their view of God's universe. Job's suffering becomes the means by which they justify themselves, and their guilt about their own motivation is blindly projected onto Job. To avoid confronting his own potential limitations and self-knowledge, Zophar says to Job:

> Come now, repent of your sins;
>   open your heart to God.
> Wash your hands of their wickedness;
>   banish crime from your door.
>
> (Job 32)

The failure of his friends' empathy is as painful to Job as is the abyss of inscrutability between Job and his God.

Job is aware of the irony of Zophar's arrogance, as his sardonic response reveals:

> You, it seems, know everything;
>   perfect wisdom is yours.
> But I am not an idiot:
>   who does not know such things?
>
> (Job 33)

Job does not lack humility before God's wisdom, and he fully understands that power belongs to Him only, but Job will not be cowed into denying that he is innocent. He will not sentimentalize the idea of guilt by assuming that he is guilty merely because he is human, for real distinctions must be made between human goodness and human evil. Thus, Job insists on having his day in court, on being heard by God: "But I want to speak before God, / to present my case in God's court."

If Job is to be tried by God, he wants his friends to testify in his behalf, not to perjure themselves as his accusers in order to win God's approval. As Job has combined his roles as defendant and accuser of God, so, too, he becomes the accuser of the comforters when he says:

> Will you lie to vindicate God?
>   Will you perjure yourselves for him?
> Will you blindly stand on his side,
>   pleading his case alone?
>
> (Job 34)

In his courage to stand alone before God and man, Job has found strength that supersedes his earlier nihilism. In defiance, holding to the truth as he knows it, Job has advanced in what Stephen Mitchell calls his "spiritual transformation." Job declares:

> He may kill me, but I won't stop;
> > I will speak the truth to his face.
> Listen now to my words;
> > pay attention to what I say.
> For I have prepared my defense,
> > and I know that I am right.
>
> > (Job 35)

The pain of isolation will not deter Job from holding to his last possession—his integrity. Nothing can ameliorate this isolation since Job views death for humankind as absolute, unlike nature's cycles of renewal:

> Even if it is cut down,
> > a tree can return to life.
> Though its roots decay in the ground
> > and its stump grows old and rotten,
> it will bud at the scent of water
> > and bloom as if it were young.
> But man is cut down forever;
> > he dies, and where is he then?
>
> > (Job 36)

The debate between Job and his comforters is elaborated with the comforters' accusation about Job's blasphemy: "You are undermining religion / and crippling faith in God," and Job's counter accusations about the comforters' hypocrisy: "I am sick of your consolations! / How long will you pelt me with insults? / Will your malice never relent?" Technically, the comforters are correct in accusing Job of blasphemy and in claiming that he is undermining religious faith, but, in the deeper sense, they fail to see that Job is justified, even heroic, in challenging God. And Job is also right in attacking the comforters' malice even though they are unconscious of their motivations, particularly since Job wants to receive compassion and empathy from them, to have them acknowledge their common human predicament:

> My breath sickens my wife;
> > my stench disgusts my brothers.
> Even young children fear me;
> > when they see me, they run away.
> My dearest friends despise me;
> > I have lost everyone I love.

> Have pity on me, my friends,
> for God's fist has struck me.
> Why must you hunt me as God does?
>
> (Job 49)

Job asks his friends to ally themselves with him according to their human bond, not add to his torment by condemning him as if they represented God's punishing judges.

Throughout his ordeal Job, claiming innocence, continues to wish for a fair trial in God's court:

> If only I knew where to meet him
> and could find my way to his court.
> I would argue my case before him;
> words would flow from my mouth.
> I would counter all his arguments
> and disprove his accusations.
>
> (Job 59)

But in this invocation to justice, Job still is caught in a structure of rational thought, as are the comforters. Although by now Job has realized that the logic that argues that God rewards the virtuous and punishes the wicked is false and does not pertain to human affairs, Job has not yet relinquished his conviction that God can be comprehended in moral and rational terms: "Surely he would listen to reason," Job declares. In his journey of spiritual transformation, Job has not yet accepted God's morality—if it is such—as something completely different from human morality. Job has not yet understood that God's commandments, His laws, apply only to human behavior and not to God's managing of nature and the universe. Although Job knows that "I have kept all his commandments, / treasuring his words in my heart," he knows, too, that God, in His infinite power, permits evil to thrive in the world:

> In the city the dying groan
> and the wounded cry out for help;
> but God sees nothing wrong.
> At twilight the killer appears,
> stalking his helpless victim.
> The rapist waits for evening
> and roams through the darkened streets.
> The thief crawls from the shadows
> with a hood over his face.
>
> (Job 60)

In Zophar's final speech, before Job's summary response to them all, Zophar asks: "What can the sinner hope for / when God demands his life?" But Job perceives himself as having been convicted of a crime that has not been proven, for which there is no evidence. The comforters' whole case for Job's guilt is that misfortune has befallen him. The question of hope that Zophar raises, however, is the appropriate one because only hope remains to Job. Until Job is confronted by the voice of God from the whirlwind, he continues to hope that he will be fairly judged; his faith persists that God will reveal Himself in ethical terms. In contrast to Job's passionate adherence to the truth of his own moral innocence and his refusal to submit to a logic that would force him to lie: "I will hold tight to my innocence; / my mind will never submit," Zophar's imagination is morbidly inspired by the vision of punishment for the sinner he considers Job to be:

> Waves of terror flood over him;
>   panic sweeps him away.
> The east wind flings itself on him,
>   whirls him out of his bed,
> claps its hands around him
>   and whistles him off in the dark.
> (Job 65)

In his summation to the comforters, as if in a court of law, Job pleads his case on the basis of his history of upright behavior:

> For I rescued the poor, the desperate,
>   those who had nowhere to turn.
> I brought relief to the beggar
>   and joy to the widow's heart.
> Righteousness was my clothing,
>   justice my robe and turban.
> I served as eyes for the blind,
>   hands and feet for the crippled.
> To the destitute I was a father;
>   I fought for the stranger's rights.
> (Job 70)

There is every reason to believe—though the comforters do not—that Job is giving an accurate account of his life, and the only fault that one might find in Job, from a moral perspective, is that he has behaved well for the sake of reward, rather than for the sake of virtue:

> And I thought, I will live many years,
>   growing as old as the palm tree.
> My roots will be spread for water,
>   and the dew will rest in my boughs.
> (Job 70)

Job has not been made to suffer because God has found fault with him. Indeed, Job is prepared to answer any charges against him. His agony resides in the appalling fact that no charges have been made; there is only silence on God's part.

Job's losses, his physical suffering, and the alienation of his friends, all torment him, but his anguish comes also from the violation of his moral imagination. The concept, based on the evidence of his own life, that God is not just becomes Job's obsession: "Yet instead of good came evil, / and instead of light there was darkness." Job feels himself to be an outcast—as remote from God as the wild animals; he is part of nature but not one with nature because his consciousness separates him from the animals, who follow the laws of their instincts:

> I despair and can find no comfort;
>   I stand up and cry for help.
> I am brother to the wild jackal,
>   friend to the desert owl.
> My flesh blackens and peels;
>   all my bones are on fire.
> And my harp is tuned to mourning,
>   my flute to the sound of tears.
>   (Job 72)

So Job is driven to the final blasphemy: he sees God as his ethical inferior, a vast power not in control of his own designs: "Can't he tell right from wrong, / or keep his accounts in order?" Yet Job still cannot relinquish his need for justice, his need to be heard, his supreme demand of the cosmos—that it respond to him:

> Oh if only God would hear me,
>   state his case against me,
> let me read his indictment.
>   I would carry it on my shoulder
> or wear it on my head like a crown.
>   I would justify the least of my actions;
>   I would stand before him like a prince.
>   (Job 75)

Eventually God does respond to Job, but not in the ethical terms on which Job has insisted. God presents Himself only as the designer of the universe. Where Job has challenged God in the name of justice, God replies in the amoral terms of the joy and grandness of creation itself:

> Where were you when I planned the earth?
> Tell me, if you are so wise.

Do you know who took its dimensions,
   measuring its length with a cord?
What were its pillars built on?
   Who laid down its cornerstone,
while the morning stars burst out singing
   and the angels shouted for joy?

                              (Job 79)

God does not even expatiate about the creation of humankind; rather, He evokes existence itself, physical matter, elements such as snow, hail, wind, and rain, the patterns of heaven, thunderclouds, and the storm that turns dust to mud.

Most prominently, God presents Job with a catalog of the animals He has set upon the earth; He describes their characteristic behavior, making no distinctions among them according to virtues. They are all equally beautiful in God's eyes: the lioness who finds her prey at nightfall; the wild ass who ranges the open prairie; the wild ox who must be forced to harrow the fields; the ostrich who treats her children cruelly as if they were not her own; the horse who laughs at the sight of danger; the vulture who makes his home on the mountaintop: "on the unapproachable crag. / He sits and scans for prey; / from far off his eyes can spot it; / his little ones drink its blood." God makes no excuse for the Darwinian cruelty and death that is depicted here. Only God's ecstatic pride in the plenitude of His creation is expressed. Even though He has not answered Job's accusation that He has been unjust, God challenges Job: "Has God's accuser resigned? / Has my critic swallowed his tongue?" and Job, dumbfounded, replies, "I am speechless: what can I answer? / I put my hand on my mouth."

God's paradoxical question, "Am I wrong because you are right?" is the baffling challenge that Job must somehow meet. This paradox is wonderfully highlighted in Stephen Mitchell's rendering of the more literal version of the King James Bible, "Wilt thou also disannul my judgment? Wilt though condemn me, that thou mayest be righteous?" (Job 40.8) In both versions, God reveals that He cannot be comprehended by reason; He cannot be circumscribed by moral categories or ordinary human logic. From an ethical point of view, God is wholly other; what is right for humans does not apply to God. God's medium is power and creation; man's medium is morality and social law, which God has assigned to humankind so that humans might govern themselves. Man does not have the power to save himself through his own attempts at government, his own ethical systems. God ironically reminds Job that only He possesses the power to save:

> Unleash your savage justice.
>   Cut down the rich and the mighty.
> Make the proud man grovel.
>   Pluck the wicked from their perch.
> Push them into the grave.
>   Throw them, screaming, to hell.
> Then will I admit
>   that your own strength can save you.
>   (Job 85)

God's concluding revelation of Himself to Job comes through His description of His two primal creatures, the Beast and the Serpent. The style of their evocation differs from God's earlier catalog of the animals because the Beast and the Serpent are depicted both as they occur in nature and as symbols of universal forces. The Beast is an emblem of procreative power, the source of God's fundamental delight in creating creatures that also have the power to create through Darwinian replication. In this sense, the Beast represents the ongoing creativity of nature itself:

> Look now: the Beast that I made:
>   he eats grass like a bull.
> Look: the power in his thighs,
>   the pulsing sinews of his belly.
> His penis stiffens like a pine;
>   his testicles bulge with vigor.
> His ribs are bars of bronze,
>   his bones iron beams.
> He is first of the works of God,
>   created to be my plaything.
>   (Job 85)

The awesome Serpent is presented as a model of nature's destructiveness, inseparable from nature's fecundity. Although the Serpent embodies what Mitchell calls the "forces of chaos," chaos and destructiveness are evoked as essential aspects of ongoing creation. The Serpent represents the elements of nature that cannot be tamed or rationalized by man into any moral system based on compassion or justice. A symbol for those natural forces which surpass all human powers, the Serpent is a kindred aspect of the whirlwind itself out of which God speaks to Job:

> Who would dare to arouse him?
>   Who would stand in his way?
> Who under all the heavens
>   could fight him and live?
> Who could pierce his armor
>   or shatter his coat of mail?

> Who could pry open his jaws,
>   with their horrible arched teeth?
> He sneezes and lightnings flash;
>   his eyes glow like the dawn.
>
> (Job 86)

There is no doubt about the significance of God's description of the Serpent: God delights in his creation, in his abiding power. God makes no apologies to Job for the dominance of the destructive Serpent:

> No one on earth is his equal—
>   a creature without fear.
> He looks down on the highest.
> He is king over all the proud beasts.
>
> (Job 87)

Job's culminating realization of his relationship to God has nothing to do with the question of justice: he does not stand before God in a court of morality or law. Job's revelation is of God's power, His incomprehensible vastness. Before God's bewildering magnitude, Job humbles himself: "I have spoken of the unspeakable and tried to grasp the infinite."

The spiritual transformation from Job's earlier despair—"let there be darkness"—is clear, and nihilism—wishing to revoke creation itself—is finally overcome with his awareness of the mystery and vastness of God's design. This awareness requires of Job's imagination that he take "the long view" of nature and its unfolding in evolutionary time. Job does not have to relinquish his own ethical concerns and his demand for justice, but he has to set them in the larger context of a cosmic order in which he plays only a small part.

Job's new humility, however, is neither self-despising nor self-castigating, but rather detached and objective. As Mitchell says, "Anyone who acts with genuine humility will be as far from humiliation as from arrogance." Job's abstract concept of justice, connecting virtue with reward, has collapsed in the face of experience itself, but Job, unlike his friends, has had the courage and integrity to acknowledge the indifference of reality to human desires and at the same time to find something worthy of awe in that indifference. God's direct and immediate appearance to Job, literally presented in the poem, can be regarded as a metaphor that expresses the clarity of Job's enlarged perception of reality:

> I have heard of you with my ears;
>   but now my eyes have seen you.
> Therefore I will be quiet,
>   comforted that I am dust.
>
> (Job 88)

Resignation to silence, Job's culminating act of will, acknowledges that he is God's creation out of the dust; it acknowledges his finitude, against which he no longer rebels. Like everything in nature, he, too, is subject to extinction. His comfort finally comes from his acceptance of this ineluctable fact. Unlike Job's opening curse in which he sought death as an escape from existence, he now has only to accept his mortal condition, the condition of his humanity. Through all his agony, Job does not renounce or relinquish his human understanding, his morality, his otherness from God; rather, he accepts it within a larger context of power and magnitude of existence. As Darwin also saw, man cannot be understood as having been created in God's image:

Astronomers might formerly have said that God ordered each planet to move in its particular destiny. In the same manner God ordered each animal created with a certain form in a certain country, but how much more simple & sublime [to imagine God's] power let attraction act according to certain laws [so that as an] inevitable consequence the animals [would] be created.[4]

To contemplate the diversity and plenitude of God's nature is to free one's thoughts from one's own fate, even the fate of one's own species into a larger sublimity. For Darwin, an enlarged sense of "grandeur" is inherent in viewing creation as ongoing and dynamic, as a process of endless evolution, rather than as static and complete. Even though moral law is apparently removed from God's creative intent, just as it was removed in Job's experience of suffering, a cosmic sense of values does not disappear.

[In time] instincts alter, reason is formed, & the world is peopled with myriads of distinct forms from a period short of eternity to the present time to the future. How far grander [is this idea] than the idea from a cramped imagination that God created . . . the Rhinoceros of Java & Sumatra, that since the time of the Silurian, he has made a long succession of vile Moluscous animals. How beneath the dignity of him, who is supposed to have said, "Let there be light & there was light."[5]

Though God has refused to respond to Job's accusation that he has been punished despite his innocence, that the world of God's creation is unjust, God does express His anger to the comforters for having borne false witness: "I am very angry at you and your two friends, because you have not spoken the truth about me, as my servant Job has." Here, with stunning irony, God makes it explicit that human beings must adhere to the tenets of morality; they must pursue justice, despite the fact that such ethical restrictions do not pertain to God Himself. Man and God remain in different realms. Human caring and compassion may be seen, however, as compensation for God's otherness and nature's indifference. And so, finally, Job is blessed with the commiseration of his relatives and friends: "All his relatives and everyone who had known him came to his house to celebrate. They commiserated with him over all the suffering that the Lord had inflicted on him."

Ultimately, when God's otherness is understood and accepted, His creation, physical existence itself, can be perceived in the fullness of its beauty. This acceptance is represented in the spirit of fable by God's restoration of Job's sons and daughters: "He also had seven sons and three daughters: the eldest he named Dove, the second Cinnamon, and the third Eye-Shadow. And in all the world there were no women as beautiful as Job's daughters" (Job 91). Mitchell emphasizes the importance of this naming of Job's daughters: "The names themselves—Dove, Cinnamon, and Eye-Shadow—symbolize peace, abundance, and a specifically female kind of grace. The story's center of gravity has shifted from righteousness to beauty." This shift completes the poem's transformation from Job's curse to his blessing in which natural death is experienced as benign: "Job lived to see his grandchildren and his great-grandchildren. And he died at a very great age." Man's individual, daily imagination, however, cannot be maintained at the level and intensity of "the long view," on Darwin's spectacle of evolution into an indefinite and undisclosed future, but must return to the scale of more immediate concerns, to human justice and the search for human happiness. And so Job, having been rewarded with the ecstasy of God's revelation from the whirlwind of ongoing and endless creation, is relieved of that intensity, which his mind can only briefly contain, and he is allowed to die comfortably within the finite scope of family love.

III

Darwin was aware that his theory of evolution would be seen as blasphemous by the pious, just as Job's utterances questioning God's justice were condemned by his comforters. Stephen Jay Gould points out in his essay "Darwin's Delay" that Darwin gave vent to his beliefs only when he could hide them no longer, in the *The Descent of Man* (1871) and the *The Expression of the Emotions in Man and Animals* (1872). Further, Gould quotes Darwin's letter to Karl Marx in which Darwin writes:

It seems to me (rightly or wrongly) that direct argument against Christianity and Theism hardly have any effect on the public; and that freedom of thought will best be promoted by that gradual enlightening of human understanding which follows the progress of science.[6]

At the end of *The Descent of Man* Darwin acknowledges his iconoclasm when he says: "I am aware that the conclusion arrived at in this work will be denounced by some as highly irreligious," and then he goes on to argue that if we can accept natural childbirth as part of a divine plan, we should be able to accept evolution also as within the parameters of religious belief. Thus, for Darwin, it is not more irreligious to explain the origin of man as a distinct species by descent from some lower form, through the laws of variation and natural selection, than to explain the birth of the individual through the laws of ordinary reproduction (Darwin 202). Darwin's Jobian perspective in which God's morality is brought into question strongly resembles the view that will be adopted by Robert Frost. And yet, even though God cannot be comprehended as having created the human race in his own image, or as having a purpose that corresponds to the human longing for justice, Frost does not entirely abandon all belief in divinity. Darwin's key statement regarding this issue reads: "The birth both of the species and of the individual are equally parts of that grand sequence of events, which our minds refuse to accept as the result of blind chance."

This statement by Darwin, however, is not entirely unambiguous. It might be interpreted to mean that, even though our minds refuse to accept evolution as the result of blind chance, that is nevertheless precisely what we must learn to accept. Or the statement might imply—as I think is the case in Robert Frost's poetry—that our minds are right to refuse to accept evolutionary theory as the result of blind chance unequivocally only because no certainty about divine intention or creation is possible. If the refusal of certainty is justified for reasons that go beyond scientific inquiry, such refusal must necessarily require an openness of speculation, allowing even for the existence of a God of creation—a creation, however, that takes evolutionary time as the medium in which it unfolds. Evolution, in other words, may be seen as the law that describes the infinitude of a creation that is thus never completed. Darwin argues that the general public rejection of evolution as the result of blind chance is due to the fact that our understanding revolts at such a conclusion. Perhaps something of this revulsion lies beneath the surface of Frostian thinking, his unwillingness to take a wholly atheistic stance, yet this revulsion of living in a world whose design is a "design of darkness," or one in which God is "kindred" to a spider does not really undermine his essential skepticism.

Darwin comes to place his primary faith, however, in that gradual enlightening of human understanding which follows the progress of science, and his writing is replete with phrases that reveal both his aesthetic and his moral sense. He refers, for example, to the "dignity of mankind" or to the "wonderful advancement that has come from the development of articulate language." For Darwin this advancement is to be found in the appearance of the human capacity for sympathy. He speaks, for example, of the acquirement of the higher mental qualities, such as sympathy and the love of his fellows, whose foundation lies in social instincts and family ties. The distinct emotion of sympathy and the moral sense are related by Darwin to the high activity of man's mental faculties. When Darwin writes of an advance in morality or in man's reason, he is not using such words as "higher," "qualities," or "advance" only to indicate man's power of adaptation to his environment; rather, he makes an evaluation that is spiritual, as well as pragmatic. His concept of human advancement is not bound to his concept of the survival of the fittest.

Darwin says that the conclusion he has come to in *The Descent of Man* will be offensive: "that man is descended from some lowly organized form, will, I regret to think, be highly distasteful to many." From our contemporary vantage point, we must include him in that many. Darwin's repugnance for the behavior of his human ancestors is unmistakable in his description of the savage "who delights to torture his enemies, offers up bloody sacrifices, practices infanticide without remorse, treats his wives like slaves, knows no decency, and is haunted by the grossest superstitions," but his hope for advancement is not based on an appeal to divinity, only on the evolutionary fact of our species having thus risen as a conglomeration of social animals, instead of having been aboriginally placed on earth by God. Thus Darwin's hope for a still higher destiny in the distant future resides entirely in the human capacity for sympathy that feels for the most debased, with benevolence that extends not only to other men but to the humblest living creatures as well.

Darwin, like Job, turns back to the plenitude of creation, to the animals, and takes his comfort both from the spectacle of existence and from man's god-like intellect, which provides the sympathy that nature itself, and perhaps even the God of nature, is lacking. Darwin ends his book, however, with a note of warning, reminding us of our human history of having evolved from lower forms, a history that we must vigilantly keep in mind: "Man still bears in his bodily frame the indelible stamp of his lowly origin." Without the humility of such remembrance, Darwin's words imply, we are doomed to an arrogance that belies our nature.

Those who suffer, as Darwin believes some individuals must, from the war of nature, from famine and death, and those who are washed away, or crushed, or scorched, or blasted by flood, earthquake, fire, or whirlwind are not likely, in the agony of their unmerited fates, to sing praises to the designer of the universe. A human being, who possesses reason and language with which to cry out, will be tempted, rather, to appeal to a merciful God who empathizes with his or her suffering, a

humanly comprehensible God who offers comfort. The universe, how-
ever, has never offered such comfort, as the Book of Job definitively dra-
matizes. If comfort is to be offered at all, it is only within the capacity of
other human beings to make such an offering. Although the wondrous
beauty of the universe has always been a primal source of poetic inspira-
tion, the magnificence of the created world will not appear to be sufficient
compensation for the unwarranted pain of a random death, either at the
hands of other humans or as a result of worldly conditions, unless one can
embrace the long view as expressed by the Book of Job or by Darwin's the-
ory. Should one choose protest or outcry, rather than acceptance and
praise, one's adversarial words against the conditions of nature, no matter
how poetically eloquent, would not reach even the nearest stars. One's
human voice would be too small, too fleeting, too personal. Other cries of
other voices always are awaiting their turns to live and to die.

IV

In the poetry of Robert Frost the profound influences of Darwin and the
Book of Job converge. In *A Masque of Reason,* Frost creates a witty di-
alogue between God and Job about the relationship between justice and
power, behavior and reward. By keeping these issues at the level of intel-
lectual debate, however, Frost presents his readers with a comic work
that is deliberately devoid of the terror and bafflement of the main body
of the Book of Job. In doing so, Frost, in a way, takes on the role of a
comforter by offering intellectual detachment as an amelioration for
physical suffering and the awareness of worldly injustice. Frost's masque
is more in the spirit of the Epilogue of the Book of Job, in which, after the
grim reality of the poem's main drama—Job's exchanges with his friends
and his confrontation with God—is completed, the poem turns into a
kind of fairy tale of resolution in which, so it seems, all losses are restored
and sorrows end.

Frost offers comfort as entertainment through punning wit (a doctor
joke on Job's famous patience) and playful banter. God's first words to
Job in Frost's poem are casual and jaunty:

> Oh, I remember well: you're Job, my Patient.
> How are you now? I trust you've quite recovered,
> And feel no ill effects from what I gave you.
>
> (Frost 474)

Job's reply is appropriately sassy as he continues the repartee with the
tacit assumption that he and God are intellectual equals:

> Gave me in truth: I like the frank admission.
> I am a name for being put upon.
> But, yes, I'm fine, except for now and then
> A reminiscent twinge of rheumatism.
> The letup's heavenly. You perhaps will tell us
> If that is all there is to be of Heaven,
> Escape from so great pains of life on earth
> It gives a sense of letup calculated
> To last a fellow to Eternity.
>
> (Frost 474–75)

Here, Job's ironic reply to God, particularly in reference to his rheumatic twinge, is at the other end of the emotional spectrum from Job's curse of God in the biblical account.

Although God's rejoinder to Job retains the mood of jocularity, it has a serious undercurrent: it addresses the great theme of the separation between man and God, in which God's otherness cannot be spanned by human reason:

> I've had you on my mind a thousand years
> To thank you someday for the way you helped me
> Establish once for all the principle
> There's no connection man can reason out
> Between his just deserts and what he gets.
>
> (Frost 474)

Frost's God gives Job his due, just as God in the Bible acknowledges that Job has spoken the truth about him, but the whirlwind of God's voice has been diminished into a philosophical argument—the reasonable principle that human reason has its limits: "My thanks are to you [Job] for releasing me / From moral bondage to the human race." On the conceptual level, these words by God philosophically clarify the import of the Book of Job. With the dread of God removed from the confrontation between Job and God, however, the glibly comforting effect of these lines is antithetical to the toughness of God's speech from the whirlwind, which offers awe and wonder without the concern for human physical well-being and moral meaning.

Frost's God, however, unlike Job's, is not prepared to avoid the issue of "meaning" altogether and so He resorts to what appears to be a paradoxical formulation:

> Too long I've owed you this apology
> For the apparently unmeaning sorrow
> You were afflicted with in those old days.
> But it was of the essence of the trial

> You shouldn't understand it at the time.
> It had to seem unmeaning to have meaning.
>
> (Frost 475)

This is really just a clever argument in defense of the idea of faith, that man is always on trial to believe in the goodness and justice of God even when there is no worldly evidence to support such belief. God here is claiming that Job's trial would, and did, simply take time to make sense. So here, too, in his comic mode, Frost continues to be closer to the biblical comforters than the biblical Job to whom God offers no reasonable or meaningful explanation. God's motivation, rather, for testing Job seems to be simply based on winning a wager with the Devil without respect to Job's welfare or any universal principle of justice.

In Frost's poem, Job's wife is much less ready to accept God's rationalization for faith—that it had to "seem unmeaning to have meaning"— than does Job, who appears to enjoy the discussion with God mainly for the pleasure of theological conjecture. Job's wife is directly critical of God when she declares, "All You seem to do is lose Your temper / When reason-hungry mortals ask for reasons," and then, as feminist reformer, she continues: "still its mostly women / Get burned for prophecy, men almost never." At such a moment, Frost's poem moves closer to Job's heartfelt cry for justice in the Bible, in which Job's wife's excruciating words were: "Curse God and die."

Frost's God wants to make it clear that he is up to date on the latest Darwinian thinking when he says, displaying his erudition, "look at how far we've left the current science / Of Genesis behind." But Job, it turns out, has been biding his time, waiting for the right moment to return to the themes of reason and meaning, and, in particular, God's reason for tempting and torturing him. The earlier formulation that the test had to "seem unmeaning to have meaning" is now revisited by Job:

> Because I let You off
> From telling me Your reason, don't assume
> I thought You had none. Somewhere back
> I knew You had one.
>
> (Frost 482)

And so Frost's Job turns out to be closer to the original in his rebelliousness than had appeared earlier in the poem since he clearly expresses his dissatisfaction with the paradox of taking God's meaning on faith. Frost's Job, now emboldened, goes even further in accusing God of using the argument according to faith and unmeaning as an excuse contrived after the fact of God's mistreatment of Job merely to win a bet:

> It seems to me
> An afterthought, a long-long-afterthought.
> I'd give more for one least beforehand reason
> Than all the justifying ex-post-facto
> Excuses trumped up by You for theologians.
>
> (Frost 482)

Frost's Job, it becomes clear, wants two things: he wants some grand sense of design that he can appreciate, not obfuscation: "The artist in me cries out for design." But Frost's most Jobian/Darwinian version of "design" will be put forth in Frost's poem "Design," to be examined shortly. The second thing Frost's Job wants, more personally, is to know the answer to the question, "Why did You hurt me so? I am reduced / To asking flatly for the reason—outright." The pained tone of these lines is remarkably close to the biblical Job's: "I cry out, and you do not answer." So nothing has really changed as Job's wife sees with such clarity and expresses with such succinctness: "You won't get any answers out of God."

Job's wife is then given the speech that expresses the religious skepticism that pervades Frost's poetry, a skepticism that insists on remaining uncertain about divine revelation, yet maintains its attention on humankind's deepest hope, its stubborn desire for immortality:

> Perhaps that earth is going to crack someday
> Like a big egg and hatch a heaven out
> Of all the dead and buried from their graves.
>
> (Frost 484)

Job's disbelieving wife suggests to God that He could put an end to such fantastic nonsense, but God, rather, falls back upon a confession of a motive that any attentive reader of the Book of Job has suspected all along. God admits that "I was just showing off to the Devil, Job." Frost's intellectual comedy here is right at the edge of bitter satire, and, indeed, what Job sardonically replies reveals the immensity of his disappointment at having only the obvious revealed to him: "I expected more / Than I could understand and what I get / Is almost less than I can understand."

God attempts one more recovery of self-justification, even a plea for sympathy, in acknowledging that He was the one who succumbed to temptation when He says that "The tempter comes to me and I am tempted." He tells Job what He, just like the biblical Job, already knows:

> I trust I made it clear I took your side
> Against your comforters in their contention
> You must be wicked to deserve such pain.
>
> (Frost 486)

But just as the Book of Job modulates into the mode of a fairy tale with its literary allusions in the name of Job's new daughters and its happy ending, Frost's poem diminishes into a kind of literary farce with the entrance of Satan, whose main role at the poem's conclusion is to have his picture taken by Job's wife with her Kodak. Both Job and Job's wife are fully aware of Satan's literary antecedent in Milton's *Paradise Lost* as Job refers to Milton as "the greatest Western poem yet." Appropriately, Job's wife expects Satan to be a great talker and confronts Satan with the question, "what ails you? Where's the famous tongue, / Thou onetime Prince of Conversationalists?"

Frost's masque (a highly literary form itself) satirizes itself by turning into drawing room comedy as if nothing mattered but our manners, as Job's wife remarks. The awareness of the immediate reality of evil in the world, the urgent questioning about justice and meaning, is too painful and cannot be sustained—a truth God Himself recognizes when He describes the demise of Satan into a literary construct: "figurative use [has] pretty well / Reduced him to a shadow of himself." Wallace Stevens cogently made the same point in the same ominous undertones about the diminishment of the human ability to confront actual evil, when he declared that "The death of Satan was a tragedy / For the imagination." And so Frost's poem ends with an intensified awareness of its own artifice. Jobs wife says: "Now someone can light up the Burning Bush / And turn the gold enameled artificial birds on." Beyond human metaphor, God's "design" remains unknown.

V

The concept of "design" that inspires the artist in Frost's *A Masque of Reason* nevertheless brings forth in Frost's poem "Design" the darkest vision of what the design of nature—and thus the design of the creator of nature—might be within the context of Darwinian evolutionary understanding. In this intense and compact sonnet, Frost rejects the impulse to offer his readers the comfort of humor or intellectual play. Rather, "Design" exemplifies the essential Jobian spirit in the Bible in which terror and awe are combined. The Argument from Design, as set forth by William Paley in 1802, as Frost well knew, contended that the organization and order seen everywhere in nature implied an intelligent creator. In his famous analogy of nature to a watch, Paley imagined what one would necessarily have to assume about the watch if one discovered it by the wayside:

that the watch must have had a maker: that there must have existed, at some time, and at some place or other, an artificer or artificers, who formed it for the purpose which we find it actually to answer; who comprehended its construction, and designed its use.[7]

It is precisely this view of nature as having a deliberate design like a watch that Darwin's theory of evolution refutes. In the words of Richard Dawkins, one of Darwin's leading contemporary expositors:

Natural selection . . . has no mind and no mind's eye. It does not plan for the future. It has no vision, no foresight, no sight at all. If it can be said to play the role of watchmaker in nature, it is the blind watchmaker. (Dawkins 5)

In his poem, Frost examines a minute scene in nature and asks himself what design is to be perceived there, and what kind of creator, with what intent, would choose to create such a design.

Design

I found a dimpled spider, fat and white,
On a white heal-all, holding up a moth
Like a white piece of rigid satin cloth—
Assorted characters of death and blight
Mixed ready to begin the morning right,
Like the ingredients of a witches' broth—
A snow-drop spider, a flower like a froth,
And dead wings carried like a paper kite.

What had that flower to do with being white,
The wayside blue and innocent heal-all?
What brought the kindred spider to that height,
Then steered the white moth thither in the night?
What but design of darkness to appall?—
If design govern in a thing so small.

(Frost 302)

The poem is divided into two stanzas: the first is written in a style dependent upon similes that attempt to offer consolation by presenting images of destruction in pleasingly aesthetic terms, while the second stanza rejects the illusion that nature is benign by questioning every assertion previously made in the mode of poetic description which, through simile, depicted nature as benign. Thus, the central rhetorical term of the first stanza, "like," is replaced in the second stanza with the repetition of "what," a word that evokes uncertainty and bafflement.

Frost's spider is introduced to the reader as being dimpled—hardly a word that evokes fear, since it connotes cherubic cuteness. The description of the spider as fat and white augments the first impression that this chubby spider is not dangerous; rather, it is an innocent creature going about its morning business. The image of the spider sitting on a white heal-all further evokes an atmosphere of innocent enchantment. The heal-all, normally a blue flower, becomes part of the apparent design of white the poet perceives in the scene, so its name, suggesting curative powers, is concordant with its color. Although the spider is holding up a moth, an ominous image, the poet compares this moth to a white piece of rigid satin cloth as if to insist that this image, too, can be viewed as part of a pattern of innocent whiteness. The awareness of the moth as a dead creature is further suppressed by the simile of satin cloth, and the effect of the line is thus one of aesthetic loveliness. The word "rigid," however, undermines the poet-speaker's attempt to render the scene in comforting terms because it functions as a breakthrough of the speaker's repressed awareness, shared by the temporarily deceived reader, of the moth's rigor mortis.

The poet's denial (the denial, rather, of the poem's narrator as contrived by Frost) continues in the next two lines through tonal means. Although the lines "Assorted characters of death and blight / Mixed ready to begin the morning right" appear to confront the spectacle of death, they are facetiously mocking, culminating in the pun on "right," which suggests both rite and write (the poet's morning exercise of writing a poem). The poet, creating a ritual of linguistic display, appears to be in control, and it is exactly this false appearance that must be dispelled in the course of the poem, revealing the speaker's naked uncertainty about how to interpret the appearance of design in the universe.

Before this revelation of uncertainty is accomplished, however, the speaker offers the reader (and himself) another simile: "Like the ingredients of a witches' broth." Since the poet knows that we no longer believe in witches, this line serves as a parody of the possibility of malevolent forces at work; it is a defunct metaphor like Stevens's "death of Satan." Nor can the spider and white heal-all substitute for the equivocating witches in *The Tragedy of Macbeth* to whom Shakespeare's audience, unlike Frost's, would give credence. The speaker resolves the stanza, seemingly content, by returning to decorative images: the "snow-drop spider," the flower "like a froth," and the "paper kite." And if we gloss over the word "dead" in the rushed movement of the last line of the stanza, as we are tempted to do, the wings of the moth would seem like a light-hearted image evoking a child's game as suggested by the simile "like a paper kite." The poetic narrator's attempt to master nature and impose upon nature's design the willfully cheerful design of his own poetic description seems momentarily to make him sovereign over the circumstances of the physical world.

But the reality of death and blight that the poet-speaker has struggled to repress in the first stanza reasserts its power in the second as the poet's tone changes from playful to grim. Because the poet realizes that he cannot control the design of nature through consoling similes, he is left only with the unguarded honesty of asking questions. The poet now admits that the extraordinary whiteness of the scene cannot imply nature's innocence, and that the attribution of innocence to the spider or the flower cannot have curative power for a mind searching for meaning in the physical world. Since the speaker can provide no answer to his own question, "What had the flower to do with being white?" he can only pose more questions that begin to acknowledge his previously repressed terror. With the following line, "What brought the kindred spider to that height?" the presence of a controlling force in a universe with its own design or intent is implied and, horrifyingly, this power may be kindred to that of the predatory spider. This meditation on design, then, is as close as Frost comes to Jobian blasphemy: the designer of nature, God, is predatory like his creation, the spider, and nature, thus, is God's web which entraps us all in our ultimate human vulnerability.

The suggestion of the presence of an omnipotent controlling force in nature becomes even more explicit in the line, "Then steered the white moth thither in the night." The stressed word, "steered," emphasizes what appears to be the designer's deliberate intent: this force has chosen the white moth as victim just as it has chosen the spider as agent. Everything—so the awe-struck speaker now speculates—seems to have been determined according to a plan whose purpose, if indeed there is one, remains unknown, just as divine purpose remains unknown in the book of Job and plays no part in Darwinian evolution. With the repetition of the third "What," the speaker ventures the dreadful guess: "What but design of darkness to appall?" The images of whiteness, which in the first stanza had appeared to symbolize innocence, now appear to have been a deception, a disguise for the design of darkness. Whiteness turns out to be a disguise for its opposite. The only discernible purpose of this design is to terrify those human beings who are capable of perceiving it, those human beings who have the courage of their skepticism to reject their need to be comforted by the belief in a benevolent and just deity. The alternatives suggested by Frost's poem are either that a God of creation is like a spider, or that nature, as Darwin saw it, has evolved with no purpose at all, in which competition within and between species, and adjustment to environmental conditions, along with random mutation, are the engine of endless change toward no particular end. Transience and transformation are all.

In Frost's earlier version of "Design," called "In White," the above line read "What but design of darkness and of night?" Frost's revision, which replaces "night" with the explosive word, "appall," with its multiple allusions, expresses the personal aspect of his cosmic dread. In this moment of speculative revelation, the blood drains from the speaker's face, so he is left with a deadly pallor, as if he envisions himself on his own pall; literally, he has turned white. His is surely not the whiteness of some redeeming innocence, but rather the fearfulness of Melville's albino whale in *Moby Dick*. This is the same terror experienced by Job as he stands dumbfounded before his God who speaks of the grandeur and diversity of creation from a whirlwind, but will not reply to Job's challenge that God reveal himself in moral and ethical terms.

The concluding speculation, "If design govern in a thing so small," seems almost confirmed—yes, such design does govern—by ending in a period rather than a question mark, and it throws the poem back on itself because of the uncertain reference to the word "thing." The uncertain reader might speculate that "thing" alludes to the spider in its action of catching the moth, but "thing" might refer as well to the poem's speaker, who has designed his sonnet with the deliberate intent to appall his readers with his own dark revelation. Trapped in the intricate web of the poem by the poet—who must then also be seen as kindred to the spider—the reader, too, becomes a victim in the larger design of a spider-like deity. Such an encompassing design—in which creatures imitate both the creative and the destructive aspects of their creator, whether it be God or evolutionary nature, in the making of webs or the making of poems—is indeed awesome. The beauty of nature, humanized in poetic similes, and the terror and predatory vileness of nature apprehended in the breaking down of these protecting similes are Jobian in the sublimity of their juxtaposition.

Frost's courage, like Job's, is to look directly at nature, the spider, the heal-all, to be appalled and yet finally not to flinch. His only true comfort comes from his ability to reject any innocent or untenable form of consolation; his courage lies in his stripping away the temptations of rationalization and denial. Nature—and the God of nature if such a God exists—are both beautiful and terrible and thus the onlooker's ambivalence must be absolute. As with both Job and Darwin, the main virtue of the poem's speaker lies in his integrity, his willingness to bear witness to a universe of unending change, not as he wishes God to have made it, but according to the testimony of his own senses and his own equivocal experience. Such hard-headed skepticism returns Frostian speculation back to this transient world where, if one is to ask questions about the design of nature, one would do well to emulate Frost's old woman in "Wild Grapes," who, seeking to take another step in knowledge, says to her attendant friends, "You'll have to ask an evolutionist."

Chapter 3

Loss and Inheritance in Wordsworth's "Michael" and Frost's "Wild Grapes"

I

"I am what survives me" is the pithy and poignant phrase that Erik Erikson[1] uses to describe the attitude of an aged person who has achieved a sense of personal integrity in the face of the possible despair that final annihilation, death without a belief in an afterlife, can cause. With such an attitude of integrity and relinquishment, the border between self and other may be broken down: If so, the parent's sense of self is extended to include the life of the child as he or she is imagined even beyond the parent's life. So, too, the poet may see his or her poem as a parental gift to the reader—a gift of affirmed continuity and self-relinquishment, in which one's ego merges into someone else's life through identification, so that cherished values can pass from one generation to the next, forming a kind of covenant, despite the inevitable change in circumstances and conditions that time brings.

Scrutinizing poems that are not merely fashionable artistic posturing, whose technical means of expression reflect their philosophical seriousness, is the necessary way in which we, the living inheritors, cherish these poems and keep their memory vital within us. In doing so, we extend the covenant that binds the generations together, transcending the temptations of which Yeats warned the poets who would succeed him, fearing that they would be inclined to take liberties with the formal aspects of poetry and fail to "learn their trade." With frustration and even anger, Yeats excoriated the poets who would break with the past and its noble tradition of high artistic seriousness, and he castigated them for their "unremembering hearts and heads." If poets possess the filial qualities of gratitude toward their own poetic fathers, to cherish and remember, then, in a parental spirit, they could pass on the same values of "unaging intellect." Likewise, as Wordsworth said to Coleridge at the conclusion of *The Prelude:* "what we have loved, others shall love, / And we shall teach them how." Through patience and cultivated skill, the younger poets, overcoming the ambivalence that sometimes can result from influence, may achieve a maturity of perspective. The composure to be found in such perspective is often expressed by Wordsworth in those expanded moments of stillness that resist what Wordsworth calls "the disturbances of space and time" and Frost calls "the rush of everything to waste." Frost's nonteleological view of time, seeing "waste" as its inevitable result, is a central aspect of his Darwinism in which "More individuals are produced than can possibly survive." From this grim perspective, "waste" must be taken into account in one's view of nature as a process, however grand and inspiring nature may seem in moments that are not experienced as threatening. Again and again in his poetry Frost seeks to find meaning or believable consolation that runs "counter" to natural entropy.

II

Defending against the noisy rush of time, moments when the landscape is silent and still are vital for Wordsworth, as they will be for Frost, when, for example, he addresses his daughter in a poem for her wedding, "The Master Speed," and wishes her "the power of standing still." Such moments in nature are precious for both poets because they evoke a corresponding "calm" from one's innermost being. God speaks to Wordsworth mainly during the pauses in the normal flow of discord and distracting sound. For Wordsworth, to respond fully to the imagery of nature—as if nature were God's book—required that he respond as well to the mystery of what God withholds: the purpose of suffering, as Job experiences its random appearance, or the uncertainty of whether one will receive God's mercy in the end. Just as Jesus used the language of metaphor and mystery—"And he spake many things unto them in parables"—so, too, the language of nature, for Wordsworth, was like that of a parable, and part of the grammar of that language, perhaps even its essence, was silence. To be in touch with the restorative power of divinity, Wordsworth needed to recollect and cherish the youthful experiences of silence that evoked in him a sense of the holy:

> Transcendent peace
> And silence did await upon these thoughts
> That were a frequent comfort to my youth.
> (*Prelude* VI, 139–41)[2]

Wordsworth responds to a landscape as if he were a reader perusing a text that invited his own interpretation. In the education of the young, landscape and books are inextricably linked, and Wordsworth wishes on behalf of all children: "May books and Nature be their early joy!" A direct analogy exists for Wordsworth between the landscape as parable and the poem as parable. The poem, in effect, extends the natural landscape into the landscape of the mind, and God's presence is made manifest in the human imagination as it responds to and interprets "Nature's self, which is the breath of God, / Or His pure Word." The "visionary power" that enables Wordsworth to have glimpses of divinity abides in the "motions of the viewless winds, / Embodied in the mystery of words." For Wordsworth, the natural landscape and the Bible are alike as symbolic forms and as sources of revelation, and the imagination is the God-given power to see nature in its symbolic and instructive aspect.

Wordsworth's masterpiece, "Michael," is a framed story in which the narrator first addresses the reader, then tells the story of Michael and his son, Luke, who leaves home never to return, and finally addresses the reader once again. The reader is invited into the story by being identified with the travelers on the "public way," who are given the choice to follow the narrator-guide into the "hidden valley" where Michael's story had been enacted. The relationship between the narrator-guide and the reader-traveler is crucial to the poem because it both parallels and contrasts with the relationship between Michael and Luke. The reader must decide whether to enter the landscape of the poem and listen to the story, and, finally, must determine how to interpret the story. The poem opens with the word "If"—"If from the public way you turn your steps / Up the tumultuous brook"—and everything that follows is seen as the consequence of choices, though mysterious forces from the past affect the outcome of those choices.

The identity of the reader-traveler is doubly complex. At the end of the poem's first paragraph, which completes the prologue before the story itself begins, the narrator says that he will relate Michael's history "for the delight of a few natural hearts." Here, the narrator assumes that some special bond exists between himself and his self-chosen readers that is like the bond John Milton describes between himself and his reader when he says, "fit audience find, though few" (a line that Wordsworth echoes exactly in *The Prelude*). But Wordsworth goes even further in identifying his reader by extending the image of his reader to include the "youthful poets" who will survive him. The major themes of transience and inheritance, for Wordsworth, are ineluctably bound together. Thus, the narrator's story (and Wordsworth's poem) will be written "with yet fonder feeling, for the sake / Of youthful Poets, who among these hills / Will be my second self when I am gone." In telling Michael's story, the narrator is, in effect, writing his will, leaving his inheritance to the future generations of poets. The main issue of the poem therefore lies in the question of how the narrator's telling of Michael's story will affect his readers and the successor poets yet to enter this landscape. The implied question that underlies "Michael" can be expressed as the following contingency: if the story about Michael and his son describes the breaking of a covenant, how does the *relating* of the story provide the means for the reestablishment of the same covenant?

Through his narrator, Wordsworth tells the story of Michael as if it were a parable. The narrator-guide says of Michael and his wife that "they were as a proverb in the vale / For endless industry," and, most important, the entire poem is suffused with allusions to and echoes of the Twenty-third Psalm with imagery of green pastures, paths of righteousness, valley, staff, and dwellings.

> *Psalm 23:* The Lord is my Shepherd
> *Wordsworth:* There dwelt a Shepherd, Michael was his name
> *Psalm 23:* He maketh me to lie down in green pastures
> *Wordsworth:* the tumultuous brook of Green-head Ghyll
> *Psalm 23:* the paths of righteousness
> *Wordsworth:* with an upright path / Your feet must struggle
> *Psalm 23:* the valley of the shadow of death
> *Wordsworth:* a hidden valley
> *Psalm 23:* thy rod and thy staff
> *Wordsworth:* a perfect shepherd's staff
> *Psalm 23:* thy rod and thy staff they comfort me
> *Wordsworth:* There is a comfort in the strength of love
> *Psalm 23:* I will dwell in the house of the Lord for ever.
> *Wordsworth:* at her death the estate was sold, . . . yet the oak is left . . .

Psalm 23 is the underlying text of Wordsworth's poem, just as the presence of God is inherent in the very landscape that Wordsworth describes: "And in the open sunshine of God's love / Have we all lived." Michael never prays directly to God, for what he knows of divinity is to be found abundantly in physical nature. Even after Michael realizes that his son will not return, the narrator tells us that "Among the rocks / He went, and still looked up to sun and cloud, / And listened to the wind." Michael seeks "comfort" after his son goes to the "dissolute city" and "slacken[s] in his duty," then vanishes from the poem and from Michael's life, never to return. But that comfort depends upon an interpretation of what the landscape reveals. Consolation, for Wordsworth, is the work of man, yet man always has available to him the palpable aid of nature as God's book, which always is present as an available source of both beauty and comfort. The physical world itself and the story within the poem contain twin aspects of God's immanence, His presence in nature where objects become also symbolic forms. Both world and poem thus come together as a recorded parable in which the mystery of suffering and redemption is to be accepted and embraced. The actual landscape, the Bible, the story of Michael and Luke, and Wordsworth's poem, all form a continuum of divinity, flowing through time and history, and that divinity, Wordsworth hopes, is there to be received by the reader, who also is a traveler in "the valley of the shadow of death."

The reader-traveler, having entered the poem and its valley "hidden" from the "public way," is shown the "straggling heap of unhewn stones" which inspires the telling of Michael's story. Without the narrator-guide to interpret them, the stones would have no meaning, and the reader-traveler " might pass by, / Might see and notice not." To understand these stones is to remember and keep alive the story of the broken covenant, the separation of father and son. Through no fault of his own, Luke must leave home in order to earn money to help pay off a family debt from the forgotten past:

> The Shepherd had been bound
> In surety for his brother's son, a man
> Of an industrious life, and ample means;
> But unforeseen misfortunes suddenly
> Had prest upon him; and old Michael now
> Was summoned to discharge the forfeiture.
> (Wordsworth 150)

The "patrimonial fields" that had bound Michael and Luke together in love are now seen to carry a burden and an ancestral curse, a blight that resembles "original sin." Ominously, when Luke leaves home, he disappears into the same "public way" where the reader has entered the poem: "when he [Luke] had reached / The public way, he put on a bold face." The bond between father and son, the link between Michael's happy family and the landscape that nurtured them, is broken, and Luke vanishes into a "hiding place beyond the seas."

What is the cause of this breaking of the family covenant? Who is at fault? Wordsworth has portrayed Michael's deep love for his son by depicting the motherly aspects of Michael's devotion and caretaking: "For oftentimes / Old Michael, while he [Luke] was a babe in arms, / Had done him female service, . . . and he had rocked / His cradle, as with a woman's gentle hand." Michael's physical powers ("His bodily frame had been from youth to age / Of an unusual strength") are enhanced and made complete by his tenderness and his capacity to express emotion, as when he and Luke together lay the first stone of the sheepfold: "The old Man's grief broke from him; to his heart / He pressed his Son, he kissed him and wept." Michael has been an ideal father to Luke, nurturing him, teaching him, working with him, and the reader is likely to agree with Michael's own representation of himself to his son: "Even to the utmost I have been to thee / A kind and a good father." And yet, the reader still wonders, might there have been a flaw in Michael's fathering?

The narrator tells us that Luke had been "prematurely called" to help Michael with the herding of the sheep. But we cannot demand inhuman perfection from Michael in the timing of the initiating process of his son in order for us to feel that Michael had been good to the "utmost." Wordsworth has portrayed Michael's humanness, but Luke's failure to maintain his father's values of loyalty and piety remains clouded in mystery. Wordsworth's description of Luke's fate is factual, without explanation, and astonishingly brief:

> Meantime Luke began
> To slacken in his duty; and, at length,
> He in the dissolute city gave himself
> To evil courses: ignominy and shame
> Fell on him, so that he was driven at last
> To seek a hiding-place beyond the seas.
>   (Wordsworth 155)

The city itself is not the sufficient cause of Luke's fall—since Luke, as Wordsworth insists, "gave himself"—but, rather, the city represents the unexplained presence of evil in the world. The city is a sign of the consequence of the broken covenant between man and the natural landscape, a manifestation of man's fallen condition, his predilection toward self-deception and lying, toward offering hypocritical "greetings where no kindness is," as Wordsworth describes alienation in this incisive phrase from "Tintern Abbey."

Despite his goodness and his piety, Michael is not unaware of the fact that there is evil in the world. He is exceptional in not succumbing to a self-deceiving sentimentality, yet open to the direct expression of emotion. The day before Luke must leave home, Michael takes him "Up to the heights," where the sheepfold is to be built, and instructs him:

> Lay now the corner-stone,
> As I requested; and hereafter, Luke,
> When thou art gone away, should evil men
> Be thy companions, think of me, my Son.
>   (Wordsworth 155)

Michael's words are disturbingly prophetic, for beneath their ominous warning lies the suggestion that somehow Michael knows that "evil" will break the "links of love" that have "bound" father and son. Nevertheless, Michael takes hope, and he promises Luke that "When thou return'st, thou in this place wilt see A work which is not here: a covenant / 'Twill be between us." The sheepfold which Michael plans to complete during Luke's absence will symbolize this "covenant," binding together father and son, man and landscape, the present and the future. The continuity of values from generation to generation is, precisely, what Wordsworth means by "hope," for it is the goodness of God's original creation of nature, according to His own proclamation, "and God saw that it was good," that forever defines what is valuable and is to be cherished. And yet, despite the hope inherent in laying the first stone of the sheepfold, Michael darkly concludes his last speech to Luke by saying that "whatever fate / Befall thee, I shall love thee to the last, / And bear thy memory with me to the grave." In a sense, Michael must take "fate" into his own hands, paradoxically, by accepting the fate of separation and loss, the fate that the covenant will be broken again as it has been repeatedly in the biblical past. Yet in accepting that fate of broken connection, love ceases to be dependent on a happy outcome, on rewarding circumstances; rather, the emotion of enduring love becomes its own fate.

To seek consolation simply in defeat, however, might seem somewhat perverse. Wordsworthian hope, though often threatened and challenged in his poetry, at its strongest is based on a covenant of sustained values and commitments. The building of the sheepfold, the manifestation of Michael's hopefulness, is his testament to the values of love and continuity that he has always cherished. As the symbol of the covenant, it represents Michael's will, his symbolic inheritance. The original covenant, which is the model for Michael, was reaffirmed between God and Noah when God promised that he would never send another flood to punish humankind for disobedience.

And I will establish my covenant with you; neither shall all flesh be cut off any more by the waters of a flood; neither shall there any more be a flood to destroy the earth. (Genesis 9:11)

And just as Michael needed a visible symbol of his covenant with Luke, so, too, the Lord before him had chosen to make visible his covenant with Noah in the image of the rainbow: "I do set my bow in the cloud, and it shall be for a token of a covenant between me and the earth." Throughout Wordsworth's poetry, with the biblical covenant in mind, the presence of God is to be found in "natural objects." Every image in a landscape, as in a poem, is therefore replete with symbolic implications that suggest God's presence in nature and invite each human observer to respond to God through his or her own interpretation of what the landscape is able to reveal to the active imagination.

In the biblical account, God continues to renew his covenant with his chosen people throughout the generations. It is of particular significance in Genesis 17:4–5, when God says to Abram: "Behold, my covenant *is* with thee, and thou shalt be a father of many nations. Neither shall thy name any more be called Abram, but thy name shall be Abraham." Abram is renamed to indicate his role as a "father of many nations" and thus as the carrier of God's covenant. God then further instructs Abraham:

And ye shall circumcise the flesh of your foreskin; and it shall be a token of the covenant betwixt me and you . . . and my covenant shall be in your flesh for an everlasting covenant. (Genesis 17:11–13)

Not only is God's covenant placed in nature, it is placed in the "flesh," so that the human body, like the landscape, also can be seen as revealing the immanence of God. Like God's reminder to Noah that he possesses destructive power to flood the earth that *he will not use,* God's decree of circumcision conveys the same message to Abraham: God could cut off the power of Abraham's paternity, but he chooses contingently not to do so. God's covenant through the use of circumcision is the alternative to God's punishment, and God's blessing to Abraham to become a father himself is God's reward for Abraham's maintaining of the covenant. Circumcision has the same function for Abraham as Michael's "threatening gestures" have for Luke; both are reminders of the potential aggression and destructiveness that love must subsume and overcome in order to make a covenant of continuity.

The story of father and son ends with Luke's disappearance to a "hiding-place beyond the seas." The covenant between them has been broken, but the cause of that rupture remains mysterious, even absurd. All we can say is that the cause seems to lie in the obscure family past as the result of an "evil choice" by an "evil man," whom Michael somehow must "forgive"; or the cause lies in the "burthened" fields, which seem to have a curse upon them—something like the rift between God as father and Adam as the disobedient son who must leave Eden, just as Luke must depart from the hidden valley. After the story's apparently hopeless conclusion, the narrator again addresses the traveler-reader, who is still looking at the pile of stones. But at least the reader now knows the history of those stones and what they were intended to be. The story of the stones, like the name given to a person, becomes inseparable from the objective fact of the stones themselves. It is astonishing that the narrator's tone, despite the tragic tale, maintains a quality of tranquility, as if a long process of mourning already has been completed.

The narrator begins the poem's epilogue by speaking of "comfort," when we might have felt that no comfort was to be found. He says: "There is a comfort in the strength of love," and we are reminded of Michael's last words to Luke, "I shall love thee to the last," as if the reader, too, is now able to partake of such love and, in turn, be strengthened by it. This comfort is grounded in communal memory, beginning with the narrator and Michael's neighbors—"I have conversed with more than one who well / Remember the old Man"—and now including the traveler-reader as well. Although the story is one that, without the strength of love, could "overset the brain, or break the heart," the telling of the story, astonishingly, has an opposite effect: it strengthens by releasing the source of human sympathy and compassion. The narrator asserts, "Tis not forgotten yet / The pity which was then in every heart / For the old Man!" Michael's neighbors, and now the readers of Wordsworth's poem, are all enlarged, their humanity expanded, by the hearing of Michael's story.

In "Elegiac Stanzas Suggested by a Picture of Peele Castle," Wordsworth's poem about the drowning of his brother, the same crucial idea of the strength to be found in shared sympathy is expressed in the line: "A deep distress hath humanized my soul." And this strength is also the source of the thoughts, transfiguring the tears of grief, that conclude the "Ode: Intimations of Immortality": "To me the meanest flower that blows can give / Thoughts that do often lie too deep for tears." Like Hamlet's mysterious evocation of one "who in suffering all, suffers nothing," Wordsworth's thoughts take him to a depth from whose perspective suffering somehow finds its acceptance as part of a larger and more encompassing vision of human life.

The poem's final image is of Michael "Sitting alone, or with his faithful Dog," beside the sheepfold, though we are told that "from time to time" he did continue to work at it. Nevertheless, the sheepfold does not get completed, and, looking at the pile of stones, we are forced to face the fact that Michael "left the work unfinished when he died." Michael's worst fears are realized when, after the death of his wife, the land is sold, their cottage is torn down, and "great changes," the inevitable effects of transience, make the neighborhood almost unrecognizable. Almost unrecognizable, but not totally so, for "the oak is left / That grew beside their door," and, above all, the "straggling heap of unhewn stones" is still there. We—the reader or the youthful poets Wordsworth imagines who follow after him—have left the "public way" and entered the "hidden valley" in order to learn of the history of these stones. The narrator-guide concludes, without explicitly drawing a moral, that "the remains / Of the unfinished Sheep-fold may be seen," though his voice intensifies into alliteration when he names the landscape in the final line, "Beside the boisterous brook of Greenhead Ghyll." And we, the inheritors, are left to make our own interpretation of what we have seen and heard.

Without the narrator, the pile of stones would have appeared merely as a pile of stones without symbolic import, nothing more. We have paused in our traveling through Wordsworth's version of "the valley of the shadow of death" in order to see "the remains / Of the unfinished Sheep-fold." "Remains" is the luminously suggestive word here. First of all, it means ruins, but after that another meaning of the word begins to resonate, for "remains" also implies that which endures and continues. Just as Michael bears Luke's memory to the grave, the reader now carries with him the memory of Michael's trial of endurance, his suffering, and the comfort of love that suffered no diminishment. In effect, the broken covenant is replaced by the *story* of the broken covenant, and it is now the reader's option to keep this story alive as both Michael's and Wordsworth's inheritance if he or she takes the story to heart. The poem as story and parable becomes the enlarged essence of an imagined identity, Erikson's "I am what survives me," through cherished remembrance. And should the reader be a "youthful Poet," he or she may, indeed, become the narrator's "second self," as proposed hopefully at the poem's beginning, through the transfiguring power of shared suffering and enduring love.

Wordsworth has given us a double story whose two lines are potentially parallel: Michael is to Luke as the narrator is to the reader. The covenant between Michael and Luke is broken, but the fate of the covenant between the narrator and the reader remains undecided. The reader or the youthful poet, should he so choose, can accept Michael's inheritance and thus replace Luke as the failed son, to become the son who does not break the continuity of the generations. By honoring the narrator's story, by electing to remember it and perhaps retell it, the reader, in effect, restores the covenant and completes the unfinished sheepfold. By making this free choice—which is just as mysterious as an act of will as Luke's inexplicable giving himself to "evil courses"—not only is Wordsworth's own pastoral poem kept alive, but Michael's story within Wordworth's poem is revivified as well. As we remember the shepherd, Michael, with the "perfect Shepherd's staff" made by his own hand, the comforting words of the ancestral Bible are reflected in the landscape itself, in the enduring oak tree, the boisterous brook, and the stones: "Yea, though I walk through the valley of the shadow of death, I will fear no evil: for thou *art* with me; thy rod and thy staff they comfort me." And thus, for Wordsworth, is the capacity for comfort passed on through the ages as a covenant composed equally of memory and of hope.

III

Wordsworth's "Michael" is a model for Robert Frost's "Wild Grapes" in several significant ways. One might well regard Frost here as Wordsworth's "second self." Both poems take as their protagonist an old person who is facing loss and death: the shepherd, Michael, and Frost's old woman who is the narrator in "Wild Grapes." Both poems are framed stories in which the narrator first addresses the reader, then tells a story, and finally addresses the reader again directly. In Wordsworth's poem, the reader is identified with the travelers on the "public way" who are led into a "hidden valley," and in Frost's poem, the reader is identified with the friends who are attending the old woman's birthday party at which she recounts having picked wild grapes with her older brother when she was five years old. Both narrators tell their stories as if they were parables of both nature's bounty and its power to take away everything one loves. Where the underlying text of Wordsworth's poem is the Twenty-third Psalm, the biblical text alluded to in Frost's poem is Luke 6:44: "For every tree is known by its own fruit: for of thorns men do not gather figs, nor of a bramble bush gather they grapes."

At the beginning of Frost's poem, in a spirit of enigmatic teasing, the old woman declaims to her friends who have gathered to celebrate her birthday:

> What tree may not the fig be gathered from?
> The grape may not be gathered from the birch?
> It's all you know the grape, or know the birch.
>
> (Frost 196)

The point of her joke is that in New England wild grape vines climb up birch trees, so that it is possible for grapes to be gathered from birches. Thus, it seems, contrary to the Bible, not every tree can be known by its own fruit. To understand the metaphorical truth of the Bible, therefore, requires local interpretation. (As Frost says elsewhere: "It takes all sorts of in and outdoor schooling / To get accustomed to my kind of fooling.") Beneath the old woman's natural lore, beneath her genial chiding, lies a serious need to tell a story and, finally, to make a statement about life and death, to sum up what she knows and pass her wisdom on to her friends as her inheritance to them.

Her initiation into knowledge as a child is achieved through a long process of self-projection and identification with others. This empathy commences with the old woman's depiction of her childhood self as if she were a grape:

> As a girl gathered from the birch myself
> Equally with my weight in grapes, one autumn,
> I ought to know what tree the grape is fruit of.
>   (Frost 196)

In relating how she was whisked up into the birch tree from which she was gathering grapes, couldn't get down by herself, and had to be rescued by her brother, she describes that historical day as if it were a second birthday, since her first "beginning" had been "wiped out in fear / The day I swung suspended from the grapes." In a sense her new life, which she comically calls her "extra life," having begun when she descended from the birch tree on the day she and her brother went grape collecting, finds its genesis in the fear that wipes out her first life, her innocence which was devoid of the sense of danger and the "weight" of mortality. Fear will come to be seen as a source of rebirth into necessary knowledge, and this fear will form the basis for Frost's later expressions, as in "The Masque of Mercy," of what he will call "The Fear of God." Continuing her joke, her in and outdoor fooling, the aged speaker says, "So if you see me celebrate two birthdays," and, drawn into her circle of intimacy, we, the readers, like her birthday party friends, await her story, which will become her gift to us to counter our own fears of transience and loss.

The story of the grape gathering is a parable of the passing-on of knowledge in which the older brother, acting as a guide, leads the young initiate into a special landscape that she must learn to interpret. In his function as a guide and teacher, the brother resembles Wordsworth's narrator in "Michael" who also leads us into the landscape and its history. Similarly, the bond between Frost's guiding brother and neophyte sister will develop into a covenant that, as in Wordsworth's poem, will not be completed. The old woman's prologue address to her birthday party friends shifts abruptly back into the past, which, in recollection, takes on the resonances of an anthropomorphic nature myth:

> One day my brother led me to a glade
> Where a white birch he knew of stood alone,
> Wearing a thin headdress of pointed leaves,
> And heavy on her heavy hair behind,
> Against her neck, an ornament of grapes.
>   (Frost 196–97)

The brother possesses knowledge of the landscape that the young girl desires, and the special "white birch he knew" is described as a kind of mother/earth goddess, a source of fertility and pleasure whose bounty the brother is willing to share with his sister, despite a measure of competitive sibling reluctance. In "climbing" the tree, the brother seems to master it with proud male domination, just as in Frost's companion poem, "Birches," the boy "subdued his father's trees / By riding them down." In "Wild Grapes," however, Oedipal rivalry between son and father for Mother Nature is, at most, implied, and the authoritative role played by the brother seems to combine father and brother in one. To further prove his prowess and mastery, the manifestations of his knowledge, the brother

> climbed still higher and bent the tree to earth
> And put it in my hands to pick my own grapes,
> "Here, take a treetop, I'll get down another.
> Hold on with all your might when I let go."
>
> (Frost 197)

With these resounding words of command, as if from the resident god of the mother tree, the brother has provided his sister with a holy text that, eventually, will require her own interpretation. She will have to make those words, "Hold on," her own, and, indeed, the dialectical phrases, "hold on" and "let go," which seem so casual and colloquial when first uttered, will become a kind of refrain and form the parabolic heart of the poem.

When her brother lets go of the tree branch the girl is holding, she is whisked up into the air like a caught fish. Her brother calls to her, "Let go! / Don't you know anything, you girl? Let go!" But the little girl, out of some primal instinct for survival not yet refined by knowledge, continues to hold on

> with something of the baby grip
> Acquired ancestrally in just such trees
> When wilder mothers than our wildest now
> Hung babies out on branches by the hands . . .
>
> (Frost 197)

Again the tree is represented as a mother, but now, by analogy, the implication is that the child soon must learn how to let go of parental protection, and we are told: "I held on uncomplainingly for life." What her brother teaches her about laughter is the next essential step in the process of her initiation, her learning to let go:

> My brother tried to make me laugh to help me.
> "What are you doing up there in those grapes?
> Don't be afraid. A few of them won't hurt you.
> I mean they won't pick you if you don't them."
>
> (Frost 197–98)

We may assume that the good-natured humor we see in the old woman at the poem's beginning is, at least in part, the gift of laughter she learned from her brother when in danger—the danger, it seemed, of being snatched off the face of the earth, "not to return," as Frost says of the boy in the same situation in "Birches."

The ability to confront fear with laughter is a revelation for the young girl, and it releases a new capacity for understanding in her that will enable her to comprehend her brother's next lesson—the concept of empathy which her brother introduces to her in comic form: "'Now you know how it feels,' my brother said, / 'To be a bunch of fox grapes.'" Partaking of her brother's identification of her with the bunch of hanging grapes that "thinks it has escaped the fox / By growing where it shouldn't—on a birch" foreshadows the empathy the old woman will have for the distress of the "others" at the end of the poem, the others who wish they could be spared the burden of consciousness when they are forced to face death.

Clinging to the tree, not knowing how to let go, the young girl loses her "hat and shoes," and this image of her being stripped of her human vestments suggests a reversal back from her human status to primal nakedness and her Darwinian monkey ancestry as suggested earlier in the poem. Her reversal back toward nakedness reminds the reader of our common creaturehood and our bodily vulnerability when confronted with natural danger in the physical environment. At first, her brother adds to the element of threat when he says, "'Drop or I'll shake the tree and shake you down,'" but then he realizes that her fear is genuine, and for a moment he is puzzled: "'Hold tight awhile till I think what to do / I'll bend the tree down and let you down by it.'" This descent marks her second birth, and with it the fall into her first realization of mortality. The echo on the word "down" in her brother's voice is sustained in the old woman's comment, "I don't know much about the letting down." However, when she feels the revolving earth again under her stockinged feet, she knows now how to look deeply: "I know I looked long at my curled-up fingers." That quintessential image intimates the Darwinian knowledge of her monkey ancestry, her future old age, and, above all, her power to hold on. Her brother, aware of his own responsibility in getting her up into the tree, and no doubt somewhat fearful himself, comically projects the blame onto her: "'Don't you weigh anything? / Try to weigh something next time, so you won't / Be run off by birch trees into space.'" This frightening moment is remembered in the spirit of the brother's comic teasing from the distant perspective of present time, and the reader, too, enjoys the humor. The brother, however, has taken his sister as far as he can in his role of comic guide, and it remains for the old woman to make her own interpretation in the epilogue of her brother's crucial distinction between "weight" and "knowledge," and her own interpretation of the symbolism inherent in the incantatory phrase, "letting go."

Commemorative; of life & death

Once again she directly addresses her friends at the birthday party, just as Wordsworth's narrator at the end of "Michael" directly addresses the readers as characters who have come to the hidden valley, where the story takes place, from the public way. Contrary to her brother's tease, "Try to weigh something next time," it was her weight that brought her back to earth, to her own "extra" life, which she now celebrates. What she lacked was not "weight," but the knowledge of weight—the knowledge of mortality: "My brother had been nearer right before. / I had not taken the first step in knowledge." Mortality returns everything to the earth. Learning is likened to walking, and the hike into the woods to gather grapes has its equivalent in an inner journey of the mind, making the literal landscape a symbolic one as well. The first step in knowledge, with its concomitant fear, is the awareness of death. To "let go with the hands" thus implies the necessity and inevitability of relinquishing one's own body back "down" to the "revolving" earth. Physically, one cannot hold on to life for long even if one is blessed with "extra life." The awareness of death does not require, however, that one stop loving life. Caring about ongoing life even at the brink of death realizes Erikson's description of the triumph of identity in old age in his formula of "I am what survives me." Ceasing to care, what Erikson means by despair, should not be a defense against desiring to hold on to your one life in spirit, which nevertheless you must let go in physical reality:

> I had not learned to let go with the hands,
> As still I have not learned to with the heart,
> And have no wish to with the heart—nor need,
> That I can see. The mind is not the heart.
> (Frost 199)

The distinction the old woman makes between the mind and heart is that the mind must "let go" while the heart must "hold on," but this apparent contradiction needs to be reconciled. Both attitudes toward life and death are necessary: the mind must affirm the equally valid knowledge of the heart. Her brother's words, "Hold on with all your might when I let go," have assumed a deep meaning for her—a meaning she has appropriated as her own, and thus the covenant between brother and sister lives on in her story, just as the covenant between narrator and reader is renewed in Wordsworth's retelling of Michael's story.

The old woman's thoughts now turn in empathy to the "others"—those who desire to escape thought in order not to face the reality of death, those who wish for the oblivion of "sleep." She knows that she, too, if she gave in to despair as the result of the awareness of transience, might suffer a failure of integrity and courage:

> I may yet live, as I know others live,
> To wish in vain to let go with the mind—
> Of cares, at night, to sleep.
>
> (Frost 199)

Confronting this final fear, however—the fear of the loss of self even in life, the uncertainty of whether one has the strength to maintain one's self-possession—the old woman affirms her hardwon knowledge that "nothing tells me / That I need learn to let go with the heart." Just as the Bible says that "every tree is known by its own fruit," so, too, the old woman becomes known to us, her inheritors, by the fruit of her knowledge, by her taste of humankind's fall, embodied in her comic parable about her initiation into the knowledge of mortality and the awareness of nature as a process of unending change that demands that humans relinquish what they innately wish to possess. But it is not just the mind's knowledge of mortality that matters; equally important is the attitude that the heart takes toward the mind's intellectual knowledge. The old woman's attitude is one of humor and sustained caring, and that perspective remains—just as the "remains" of Michael's unfinished sheepfold remain—to help sustain her friends and Frost's readers as her enduring inheritance. The old woman's gift of her story qualifies as a Frostian "momentary stay against confusion" and a respite from uncertainty—not the uncertainty about ultimate meanings or the design of a deity who may or may not exist, but the uncertainty as to whether or not anything matters, like the love of nature, the physical world itself that the imagination may perceive as being invested with symbolic richness. Continuing to care about family and friends until the last moment of consciousness is the gift of inheritance, overcoming fear and uncertainty, that Frost, in identification with the storytelling old woman, leaves to his readers.

William Wordsworth
MICHAEL
A PASTORAL POEM, 1800

If from the public way you turn your steps
Up the tumultuous brook of Greenhead Ghyll,
You will suppose that with an upright path
Your feet must struggle; in such bold ascent
The pastoral mountains front you, face to face.
But, courage! for around that boisterous brook
The mountains have all opened out themselves,
And made a hidden valley of their own.   *valley of the shadow of death.*
No habitation can be seen; but they
Who journey thither find themselves alone
With a few sheep, with rocks and stones, and kites
That overhead are sailing in the sky.
It is in truth an utter solitude;
Nor should I have made mention of this Dell
But for one object which you might pass by,
Might see and notice not. Beside the brook
Appears a straggling heap of unhewn stones!
And to that simple object appertains
A story—unenriched with strange events,
Yet not unfit, I deem, for the fireside,
Or for the summer shade. It was the first
Of those domestic tales that spake to me
Of Shepherds, dwellers in the valleys, men
Whom I already loved—not verily
For their own sakes, but for the fields and hills
Where was their occupation and abode.
And hence this Tale, while I was yet a Boy
Careless of books, yet having felt the power
Of Nature, by the gentle agency
Of natural objects, led me on to feel
For passions that were not my own, and think
(At random and imperfectly indeed)
On man, the heart of man, and human life.
Therefore, although it be a history
Homely and rude, I will relate the same
For the delight of a few natural hearts;
And, with yet fonder feeling, for the sake

our home is with infinity

Of youthful Poets, who among these hills   *like Luke for him .*
Will be my second self when I am gone.

    Upon the forest-side in Grasmere Vale
There dwelt a Shepherd, Michael was his name;
An old man, stout of heart, and strong of limb.
His bodily frame had been from youth to age
Of an unusual strength: his mind was keen,
Intense, and frugal, apt for all affairs,
And in his shepherd's calling he was prompt
And watchful more than ordinary men.
Hence had he learned the meaning of all winds,
Of blasts of every tone; and oftentimes,
When others heeded not, he heard the South
Make subterraneous music, like the noise
Of bagpipers on distant Highland hills.
The Shepherd, at such warning, of his flock
Bethought him, and he to himself would say,
'The winds are now devising work for me!'
And, truly, at all times, the storm, that drives
The traveller to a shelter, summoned him
Up to the mountains: he had been alone
Amid the heart of many thousand mists,
That came to him, and left him, on the heights.
So lived he till his eightieth year was past.
And grossly that man errs, who should suppose
That the green valleys, and the streams and rocks,
Were things indifferent to the Shepherd's thoughts.
Fields, where with cheerful spirits he had breathed
The common air; hills, which with vigorous step
He had so often climbed; which had impressed
So many incidents upon his mind
Of hardship, skill or courage, joy or fear;
Which, like a book, preserved the memory
Of the dumb animals, whom he had saved,
Had fed or sheltered, linking to such acts
The certainty of honourable gain;
Those fields, those hills—what could they less? had laid
Strong hold on his affections, were to him
A pleasurable feeling of blind love,
The pleasure which there is in life itself,
His days had not been passed in singleness.

His Helpmate was a comely matron, old—
Though younger than himself full twenty years.
She was a woman of a stirring life,
Whose heart was in her house: two wheels she had
Of antique form; this large, for spinning wool;
That small, for flax; and if one wheel had rest,
It was because the other was at work.
The Pair had but one inmate in their house,
An only Child, who had been born to them
When Michael, telling o'er his years, began
To deem that he was old,—in shepherd's phrase,
With one foot in the grave. This only Son,
With two brave sheep-dogs tried in many a storm,
The one of an inestimable worth,
Made all their household. I may truly say,
That they were as a proverb in the vale
For endless industry. When day was gone
And from their occupations out of doors
The Son and Father were come home, even then,
Their labour did not cease; unless when all
Turned to the cleanly supper-board, and there,
Each with a mess of pottage and skimmed milk,
Sat round the basket piled with oaten cakes,
And their plain home-made cheese. Yet when the meal
Was ended, Luke (for so the Son was named)
And his old Father both betook themselves
To such convenient work as might employ
Their hands by the fireside; perhaps to card
Wool for the Housewife's spindle, or repair
Some injury done to sickle, flail, or scythe,
Or other implement of house or field.
Down from the ceiling, by the chimney's edge,
That in our ancient uncouth country style
With huge and black projection overbrowed
Large space beneath, as duly as the light
Of day grew dim the Housewife hung a lamp;
An aged utensil, which had performed
Service beyond all others of its kind.
Early at evening did it burn—and late,
Surviving comrade of uncounted hours,
Which, going by from year to year, had found,
And left, the couple neither gay perhaps

Nor cheerful, yet with objects and with hopes,
Living a life of eager industry.
And now, when Luke had reached his eighteenth year,
There by the light of this old lamp they sate,
Father and Son, while far into the night
The Housewife plied her own peculiar work,
Making the cottage through the silent hours
Murmur as with the sound of summer flies.
This light was famous in its neighbourhood,
And was a public symbol of the life
That thrifty Pair had lived. For, as it chanced,
Their cottage on a plot of rising ground
Stood single, with large prospect, north and south,
High into Easedale, up to Dunmail-Raise,
And westward to the village near the lake;
And from this constant light, so regular
And so far seen, the House itself, by all
Who dwelt within the limits of the vale,
Both old and young, was named The Evening Star.

Thus living on through such a length of years,
The Shepherd, if he loved himself, must needs
Have loved his Helpmate; but to Michael's heart
This son of his old age was yet more dear—
Less from instinctive tenderness, the same
Fond spirit that blindly works in the blood of all—
Than that a child, more than all other gifts
That earth can offer to declining man,
Brings hope with it, and forward-looking thoughts,
And stirrings of inquietude, when they
By tendency of nature needs must fail.
Exceeding was the love he bare to him,
His heart and his heart's joy! For oftentimes
Old Michael, while he was a babe in arms,
Had done him female service, not alone
For pastime and delight, as is the use
Of fathers, but with patient mind enforced
To acts of tenderness; and he had rocked
His cradle, as with a woman's gentle hand.

And, in a later time, ere yet the Boy
Had put on boy's attire, did Michael love,

Albeit of a stern unbending mind,
To have the Young-one in his sight, when he
Wrought in the field, or on his shepherd's stool
Sate with a fettered sheep before him stretched
Under the large old oak, that near his door
Stood single, and, from matchless depth of shade,
Chosen for the Shearer's covert from the sun,
Thence in our rustic dialect was called
The Clipping Tree, a name which yet it bears.
There, while they two were sitting in the shade,
With others round them, earnest all and blithe,
Would Michael exercise his heart with looks
Of fond correction and reproof bestowed
Upon the Child, if he disturbed the sheep
By catching at their legs, or with his shouts
Scared them, while they lay still beneath the shears.

And when by Heaven's good grace the boy grew up
A healthy Lad, and carried in his cheek
Two steady roses that were five years old;
Then Michael from a winter coppice cut
With his own hand a sapling, which he hooped
With iron, making it throughout in all
Due requisites a perfect shepherd's staff,
And gave it to the Boy; wherewith equipt
He as a watchman oftentimes was placed
At gate or gap, to stem or turn the flock;
And, to his office prematurely called,
There stood the urchin, as you will divine,
Something between a hindrance and a help;
And for this cause not always, I believe,
Receiving from his Father hire of praise;
Though nought was left undone which staff, or voice,
Or looks, or threatening gestures, could perform.

But soon as Luke, full ten years old, could stand
Against the mountain blasts; and to the heights,
Not fearing toil, nor length of weary ways,
He with his Father daily went, and they
Were as companions, why should I relate
That objects which the Shepherd loved before
Were dearer now? that from the Boy there came

Feelings and emanations—things which were
Light to the sun and music to the wind;
And that the old Man's heart seemed born again?

Thus in his Father's sight the Boy grew up:
And now, when he had reached his eighteenth year,
He was his comfort and his daily hope.

While in this sort the simple household lived
From day to day, to Michael's ear there came
Distressful tidings. Long before the time
Of which I speak, the Shepherd had been bound
In surety for his brother's son, a man
Of an industrious life, and ample means;
But unforeseen misfortunes suddenly
Had prest upon him; and old Michael now
Was summoned to discharge the forfeiture,
A grievous penalty, but little less
Than half his substance. This unlooked-for claim,
At the first hearing, for a moment took
More hope out of his life than he supposed
That any old man ever could have lost.
As soon as he had armed himself with strength
To look his trouble in the face, it seemed
The Shepherd's sole resource to sell at once
A portion of his patrimonial fields.
Such was his first resolve; he thought again,
And his heart failed him. 'Isabel,' said he,
Two evenings after he had heard the news,
'I have been toiling more than seventy years,
And in the open sunshine of God's love
Have we all lived; yet, if these fields of ours
Should pass into a stranger's hand, I think
That I could not lie quiet in my grave.
Our lot is a hard lot; the sun himself
Has scarcely been more diligent than I;
And I have lived to be a fool at last
To my own family. An evil man
That was, and made an evil choice, if he
Were false to us; and, if he were not false,
There are ten thousand to whom loss like this
Had been no sorrow. I forgive him;—but

'Twere better to be dumb than to talk thus.

'When I began, my purpose was to speak
Of remedies and of a cheerful hope.
Our Luke shall leave us, Isabel; the land
Shall not go from us, and it shall be free;
He shall possess it, free as is the wind
That passes over it. We have, thou know'st,
Another kinsman—he will be our friend
In this distress. He is a prosperous man,
Thriving in trade—and Luke to him shall go,
And with his kinsman's help and his own thrift
He quickly will repair this loss, and then
He may return to us. If here he stay,
What can be done? Where every one is poor,
What can be gained?'
                              At this the old Man paused,
And Isabel sat silent, for her mind
Was busy, looking back into past times.
There's Richard Bateman, thought she to herself,
He was a parish-boy—at the church-door
They made a gathering for him, shillings, pence
And halfpennies, wherewith the neighbours bought
A basket, which they filled with pedlar's wares;
And, with this basket on his arm, the lad
Went up to London, found a master there,
Who, out of many, chose the trusty boy
To go and overlook his merchandise
Beyond the seas; where he grew wondrous rich,
And left estates and monies to the poor,
And, at his birth-place, built a chapel floored
With marble, which he sent from foreign lands.
These thoughts, and many others of like sort,
Passed quickly through the mind of Isabel,
And her face brightened. The old Man was glad,
And thus resumed:—"Well, Isabel! this scheme
These two days has been meat and drink to me.
Far more than we have lost is left us yet.   ⅄
—We have enough—I wish indeed that I
Were younger;—but this hope is a good hope.
Make ready Luke's best garments, of the best
Buy for him more, and let us send him forth

To-morrow, or the next day, or to-night:
If he *could* go, the Boy should go tonight.'

Here Michael ceased, and to the fields went forth
With a light heart. The Housewife for five days
Was restless morn and night, and all day long
Wrought on with her best fingers to prepare
Things needful for the journey of her son.
But Isabel was glad when Sunday came
To stop her in her work: for, when she lay
By Michael's side, she through the last two nights
Heard him, how he was troubled in his sleep:
And when they rose at morning she could see
That all his hopes were gone. That day at noon
She said to Luke, while they two by themselves
Were sitting at the door, 'Thou must not go:
We have no other Child but thee to lose
None to remember—do not go away,
For if thou leave thy Father he will die.'
The Youth made answer with a jocund voice;
And Isabel, when she had told her fears,
Recovered heart. That evening her best fare
Did she bring forth, and all together sat
Like happy people round a Christmas fire.

With daylight Isabel resumed her work;
And all the ensuing week the house appeared
As cheerful as a grove in Spring: at length
The expected letter from their kinsman came,
With kind assurances that he would do
His utmost for the welfare of the Boy;
To which, requests were added, that forthwith
He might be sent to him. Ten times or more
The letter was read over; Isabel
Went forth to show it to the neighbours round;
Nor was there at that time on English land
A prouder heart than Luke's. When Isabel
Had to her house returned, the old Man said,
'He shall depart to-morrow.' To this word
The Housewife answered, talking much of things
Which, if at such short notice he should go,
Would surely be forgotten. But at length
She gave consent, and Michael was at ease.

Near the tumultuous brook of Greenhead Ghyll,
In that deep valley, Michael had designed
To build a Sheep-fold; and, before he heard
The tidings of his melancholy loss,
For this same purpose he had gathered up
A heap of stones, which by the streamlet's edge
Lay thrown together, ready for the work.
With Luke that evening thitherward he walked:
And soon as they had reached the place he stopped,
And thus the old Man spake to him: 'My son,
To-morrow thou wilt leave me: with full heart
I look upon thee, for thou art the same
That wert a promise to me ere thy birth,
And all thy life hast been my daily joy.
I will relate to thee some little part
Of our two histories; 'twill do thee good
When thou art from me, even if I should touch
On things thou canst not know of.—After thou
First cam'st into the world—as oft befalls
To new-born infants—thou didst sleep away
Two days, and blessings from thy Father's tongue
Then fell upon thee. Day by day passed on,
And still I loved thee with increasing love.
Never to living ear came sweeter sounds
Than when I heard thee by our own fireside
First uttering, without words, a natural tune;
While thou, a feeding babe, didst in thy joy
Sing at thy Mother's breast. Month followed month,
And in the open fields my life was passed
And on the mountains; else I think that thou
Hadst been brought up upon thy Father's knees.
But we were playmates, Luke: among these hills,
As well thou knowest, in us the old and young
Have played together, nor with me didst thou
Lack any pleasure which a boy can know.'
Luke had a manly heart; but at these words
He sobbed aloud. The old Man grasped his hand,
And said, 'Nay, do not take it so—I see
That these are things of which I need not speak.
—Even to the utmost I have been to thee
A kind and a good Father: and herein
I but repay a gift which I myself
Received at others' hands; for, though now old

Beyond the common life of man, I still
Remember them who loved me in my youth.
Both of them sleep together: here they lived,
As all their Forefathers had done; and, when
At length their time was come, they were not loth
To give their bodies to the family mould.
I wished that thou should'st live the life they lived:
But 'tis a long time to look back, my Son,
And see so little gain from threescore years.
These fields were burthened when they came to me;
Till I was forty years of age, not more
Than half of my inheritance was mine.
I toiled and toiled; God blessed me in my work,
And till these three weeks past the land was free.
—It looks as if it never could endure
Another master. Heaven forgive me, Luke,
If I judge ill for thee, but it seems good
That thou should'st go.'
                      At this the old Man paused;
Then, pointing to the stones near which they stood,
Thus, after a short silence, he resumed:
'This was a work for us; and now, my Son,
It is a work for me. But, lay one stone—
Here, lay it for me, Luke, with thine own hands.
Nay, Boy, be of good hope;—we both may live
To see a better day. At eighty-four
I still am strong and hale;—do thou thy part;
I will do mine.—I will begin again
With many tasks that were resigned to thee:
Up to the heights, and in among the storms,
Will I without thee go again, and do
All works which I was wont to do alone,
Before I knew thy face.—Heaven bless thee, Boy!
Thy heart these two weeks has been beating fast
With many hopes; it should be so—yes—yes—
I knew that thou could'st never have a wish
To leave me, Luke: thou hast been bound to me
Only by links of love: when thou art gone,
What will be left to us!—But I forget
My purposes. Lay now the corner-stone,
As I requested; and hereafter, Luke,
When thou art gone away, should evil men

Be thy companions, think of me, my Son,
And of this moment; hither turn thy thoughts,
And God will strengthen thee; amid all fear
And all temptation, Luke, I pray that thou
May'st bear in mind the life thy Fathers lived,
Who, being innocent, did for that cause
Bestir them in good deeds. Now, fare thee well—
When thou return'st, thou in this place wilt see
A work which is not here: a covenant
'Twill be between us; but, whatever fate
Befall thee, I shall love thee to the last,
And bear thy memory with me to the grave.'

  The Shepherd ended here; and Luke stooped down,
And, as his Father had requested, laid
The first stone of the Sheep-fold. At the sight
The old Man's grief broke from him; to his heart
He pressed his Son, he kissed him and wept;
And to the house together they returned.
—Hushed was that House in peace, or seeming peace,
Ere the night fell;—with morrow's dawn the Boy
Began his journey, and when he had reached
The public way, he put on a bold face;
And all the neighbours, as he passed their doors,
Came forth with wishes and with farewell prayers,
That followed him till he was out of sight.

  A good report did from their Kinsman come,
Of Luke and his well-doing: and the Boy
Wrote loving letters, full of wondrous news,
Which, as the Housewife phrased it, were throughout
'The prettiest letters that were ever seen.'
Both parents read them with rejoicing hearts.
So, many months passed on; and once again
The Shepherd went about his daily work
With confident and cheerful thoughts; and now
Sometimes when he could find a leisure hour
He to that valley took his way, and there
Wrought at the Sheep-fold. Meantime Luke began
To slacken in his duty; and, at length,
He in the dissolute city gave himself
To evil courses; ignominy and shame

Fell on him, so that he was driven at last
To seek a hiding-place beyond the seas.

There is a comfort in the strength of love;
'Twill make a thing endurable, which else
Would overset the brain, or break the heart:
I have conversed with more than one who well
Remember the old Man, and what he was
Years after he had heard this heavy news.
His bodily frame had been from youth to age
Of an unusual strength. Among the rocks
He went, and still looked up to sun and cloud,
And listened to the wind; and, as before,
Performed all kinds of labour for his sheep,
And for the land, his small inheritance.
And to that hollow dell from time to time
Did he repair, to build the Fold of which
His flock had need. 'Tis not forgotten yet
The pity which was then in every heart
For the old Man—and 'tis believed by all
That many and many a day he thither went,
And never lifted up a single stone.

There, by the Sheep-fold, sometimes was he seen
Sitting alone, or with his faithful Dog,
Then old, beside him, lying at his feet.
The length of full seven years, from time to time,
He at the building of this Sheep-fold wrought,
And left the work unfinished when he died.
Three years, or little more, did Isabel
Survive her Husband: at her death the estate
Was sold, and went into a stranger's hand.
The Cottage which was named The Evening Star
Is gone—the ploughshare has been through the ground
On which it stood; great changes have been wrought
In all the neighbourhood:—yet the oak is left
That grew beside their door; and the remains
Of the unfinished Sheep-fold may be seen
Beside the boisterous brook of Greenhead Ghyll.

Robert Frost
WILD GRAPES

What tree may not the fig be gathered from?
The grape may not be gathered from the birch?
It's all you know the grape, or know the birch.
As a girl gathered from the birch myself
Equally with my weight in grapes, one autumn,
I ought to know what tree the grape is fruit of.
I was born, I suppose, like anyone,
And grew to be a little boyish girl
My brother could not always leave at home.
But that beginning was wiped out in fear
The day I swung suspended with the grapes,
And was come after like Eurydice
And brought down safely from the upper regions;
And the life I live now's an extra life
I can waste as I please on whom I please.
So if you see me celebrate two birthdays,
And give myself out as two different ages,
One of them five years younger than I look—

One day my brother led me to a glade
Where a white birch he knew of stood alone,
Wearing a thin headdress of pointed leaves,
And heavy on her heavy hair behind,
Against her neck, an ornament of grapes.
Grapes, I knew grapes from having seen them last year.
One bunch of them, and there began to be
Bunches all round me growing in white birches,
The way they grew round Leif the Lucky's German;
Mostly as much beyond my lifted hands, though,
As the moon used to seem when I was younger,
And only freely to be had for climbing.
My brother did the climbing; and at first
Threw me down grapes to miss and scatter
And have to hunt for in sweet fern and hardhack;
Which gave him some time to himself to eat,
But not so much, perhaps, as a boy needed.
So then, to make me wholly self-supporting,
He climbed still higher and bent the tree to earth

And put it in my hands to pick my own grapes.
"Here, take a treetop, I'll get down another.
Hold on with all your might when I let go."
I said I had the tree. It wasn't true.
The opposite was true. The tree had me.
The minute it was left with me alone,
It caught me up as if I were the fish
And it the fishpole. So I was translated
To loud cries from my brother of "Let go!
Don't you know anything, you girl? Let go!"
But I, with something of the baby grip
Acquired ancestrally in just such trees
When wilder mothers than our wildest now
Hung babies out on branches by the hands
To dry or wash or tan, I don't know which
(You'll have to ask an evolutionist)—
I held on uncomplainingly for life.
My brother tried to make me laugh to help me.
"What are you doing up there in those grapes?
Don't be afraid. A few of them won't hurt you.
I mean, they won't pick you if you don't them."
Much danger of my picking anything!
By that time I was pretty well reduced
To a philosophy of hang-and-let-hang.
"Now you know how it feels," my brother said,
"To be a bunch of fox grapes, as they call them,
That when it thinks it has escaped the fox
By growing where it shouldn't—on a birch,
Where a fox wouldn't think to look for it—
And if he looked and found it, couldn't reach it—
Just then come you and I to gather it.
Only you have the advantage of the grapes
In one way: you have one more stem to cling by,
And promise more resistance to the picker."

One by one I lost off my hat and shoes,
And still I clung. I let my head fall back,
And shut my eyes against the sun, my ears
Against my brother's nonsense. "Drop," he said,
"I'll catch you in my arms. It isn't far."
(Stated in lengths of him it might not be.)
"Drop or I'll shake the tree and shake you down."

Grim silence on my part as I sank lower,
My small wrists stretching till they showed the banjo strings.
"Why, if she isn't serious about it!
Hold tight awhile till I think what to do.
I'll bend the tree down and let you down by it."
I don't know much about the letting down;
But once I felt ground with my stocking feet
And the world came revolving back to me,
I know I looked long at my curled-up fingers,
Before I straightened them and brushed the bark off.
My brother said: "Don't you weigh anything?
Try to weigh something next time, so you won't
Be run off with by birch trees into space."

It wasn't my not weighing anything
So much as my not knowing anything—
My brother had been nearer right before.
I had not taken the first step in knowledge;
I had not learned to let go with the hands,
As still I have not learned to with the heart,
And have no wish to with the heart—nor need,
That I can see. The mind—is not the heart.
I may yet live, as I know others live,
To wish in vain to let go with the mind—
Of cares, at night, to sleep; but nothing tells me
That I need learn to let go with the heart.

✍ Chapter 4

Mourning and Acceptance

I

Poetry is a natural medium for the expression and communication of both lamentation and celebration: each emotion provides a counterbalance to the other. Lamentation runs the risk of being self-indulgent and self-pitying, and celebration runs the risk of being sentimental and willfully blind to the inescapable causes of human suffering. In its most overt aspect, lamentation takes the form of mourning another's death, but it also can express one's mourning for one's own mortality through the identification with others. While the goal of mourning one's own death must be the acceptance of the fate of mortality and the willingness to identify with one's beloved survivors, the healthy goal of mourning someone else's death is to exorcise grief through the very act of grieving. Poetic expression, deliberate and formally controlled, can help bring mourning to an end through a process of catharsis so that one can begin again to respond to what is beautiful or good in life in an act of renewed celebration.

There is something perversely insistent, however, about mourning that seeks to perpetuate itself, that tends to feed on itself, as if the deepest goal of mourning is not to return to normal contentment or acceptance, but to immortalize grief, to be true to the loss of the departed loved one by not allowing grief to diminish. In this negative state of mind, expression, including poetic expression, will not have a cathartic effect, but will reinforce grief. Part of the healthy function of a poem is to recognize and acknowledge this temptation to prolong mourning or to make of lamentation an end in itself. This is precisely what Tennyson does in his great elegy, "In Memoriam,"[1] in response to the death by drowning of his admired and beloved friend Arthur Hallam when, late in the sequence, he cries out in astonished and sudden self-awareness, "O last regret, regret can die!" as if he were not willing to relinquish regret as the mark of his identity as a griever. He is compelled to hold on to his grief through regret so that he can maintain, in Freud's phrase, "an identification of the ego with the abandoned object" (159).[2] Without his profound psychological awareness of grief as a form of temptation, Tennyson could not go on later in the poem to relinquish this tenacious form of grief that turns in upon itself and return to the mode of natural celebration in which he finally is able to say: "and in my breast / Spring wakens too, and my regret / Becomes an April violet, / and buds and blossoms like the rest."

Just as Tennyson has to overcome his impulse to cling to regret as if it were the only way to remain faithful to his drowned friend, so, too, does Wordsworth, in his sonnet "Surprised by Joy," dwell compulsively on the memory of his daughter, Catherine, who died at age three:

> Surprised by joy—impatient as the Wind
> I turned to share the transport—Oh! with whom
> But Thee, deep buried in the silent tomb,
> That spot which no vicissitude can find?
> Love, faithful love, recalled thee to my mind—
> But how could I forget thee? Through what power,
> Even for the least division of an hour,
> Have I been so beguiled as to be blind
> To my most grievous loss!—That thought's return
> Was the worst pang that sorrow ever bore,
> Save one, one only, when I stood forlorn,
> Knowing my heart's best treasure was no more;
> That neither present time, nor years unborn
> Could to my sight that heavenly face restore.
>
> (Wordsworth 420)[3]

Caught up in a moment of joy in response to a gust of wind, the poet instinctively turns to share the transport with his daughter as if she were still alive. (Wind often was invoked by Wordsworth as an allusion to God's inspiring creative force as in the opening of *The Prelude:* "There is a blessing in the gentle breeze.") This moment of joy in response to nature's blessing is contingent on Wordsworth's having forgotten for a moment that his daughter is dead and that Wordsworth had allowed himself, in effect, to have stopped grieving for her. And then in response to his own forgetting—But how could I forget thee?—Wordsworth is smitten with a fresh pang of guilt for having ceased to grieve and for allowing his mourning seemingly to come to an end. Thus, with this guilt, his grief and his mourning resume freshly as the returned recognition of "his most grievous loss." Grief returns redoubled and renewed as the recollection of his daughter's death undoes his moment of joy and turns blessing into a curse: "That thought's return / Was the worst pang that sorrow ever bore." At the poem's end, submerged in guilt and renewed mourning, Wordsworth realizes that nothing can restore the sight of his daughter. The description of her "heavenly face" is laden with self-lacerating irony resulting from the fact that Wordsworth's earthly existence is defined by his distance from heaven, with the inescapable suggestion that for Wordsworth, so it seems here, mourning can never complete itself and achieve a resolution.

In "Elegiac Stanzas Suggested by a Picture of Peele Castle," likewise, a poem written in response to the drowning of his brother, John, Wordsworth struggles to relinquish the morbid demand within his heart to go on mourning forever: "The feeling of my loss will ne'er be old." But by the end of the poem, a willingness to loosen his grip on grief begins to emerge ever so slightly, and Wordsworth begrudgingly allows himself a glimmer of hopefulness: "Not without hope, we suffer and we mourn," he tentatively concludes. The hope Wordsworth speaks of here, however, is ambiguous. Is it simply the hope of "fortitude," that he can go on like the symbolic castle he depicts, "Cased in the unfeeling armour of old time," half numb, yet able to endure? Or is the hope closer to his previous confidence in a meaningful divine plan that Wordsworth could once see revealed in nature? The death of his brother has shattered Wordsworth's faith that "Nature never did betray the heart that loved her" ("Tintern Abbey"), and now Wordsworth has to grope his way back to recover his capacity for celebration, his delight in the immemorial forms of natural beauty that outlast human sorrow and human grieving and remain as a source of possible consolation.

II

In William Blake's poem "The Poison Tree,"[4] the speaker of the poem, as a result of repressing his anger, falls into a state of denial in which he splits himself off from his own self-awareness and, in effect, becomes his own "foe." Except for the title, which belongs to Blake the poet, the remainder of the poem is spoken by an imaginary character, and it is essential for the reader, as we shall see, to separate Blake from the poem's self-deceiving protagonist. Blake's poem appears to be set physically in the Garden of Eden, but the poem literally takes place as the malign fantasy of the speaker whose mind becomes a corrupted garden—a place of death rather than life. The whole poem then is a nightmare with a false awakening at the end—actually a nightmare within a nightmare, the mind trapped inside itself.

I was angry with my friend:
I told my wrath, my wrath did end.
I was angry with my foe:
I told it not, my wrath did grow.

And I watered it in fears
Night and morning with my tears,
And I sunned it with smiles
And with soft deceitful wiles.

And it grew both day and night,
Till it bore an apple bright,
And my foe beheld it shine,
And he knew that it was mine,—

And into my garden stole
When the night had veiled the pole;
In the morning, glad, I see
My foe outstretched beneath the tree.

(Blake 28)

We see the narrator at the poem's beginning as possessing the ability to understand his own wrath—an emotion that every human being experiences at some time—and as having sufficient knowledge to free himself from his resentful anger by giving overt expression to it. As the first two lines reveal, the narrator understands that the expression of wrath can liberate one from one's wrath. The split within the speaker has not yet taken place. What we see next, however, in lines 3 and 4, is a foe distinguished from the friend only by the way in which the speaker chooses to regard the foe. He is angry at both of them, but when the speaker fails to exorcise his anger through expression, that anger dominates and usurps his mind. In effect, the foe is the same person as the friend but without the wrath being "told." The speaker's wrathful mind, then, becomes a perverted or fallen garden; his thinking becomes twisted and paranoid: night is mistaken for day; fantasy, for reality; lies, for truth. Things that should nurture have a poisonous effect. In his mind, the speaker recreates himself as a Satanic figure, confusing Satan and God, perverting God's benevolence in the forms of water and sun into destructive forces.

The central image of the poem, the apple, now represents the speaker's own poisoned sensibility, his self-forbidden knowledge of himself that splits him off from the part of himself that is able to express and therefore dissipate wrath. The apple begins to grow, extending the effect and influence of his false knowledge, his lie. Throughout the poem we do not see an objective garden—nature as it is—we see only the speaker's projection of his own wrath and jealousy onto his surroundings. The speaker comes to mistake his own prevarication for reality; therefore, the foe continues to exist as foe, beyond forgiveness or reconciliation, because the speaker fears him as a projection of his own wrathful self. Although he does not understand that he is making such a projection—for his capability of understanding as shown in the first two lines has been repressed—the speaker suffers from the dread of his own wrath, and already we sense that unconsciously he is mourning the loss of his earlier unfallen self. Blake's ingenious parallel to the biblical story reveals that the blasphemous speaker is comparing himself to God, the true creator of the garden. It follows then that the foe who eats the apple in this revision of the biblical myth is Adam, for Blake is parodying the concept of a jealous God (called "Nobodaddy" in another poem) who takes satanic delight in poisoning mankind, his foe, the rebellious Adam. Through the depiction of the narrator's poisoned mind, Blake's satire dramatizes his belief that it is a failed imagining on the part of society to conceive of God as being jealous or wrathful. Blake shows how people can become corrupted when their imaginations become corrupted and when their religious institutions, as in "The Garden of Love," are founded on repression and false mythology. Blake takes it to be part of his role as artist to satirize these false assumptions and beliefs.

As the poem proceeds, everything the speaker sees is distorted by the darkness of his own mind, which is caused, at least in part, by his being split off from himself. In effect, the poem is the speaker's own nightmare in which his guilty wish of aggression is both enacted and punished by turning on itself. The snake of false knowledge—knowledge obscured by a disintegrated psyche—is implied in the poem through the image of the pole—since the medical insignia for cure is a pole with a snake wrapped around it, an emblem of curative force, evil acknowledged and overcome. But Blake diagnoses the cause of the failure of the mind's curative force as the failure of the imagination to overcome repression and free itself through the catharsis of expression.

At the end of the poem, the speaker seems to wake up happily; his wrath appears to have triumphed over his enemy. But there is little reason to trust anything that this speaker says by this point in the poem. He has proclaimed himself to be a deceiver and a liar, and to admit that he is lying does not make him truthful; it merely reveals to the reader that the admission itself is a kind of lie, since no repentance follows. Although we cannot trust the speaker of the poem, we can trust the poem itself and its author, Blake, who knows that a tree that is nutritious in nature becomes poisoned in the mind of the speaker when it is turned into a symbol of fatal temptation. As Blake says of the fruit of Deceit in his poem "The Human Abstract":

> The Gods of the earth and sea,
> Sought thro Nature to find this Tree
> But their search was all in vain:
> There grows one in the Human brain.
>> (Blake 27)

What is being repressed, and the consequences of this repression, is revealed to the reader, beyond the narrator, through the poem's structure, the division between friend and foe, which represents, as well, the division within the speaker's mind caused by repression. The words of the speaker, the manifest level of the poem, function as the surface of an unconscious confession and reveal exactly what the speaker is lying to himself about: that he feels good for having acted out of wrath. His poisoned mind is no longer free to acknowledge his guilt. The speaker's denial of this guilt, his repressed *mourning*—as implied by the pun (unconscious to the speaker) on the word "morning"—holds him fixed in his own self-deceit as, once again, we see how the repression of mourning perpetuates grief.

The figure of Adam at the end of the poem as the murdered foe, seemingly God's enemy, is extended into the figure of Christ (the second Adam) in the image of his crucifixion, outstretched beneath the tree. The tree of life, through repression and denial, has become the tree of death. Thus in Blake's satiric poem, the true spirit of Christianity, which embraces the virtue of forgiveness, has been sacrificed, and the speaker awakens to his own mistaken nightmare version of wrath and murder. This is not, however, truly an awakening, for the narrator is still trapped in his own guilty mind, his corrupted garden of wrath. And this nightmare will continue to replace the real world, as Blake conceives of it, until the human mind is rescued by a new imagining of an unfallen nature, of a garden with nonpoisonous fruit. Such a healthy garden is implied by the parodic perspective offered by the poem itself.

The reader comprehends the speaker's self-deception from the poem's perspective, which is the opposite of the outlook maintained by the speaker. The total effect of the poem, then, is to intensify the reader's awareness of what the speaker has falsified, and through Blake's doubling of visions, true and false, wrath exorcised and wrath repressed, the visionary poet presents an image of the mind with its capacity for imaginative understanding despite both its vulnerability to self-deception and its inclination to deceive others. With the dramatization of the divided self, in which one part of the self murders the other, Blake provides his readers with the necessary knowledge and insight to make possible the healing of the mind so that Christian forbearance (Blake's earlier title for the poem) and self-redemption may be awakened and become an actuality. Only when this true awakening is achieved will the mind be able to cease mourning its betrayal of itself and make of a fallen Garden of Eden a New Jerusalem.

III

In Gerard Manley Hopkins's poem "Spring and Fall: to a Young Child,"[5] Hopkins's narrative moves from the image of a young girl weeping at the falling of the leaves to an imagined image of the grown woman who no longer is capable of identifying with nature's imagery:

> Márgarét, are you grieving
> Over Goldengrove unleaving?
> Leáves, líke the things of man, you
> With your fresh thoughts care for, can you?
> Ah! aś the heart grows older
> It will come to such sights colder
> By and by, nor spare a sigh
> Though worlds of wanwood leafmeal lie;
> And yet you *wíll* weep and know why.
> Now no matter, child, the name:
> Sórrows spríngs áre the same.
> Nor mouth had, no nor mind, expressed
> What heart heard of, ghost guessed:
> It iś the blight man was born for,
> It is Margaret you mourn for.
> (Hopkins 19; stress markings his own)

The first pronunciation of the girl's name is diminutive—Márgarét—but by the end of the poem she will be called Margaret, her adult name. The poem's narrator is watching the girl and thinking to himself; he is not speaking to the child. A mature man, seeing a girl crying because the leaves are falling, would not approach her and tell her: "It is the blight man was born for, / It is Margaret you mourn for." Surely, the poem takes place in the mind of the speaker, for what he has to say to her in the isolation of his own mind is precisely what he cannot articulate to her out loud. Language is a barrier between them, not a means of connection, because of what the unspoken words would be compelled to convey, and thus these words will be repressed. This poem is about separation, about barriers: the leaves are to Margaret what Margaret is to the speaker—both Margaret and the speaker are watching images of a fall, yet they cannot share their similar sorrows. Their individual mourning keeps them apart.

Hopkins invents the name Goldengrove, a name suggesting that Margaret's childhood home is to be compared to the garden of Eden as a place of innocence. The poem's detached speaker is astonished that, unlike himself, Margaret is still so close to nature that she can, by weeping, mourn for the fallen leaves as if they were human presences, the "things of man." The speaker no longer can weep, for nature has become alien and hostile to him and he to it. He envisions that she will become blighted because self-indulgent mournfulness has already overtaken him: "Ah, as the heart grows older / It will come to such sights colder." Fall will become winter; Margaret's emotions will become frozen by the very process of growing up; she will be estranged from others and from the natural world. Margaret, when mature, will see the leaves crushed on the ground as "leaf meal," but she will not respond to them as she does now in childhood; she will no longer be sympathetic enough to weep for fallen leaves. The cause of her inability to weep will be a new kind of knowledge, pertaining not to the seasonal cycle of nature and the objects of the world, but merely to herself and her own loss of innocence, resulting, so it seems, from the original disobedience of Adam and Eve to which she is heir. In her inability to weep, Margaret will become trapped in her own repressed mourning and thus perpetuate that mourning. This depiction of Margaret, of course, is the projection of the speaker who, in making this projection, really describes his own fallen condition in an advanced stage. As the speaker envisions, Margaret will become imprisoned in her own self, perceiving only "Sorrow's springs" and, therefore, seeing only mortality in nature. Because Margaret will conceive of death as the end of everything, she will define nature as if nature had no life apart from her own.

In projecting Margaret's future this way, however, the speaker has forgotten the spring of the poem's title, "Spring and Fall." Limited by his own morbid gloom and grief, the speaker has depicted the seasons not as a cycle that outlasts the life of an individual, but as a fall from spring to winter, from life only to death. The word "sorrows" as misused by the narrator, with its implication of irremediable tears, describes spring as flowing always toward decay, death, and sorrow, and that movement is seen as nature's blight: mortality is the disease of all existence. The corruption of the Fall in each person seems absolute when viewed from this grieving perspective—the perspective of the self regarding only its personal fate.

The intervening spirit of the Holy Ghost, also misinterpreted by the speaker, seems to lead Margaret to guess that the Fall is irreversible and its effects are unmitigated by the sympathetic human imagination that might alleviate our suffering through the shared bond of the human condition.

The speaker sees only that we are sick unto death: "It is the blight man was born for." The only force that the nihilistic speaker sees in nature and in man is blight, and, by this grim logic, the only possible response is to mourn in isolation for one's personal death: "It is Margaret you mourn for." Nevertheless, what is deeply implied by the poem—and what the heartsick and self-indulgent narrator cannot see—is that winter always returns to spring and that the cycle of nature is renewed, inviting future celebration. For Hopkins the poet—unlike the speaker of this poem—the pattern of nature, winter returning to spring, life going on, is an analog of the resurrection, the triumph over death. Or, for the secular reader, the continuity of the seasons is a reminder that there is always life that survives one's own and that we must cultivate a generous empathy, a Darwinian "sympathy," that will allow us to identify with the sorrows and needs of others and with ongoing life. Like the fullness of the visionary imagination, the seasons unfold into infinity: they do not lead merely to death without renewal, winter without spring. Behind the speaker of this poem, then, resides the poet whose awareness is embodied as the poem's repressed but recoverable knowledge. One might even argue that the poem is the poet's act of projected empathy for the failed imagining of the speaker, who has doomed himself to a perpetual confirmation of his own mourning.

Hopkins wrote in a letter to Robert Bridges that this poem "is not founded on any real incident."[6] Hopkins has imagined the character-narrator of his poem as the most negative aspect of himself—the doubting self without faith, hope, or the ability to identify with and celebrate the spiritual capacities of others. Yet Hopkins's speaker, like Blake's speaker, also possesses the potential for empathic identification, as is portrayed in his initial response to Margaret. Thus the poem can be interpreted as a parable about the danger of despair that comes from a partial vision of nature and of the possibilities inherent in the awareness of human mortality. A failure of vision, as Hopkins shows, is the result of unmitigated mourning, of overemphasizing one's singular life rather than seeing one's life as part of a collective entity. The self cannot sustain itself only as a self, for then its fate is death, final and absolute. It may be that the death of the self is to the universe what the death of a cell is to the human body or a leaf to a tree, simply part of a whole. Proper mourning, finally, must achieve the perspective that we must grieve our way back into life and the celebration of life. In the triumphant words of William Butler Yeats in "Lapis Lazuli": "All things fall and are built again, / And those that build them again are gay." Mourning, when completed in a healthy psyche, can return to gaiety.

IV

The central paradox of Dylan Thomas's poem "A Refusal to Mourn the Death, by Fire, of a Child in London"[7] rests on Thomas's visionary speculation on whether death is permanent or temporary.

> Never until the mankind making
> Bird beast and flower
> Fathering and all humbling darkness
> Tells with silence the last light breaking
> And the still hour
> Is come of the sea tumbling in harness
>
> And I must enter again the round
> Zion of the water bead
> And the synagogue of the ear of corn
> Shall I let pray the shadow of a sound
> Or sow my salt seed
> In the least valley of sackcloth to mourn
>
> The majesty and burning of the child's death.
> I shall not murder
> The mankind of her going with a grave truth
> Nor blaspheme down the stations of the breath
> With any further
> Elegy of innocence and youth.
>
> Deep with the first dead lies London's daughter
> Robed in the long friends,
> The grains beyond age, the dark veins of her mother
> Secret by the unmourning water
> Of the riding Thames.
> After the first death, there is no other.
>
> (Thomas 112)

If death is indeed temporary, because we are resurrected at the end of time, then it is acceptable for us, Thomas proposes, to mourn, since the process of mourning is an appropriate response to temporary death. But if death is permanent, then, Thomas believes, one must repress grief by refusing to mourn and thus, paradoxically, permanently maintain oneself in a state of grief since permanent grief would be the appropriate response to permanent death. Thomas's entire poem, therefore, is contingent on his speculation about humankind's ultimate fate, a speculation that the poem cannot resolve, so that the poem's final line, "After the first death there is no other," is deliberately ambiguous. The line can be read optimistically to mean that we die only once before we are resurrected, or pessimistically to mean that we die and remain dead permanently. In either case, there is no other death. Not knowing what to believe about death, Thomas also does not know whether to grieve or not to grieve for the child killed in the bombing raid: to grieve so that grieving can be brought to an end, or not to grieve so that grieving can be maintained through repression in the psychological forever of his remaining life. Thomas assumes that his speculation cannot be resolved until the end of time when, so he hopes, he will be born again. The contingent word "until" is, therefore, the crucially pivotal word of this poem.

Thomas makes his contingent refusal—that he will never mourn *until*—by imagining God's original "fathering" power to create life, "Bird, beast and flower," at the end of time when darkness returns as it was before "Let there be light" was spoken at the beginning. So, too, at the end of time stillness replaces movement as the "still hour / Is come of the sea." Virtually simultaneously with his conceiving of the end of time, Thomas further imagines the possible personal rebirth that follows the apocalypse when he must "enter again the round / Zion of the water bead / And the synagogue of the ear of corn." These intense and powerful images convey Thomas's sense that he will reemerge from the original life-giving water and that the whole earth will then appear to him as the holy land, as Zion, and that every object, even an ear of corn, will be a source of worship, just as Blake could see "a world in a grain of sand." Only then, having experienced rebirth in his imagination, will Thomas allow himself to mourn for the dead child who will join Thomas in resurrection, because mourning, then, will allow him to pray a prayer of thanksgiving for the end of mourning. Returning to the present time, as if from the eschatological perspective of the ending and renewal of time, Thomas can now affirm and contribute to the flow of life and death by sowing his "salt seed," his fertilizing sperm. He can do so because, though he lives in the valley of the shadow of death, where mourning must continue, he can nevertheless maintain the uncertain hope that mourning eventually can come to an end. Thomas's elegiac poem about the child's innocence, offering a palliative for grief, would be a betrayal of her humanity, unless the hope of resurrection, based on Jesus' sacrificial death, suggested by the phrase "the stations of the breath," proves to be a true prophecy of things to come. If not, grief, exacerbated by repression, should be without mitigation since the human meaning of the "mankind of her going" would be the absoluteness and finality of death.

The fact of present time is that the child, "London's daughter," remains just as dead as all of mankind who have preceded her, even back to Adam and Eve, the "first dead" with whom the child now lies in the ironic fellowship of the deceased, "Robed in the long friends." Yet as part of the earth to which she has returned, she seems to be reunited with the dark veins of her mother—a posture that suggests nursing and rebirth. And so, too, she now seems to partake of the central secret of the earth and its life-giving force, which is described here as the "unmourning water of the riding Thames." It is this same "secret" of the water that Thomas, in "Poem in October," evokes in the lines: "And the mystery / Sang alive / Still in the water and singing birds." The key to Thomas's inextinguishable hopefulness for new life after death lies in his description of the water as being "unmourning." Thomas's hopefulness is closely related to Wordsworth's "faith that sees through death," which comes toward the end of the "Ode: Intimations of Immortality." According to the logic of hopefulness, as radically distinguished from Frostian skepticism, there is ultimately no need for mourning since death will be "swallowed up by victory," according to the New Testament, or, in Shakespeare's words, "So shalt thou feed on Death, that feeds on men, / And Death once dead, there's no more dying then." When dying ceases, so does the need for mourning.

And yet Thomas's uncertain belief about divine purpose, about the fate of nature and of humankind, is not entirely overcome, as we see in the equivocal final line, "After the first death, there is no other." The primal abhorrence of death, the thought of annihilation that corrupts all thinking so that "he that increaseth knowledge increaseth sorrow" (Ecclesiastes) is so powerful that it can call forth the strange and perverse response of seeking to maintain one's grief in vain protest against the unchangeable fact that natural conditions do not change. Like Yeats before him who said, "A man awaits his end / Dreading and hoping all," Thomas, in this poem, chooses not to try to resolve the excruciating dialectic of mourning that simultaneously seeks both to relieve and to sustain itself in grief.

v

An even more extreme example of the refusal to allow one's grief to be mitigated by any of the ongoing claims of life and the living is to be found in Robert Frost's "Home Burial." In this poem a woman, resenting the necessity of her husband's having to bury their child, castigates him for talking about everyday concerns, as if ongoing life should have no attraction for him. For her, it is as if the only suitable response to the death of a loved one is to die oneself, and her bitterness seems beyond relief or cure:

> Friends make pretense of following to the grave,
> But before one is in it, their minds are turned
> And making the best of their way back to life
> And living people, and things they understand.
> But the world's evil. I won't have grief so
> If I can change it. Oh, I won't, I won't!
>
> (Frost 54)

What she means is that she would like grief to go on generating more grief so that grieving allows no way back to the concerns of life. Any diminishment of mourning, for her, would be a betrayal of the dead. Yet from Frost's overriding perspective, to be forever faithful to the dead is to betray the living by rejecting life itself. Mourning can only succeed, from Frost's point of view, if it dissipates itself through its own expression and then allows the griever to return to his or her everyday activities. The failure to allow mourning to be transformed into catharsis leads not only to melancholy and gloom, but also, in Frosts poem, to misanthropy. Indeed, the wife's mourning, her faithfulness to death, exacerbates her hostility toward her husband and further perverts the sexual tension between them into a contagious hatred that seems likely to lead to overt aggression. This aggression is implicit in the husband's final words in response to his wife's threat to leave: "I'll follow and bring you back by force. I will—"

What is to be mourned in "The Death of the Hired Man" is not simply death, but something even more complex—failure in life. If what happens after death is a mystery—perhaps a judgment, as Frost sometimes fearfully wonders—so, too, is the cause of what makes an individual's life worthwhile or worthless. The dialogue between the husband, Warren, and the wife, Mary, presents two different attitudes to the hired man, Silas, who has returned to Warren and Mary's farm, supposedly to work for them again, but actually to die. Although this couple views Silas from divergent perspectives, Mary with immediate compassion and Warren more judgmentally, Mary and Warren are in good communication with each other, unlike the couple in "Home Burial," a poem written about the same time. The relationship between husband and wife in each poem is first suggested by their position on the stairs where they meet to talk. In "Home Burial" the man is seen in a dominating and threatening position above the woman, "Mounting until she cowered under him," while in "Hired Man" they sit next to each other at the same level: "She drew him down / To sit beside her on the wooden steps." This equality of position suggests their respect for each other and the complementarity of their points of view, just as in "West-Running Brook" there is a mutuality that defines the couple, a harmony that allows the woman to say of the symbolic brook that it "Can trust itself to go by contraries / The way I can with you—and you with me."

Mary's first words to Warren about Silas on his return are: "Be kind," and Warren's reply sounds a bit defensive while asserting his resistance to taking Silas back as a hired hand: "'When was I ever anything but kind to him? / But I'll not have the fellow back.'" Warren's severely judgmental attitude, "What good is he?" is based on Warren's work/survival ethic, his assertion that Silas has proven himself to be unreliable: "What help he is there's no depending on. / Off he goes always when I need him most." The question "What good is he?" will take on a theological resonance as the poem progresses, as if ultimately this is the question that God asks about each of us. When Mary describes Silas as "A miserable sight, and frightening, too," without specifying the object of this fright, she alludes to a fear that Frost describes in "A Masque of Mercy" as "the fear / Of God's decision lastly of your deeds." Mary's response to Silas is to treat him as if somehow he is the victim of his own life and therefore requires her compassion, while Warren treats Silas as the agent of his own failure and therefore to be held responsible and judged.

Silas seems to try to evade the reality of his condition by falling asleep, "he just kept nodding off," and this inclination toward sleep as an escape parallels his need to hold on to the illusion that he can still be useful, what Mary calls "Some humble way to save his self-respect." For Mary, the very need for self-respect confers some dignity on Silas even though she fully realizes that his intent to work again for Warren is an illusion; it is too late for that to happen. For Mary, however, illusion or fancy or "as if" belief is very much part of ordinary experience and reality as her astrological fantasy about the moon and cloud at the poem's conclusion fully demonstrates. Mary goes on at some length describing Silas's recollections, even though "he jumbled everything" and made her feel that "he was talking in his sleep," because she has a great capacity to identify with Silas's agitated feelings. She knows that "those days trouble Silas like a dream," and, for her, dreams like illusions and fanciful imaginings have their firm status in reality. When Mary adds, "How some things linger!" she reveals how deep her personal identification with Silas goes; she is herself aware of her identification with him, so that she claims outright, "I sympathize." For Mary, the division between one person's life and fate and another's is not complete as it is for Warren, and this merging of identities makes judgment much more uncertain and complex. Silas's belief that "He could find water with a hazel prong," something he would have liked to teach the young boy "Harold Wilson" who once pitched hay with him, also links Silas to Mary in the fancifulness of his belief. Silas, Mary recounts, would like "another chance" to teach the boy "how to build a load of hay," but this is another illusion. There are no second chances to be had.

Warren is moved by Mary's account of Silas's wish for another chance, and softens a little in his evaluation of Silas, acknowledging that Silas was good at loading and unloading hay. "Silas does that well," Warren says dryly in deference to Mary. But Mary's emotion continues to build as she says of Silas that he is "so concerned for other folk," and with this remark Mary's sense of herself and her sense of Silas converge. With pity overflowing in her voice, Mary continues her mournful account of Silas's life and current predicament with "nothing to look backward to with pride, / And nothing to look forward to with hope." At this point, almost as if to offer the reader a respite from this bleak outlook, the poem's narrator, who had begun the poem with an image of Mary "musing on the lampflame on the table," returns to a description of Mary watching the moon "falling down the west." It is appropriate that Mary's mind seems naturally to make metaphors of the sources of light since she sees so clearly into Silas's suffering and predicament.

The narrator's description of Mary is lyrical and tender as the light of the moon "poured softly on her lap." He depicts her as welcoming the moonlight: "She saw it / And spread her apron to it." Then with an image of her outstretched hand—an image that will return with great significance at the poem's conclusion—the narrator in sweet incantation says: "She put out her hand / Among the harp-like morning glory strings, / Taut with the dew from garden bed to eaves." This intensely visual portrayal of Mary is brought to its lyrical height in the exquisite lines that follow—lines introduced with the "As if" phrase that Frost so often employs to indicate the elevation of imaginative awareness: "As if she played unheard some tenderness / That wrought on him beside her in the night." At this moment, just before she addresses Warren again, some of Mary's "tenderness" passes over onto Warren.

When Mary says realistically to Warren that Silas "has come home to die," she reveals a little irritation in her ironic remark, "You needn't be afraid he'll leave you this time," but Warren's enjoinder, "Home," is described tonally by the narrator as "he mocked gently." Even so, Warren's definition of home is grimly realistic and totally devoid of sentimentality: "Home is the place where, when you have to go there, / They have to take you in." Mary, however, still going by contraries, has her own preferred definition of home as "Something you somehow haven't to deserve," as if some things come to one by virtue of a kind of natural grace. Warren's insistent use of the phrase "have to," emphasizing the idea of inflexible necessity, is directly countered by Mary's nondeterministic "haven't to."

Before Warren speaks again in response to Mary, the narrator describes a gesture Warren makes that seems to mark another change in him, and once more the reader's attention is focused on a hand: Warren "picked up a little stick, and brought it back / And broke it in his hand and tossed it by." By the poem's end, this broken stick will be replaced by Mary's hand, but for now all the reader can surmise is that Warren's thinking about home and the obligations of family has shifted. His question to Mary, "Silas has better claim on us you think / Than on his brother?" is genuinely open and exploratory, and it raises the larger question of the nature of human brotherhood and the correlative question of the claim that all human suffering has on all of us. In spite of the fact that Silas's brother is rich, as both Warren and Mary know, and in spite of the fact, as Mary acknowledges, that Silas's brother "ought of right / To take him in," the bond more powerful than blood that constitutes the reason Mary wants to accept Silas back to work or to die is the bond of pity: "But have some pity on Silas," Mary demands of Warren.

Mary's plea for pity takes on an additional psychological twist with her realization that, in actuality, families have a built-in intolerance for accepting the truth about each other, particularly about their failed members. Mary's pithy remark, generalizing from the example of Silas, that he is "just the kind that kinsfolk can't abide," reinforces her argument for why she and her husband must assume responsibility for Silas on the basis of their acceptance of the intractable fact that "Silas is what he is." The fact of Silas's identity as failure is exactly the fact that Silas's brother cannot accept. Silas's puzzlement about himself as a failure, as articulated by Mary, "He don't know why he isn't quite as good / As anybody," expresses the overriding question about universal justice. Why should it be given to some to succeed and others to fail? Can everyone equally be held accountable for their fate? At this point in the poem Mary, despite her capacity for pity, must acknowledge the seemingly inescapable truth about Silas being "worthless." And what Mary therefore is mourning here is the cruelty and apparent randomness of this existential truth.

Warren is taken aback by Mary's bluntness and tries to soften her judgment of Silas with the mitigating observation that "I can't think Si ever hurt anyone." In calling him "Si," Warren inadvertently reveals his affection for Silas, which previously he had repressed perhaps because such an admission was too painful to him. But Mary's response is stunning in the way it expands the concept of hurtfulness. It may well be true, as Warren means to say, that Silas never intended to hurt anyone, but Mary's point, "No, but he hurt my heart the way he lay / And rolled his old head on that sharp-edged chair-back," makes it clear that hurt does not necessarily come from deliberate or malevolent intent; rather, hurt can come from one person's witnessing the spectacle of human suffering or defeat in another. In this sense, we are all bound together by hurt that is in the world as the very condition of life.

For Mary the issue is not whether Silas deserves the fate of his loneliness and destitution, but the simple fact of "how much he's broken." Pity and sympathy therefore determine how Mary will treat him as she tells Warren: "I made the bed up for him there tonight." The making up of the bed is Mary's way both of making Silas at home and of accepting his immanent death. Her final instruction to her husband is to insist that Warren honor Silas's need to die with an illusion of himself intact: "But Warren, please remember how it is: / He's come to help you ditch the meadow. / He has a plan. You mustn't laugh at him." And then, as if she needs something to distract her from the hurt that Silas's very existence has caused her, Mary looks upward and turns her attention to the moon: "I'll sit and see if that small sailing cloud / Will hit or miss the moon." The question of whether the cloud will hit the moon or not is Mary's fanciful, "as if" way of projecting causation for human events onto the heavens. If the cloud will indeed hit the moon, that event will signify to Mary that Silas will die. The narrator then tells us that "it hit the moon," hinting that we now know that Silas has died even before Warren returns to inform Mary of the fact and thus seemingly to confirm Mary's intuition about human fate—that it is determined by forces beyond human understanding and human control. Mary's illusion that there is a connection between the cloud's hitting the moon and Silas's death is indeed spookily close to the actual timing of Silas's death, and in the illusion of that apparent connection—though one might call it a belief or an intuition—Mary seems to experience a kind of oneness, composed of a trinity, with the universe: "Then there were three there, making a dim row, / The moon, the little silver cloud, and she."

The narrator describes Warren's return with the news of Silas's death: He "slipped to her side, caught up her hand and waited." Earlier, Mary had put her hand out to catch the moonlight. Later, Warren breaks a stick with his hand. And, finally, Warren takes Mary's hand, uniting himself with the moonlight as well as with some kind of universal "tenderness" that her hand can be seen to represent. The poem concludes, however, with Warren's simple statement of Silas's death, "'Dead,' was all he answered," not with a psychological interpretation of Mary's and Warren's reaction. In effect, their mourning for Silas has already taken place since their grief has focused on Silas's life—a focus that makes the question of judgment after death and Silas's ultimate worthiness seem less compelling. If there is a moral implicit in this excruciating poem, it is that enough grief pervades life to exhaust our capacity for mourning without prolonging mourning through repression as Freud so well understood. The fact that life and mourning are inseparable demands acknowledgment and acceptance, though the sharing of grief, as this poem shows, may make grief more bearable and even strengthen the bond between those who are able to share their sorrow.

HOME BURIAL

He saw her from the bottom of the stairs
Before she saw him. She was starting down,
Looking back over her shoulder at some fear.
She took a doubtful step and then undid it
To raise herself and look again. He spoke
Advancing toward her: 'What is it you see
From up there always—for I want to know.'
She turned and sank upon her skirts at that,
And her face changed from terrified to dull.
He said to gain time: 'What is it you see,'
Mounting until she cowered under him.
'I will find out now—you must tell me, dear.'
She, in her place, refused him any help
With the least stiffening of her neck and silence.
She let him look, sure that he wouldn't see,
Blind creature; and awhile he didn't see.
But at last he murmured. 'Oh,' and again, 'Oh.'

'What is it—what?' she said.

                'Just that I see.'

'You don't,' she challenged. 'Tell me what it is.'

'The wonder is I didn't see at once.
I never noticed it from here before.
I must be wonted to it—that's the reason.
The little graveyard where my people are!
So small the window frames the whole of it.
Not so much larger than a bedroom, is it?
There are three stones of slate and one of marble,
Broad-shouldered little slabs there in the sunlight
On the sidehill. We haven't to mind *those*.

But I understand: it is not the stones,
But the child's mound—'

        'Don't, don't, don't, don't,' she cried.

She withdrew shrinking from beneath his arm
That rested on the bannister, and slid downstairs;
And turned on him with such a daunting look
He said twice over before he knew himself:
'Can't a man speak of his own child he's lost?'

'Not you! Oh, where's my hat? Oh, I don't need it!
I must get out of here. I must get air.
I don't know rightly whether any man can.'

'Amy! Don't go to someone else this time.
Listen to me. I won't come down the stairs.'
He sat and fixed his chin between his fists.
'There's something I should like to ask you, dear.'

'You don't know how to ask it.'

With your own hand—how could you?—his little grave;
I saw you from that very window there,
Making the gravel leap and leap in air,
Leap up, like that, like that, and land so lightly
And roll back down the mound beside the hole.
I thought, Who is that man? I didn't know you.
And I crept down the stairs and up the stairs
To look again, and still your spade kept lifting.
Then you came in. I heard your rumbling voice
Out in the kitchen, and I don't know why,
But I went near to see with my own eyes.
You could sit there with the stains on your shoes
Of the fresh earth from your own baby's grave
And talk about your everyday concerns.
You had stood the spade up against the wall
Outside there in the entry, for I saw it.'

'I shall laugh the worst laugh I ever laughed.
I'm cursed. God, if I don't believe I'm cursed.'

'I can repeat the very words you were saying.
"Three foggy mornings and one rainy day
Will rot the best birch fence a man can build."
Think of it, talk like that at such a time!
What had how long it takes a birch to rot
To do with what was in the darkened parlor.
You *couldn't* care! The nearest friends can go
With anyone to death, comes so far short
They might as well not try to go at all.
No, from the time when one is sick to death,
One is alone, and he dies more alone.
Friends make pretense of following to the grave,
But before one is in it, their minds are turned
And making the best of their way back to life
And living people, and things they understand.
But the world's evil. I won't have grief so
If I can change it. Oh, I won't, I won't!'

'There, you have said it all and you feel better.
You won't go now. You're crying. Close the door.
The heart's gone out of it: why keep it up.
Amy! There's someone coming down the road!'

'*You*—oh, you think the talk is all. I must go—
Somewhere out of this house. How can I make you—'

'If—you—do!' She was opening the door wider.
'Where do you mean to go? First tell me that.
I'll follow and bring you back by force. I *will!*—'

Chapter 5

The Modern Muse: Stevens and Frost

I

"Poetry / Exceeding music must take the place / Of empty heaven and its hymns," says Wallace Stevens in "The Man with the Blue Guitar." Stevens's poetry proceeds from the assumption that there is no God, no paradise beyond death, and that people must relinquish their traditional religious beliefs if they are to find their own mortal humanity sufficient. He hopes, in "Esthetique du Mal," that "the health of the world might be enough." Yet the rejection of religious belief and the subsequent focusing on what one can make of this world within its mortal limits does not remove the problem of belief: What kind of credence can one give, inspired by his or her muse, to one's own created structures—one's ideas, one's poems? If the poet is the maker of "fiction," the fabricator of beliefs, as both Stevens and Frost contend, what kind of validity do these fictional truths contain and celebrate?

The lovers in Frost's "Two Look at Two," for example, leave room for the spell cast by their imaginations by resisting the temptation to reach out and touch the deer that seem to mirror them, a gesture that would have the affect of a "spell-breaking." And Stevens formulates the concept of fictionalized truth paradoxically in his collection of aphorisms, "Adagia," in *Opus Posthumous:*

The final belief is to believe in a fiction, which you know to be a fiction, there being nothing else. The exquisite truth is to know that it is a fiction and that you believe in it willingly.[1]

The ability to believe in a created fiction as an "exquisite truth" is to achieve a renewed openness to language, and, in this state of credulity, ideas—including the idea of belief itself—are considered to be as real as anything in the material world. If trees grow in nature, ideas grow in the human imagination, and their actuality is sufficiently manifest in their verbal expression: "Like a book at evening, beautiful but untrue. / Like a book at rising, beautiful and true," says Stevens in "The Auroras of Autumn," describing how the reality of ideas takes hold in the mind. What exists fictively in language thus through the actual functioning of the brain also exists in nature. The speculating poet sees no unbridgeable dichotomy between verbalized thought and physical matter, and so Stevens continues to expound the existence of the reality of the idea of "innocence," which for Stevens connotes the belief that the universe contains no predetermined values or purpose and therefore is open to the imagination to design and impose meanings. The failure to do so is what Stevens calls "calamity," which for both Frost and Stevens describes the imagination's succumbing to the inexorable force of evolutionary transience in both the physical and biological world:

> There may be always a time of innocence.
> There is never a place. Or if there is no time,
> If it is not a thing of time, nor of place,
>
> Existing in the idea of it alone,
> In the sense against calamity, it is not
> Less real.[2]

Although the made things of the mind—its fictions—are not rooted in time and place, as are material things, they have their own certain forms that spring from human need for meaning and purpose, and if this need is not met, the result will be psychic "calamity." Human need for meaning or value, however, as, say, in the sense of beauty, surely is real, and the fictions that derive from that need may be given fulfilling credence for the poet or his readers as long as they do not violate what Stevens, in "Credences of Summer," calls "the limits of reality." Mortality and endless change in the physical condition of the world, seen as absolutes, are such "limits," and the belief in "Terra Paradise," of which Stevens dreams, must find its credibility within these limits, just as for Frost belief in love or art must assert itself but only within its dialectic with uncertainty.

Stevens's muse, whose benevolent power enables Stevens to give credence to his own created beliefs, to search "a possible for its possibleness," is also a muse who defines and accepts limits—the limit of mortality and worldly existence. Infinite possibility, in this deep paradoxical sense, can exist within finite reality, just as an infinite number of fractions exists between the numbers one and two. Stevens's muse represents the power within him to achieve tranquility through giving credence to his own fiction that life is good because, through an act of will, he chooses to affirm it as good, and, though death is something he has no choice about, death, too, may be seen as good because awareness can heighten the sense of the preciousness of life and therefore can be regarded as the "mother of beauty." Stevens is free to choose his attitude toward death, just as he can toward life, so that "good death replaces evil death" (evil death means death against which we rebel as a condition of nature), and thus death also can be fictionalized. Stevens calls this fictionalizing the "mythology of modern death." The fictionalization of death therefore enables Stevens to make the crucial existential choice to believe in the idea that death is good: "Be tranquil in your wounds," Stevens implores his readers. In the absence of God, Stevens profoundly believes, people may remake themselves out of their need to do so by fictionalizing their world. Stevens's capacity for fictionalization has its equivalent in Frost's concept of belief in respect to what, in his essay "Education by Poetry," Frost calls "real art . . . believing the thing into existence." In this sense, love, for example, is an idea wedded to a physiological emotion. In order to be in love, one must have in mind the concept of "love" and the word to go with it.

In *The Prelude,* Wordsworth speaks of having "a saving intercourse with my true self," and Stevens's poem "Final Soliloquy of the Interior Paramour" may be thought of as such a "saving intercourse":

> Light the first light of evening, as in a room
> In which we rest and, for small reason, think
> The world imagined is the ultimate good.
>
> This is, therefore, the intensest rendezvous.
> It is in that thought that we collect ourselves,
> Out of all the indifferences, into one thing:
>
> Within a single thing, a single shawl
> Wrapped tightly round us, since we are poor, a warmth,
> A light, a power, the miraculous influence.
>
> Here, now, we forget each other and ourselves.
> We feel the obscurity of an order, a whole,
> A knowledge, that which arranged the rendezvous.
>
> Within its vital boundary, in the mind.
> We say God and the imagination are one . . .
> How high that highest candle lights the dark.
>
> Out of this same light, out of the central mind,
> We make a dwelling in the evening air,
> In which being there together is enough.
>
> (Stevens 524)

The Interior Paramour is Stevens's name for his muse, speaking within his mind, soothing him as a mother consoles, wrapping the two of them together, as if one, in a "single shawl." Her soliloquy begins as a kind of ceremony in which she instructs the poet to light the candles of his room—which also represents his mind—as if he were lighting the "first light," Venus, the evening star. The paramour-muse, in effect, is trying to make him feel restful and at home in his own mind, and, out of emotional need, she fictionalizes the literal actuality of a thinking mind into a mind-room so that metaphorical thought becomes the "world imagined." She urges him to believe, beyond the proof of reason, that such a world may be the "ultimate good." Stevens, in *Opus Posthumous,* expresses this compelling need to believe as follows:

In an age of disbelief, when the gods have come to an end, when we think of them as the aesthetic projections of a time that has passed, men turn to a fundamental glory of their own and from that create a style of bearing themselves in reality. (Stevens, *Opus Posthumous* 289)

This inner "fundamental glory" of the Interior Paramour is invoked to light the room of the mind as if it were also the outer light from Venus.

The "rendezvous" in this literal room and in the poet's mind is the rendezvous of the poet's thoughts with his anima or female self—a concept much like that of Freud's bisexuality: "Without taking bisexuality into account," says Freud, "I think it would scarcely be possible to arrive at an understanding of the sexual manifestations that are actually to be observed in men and women" (TEOS 86).[3] (Stevens said of Freud that "Freud's eye was the microscope of potency.") This rendezvous of the different parts of the speaker's psyche can take place within the "boundary" both of the room of the poet's imagination and, simultaneously, the room and of the real world. The intensity of the rendezvous results from the realization that thought can contain itself as thought: perceptual images that mirror the physical world and ideas that respond to those images can quite naturally be brought together. In this spirit of unity, the muse says: "we collect ourselves." This gesture of synthesis is accomplished in the face of the indifference of unhumanized Darwinian reality—the natural world merely as it is as a place in which one struggles to survive—and in the face of human indifference as well.

Although poet and muse are "poor," insofar as unmediated reality offers them only indifference, they are able to find in their unity of the fictive and the real "a warmth. / A light, a power, the miraculous influence." The influence is miraculous because the poet's imagination has been able to transform the outer world he lives in by investing it with warmth and light and by giving it value. The laws of causality, however, have not been suspended—it is not a Christian miracle that is being celebrated—but the poet, through his muse, has performed a *natural* miracle, like a Frostian moment of *as if*, in creating his own mood of contentment.

In the intense immediacy of this present moment, "here, now," poet and muse "forget each other" as separate entities and forget their collective selves ("ourselves") as well in the sense that knowledge becomes feeling. This forgetting of literal reality is much like the opening of Frost's "Two Look at Two" where Frost says that "Love and forgetting might have carried them / A little further up the mountainside." So, too, Stevens and his beloved muse, his interiorized female self, become aware of "the obscurity of an order," *as if* nature, by intent, had arranged their rendezvous. Their fictive belief that nature has sponsored this moment—much like the conclusion of Frost's "Two Look at Two" in which the lovers feel certain that "earth returned their love"—has transformed the mind-room through what Stevens elsewhere calls a "style of bearing themselves in reality." The boundary of the room has become the boundary of their collective mind, yet, though the boundary is a recognition of a limit beyond which thought cannot go, it is felt, nevertheless, to be a "vital boundary," a limit that inspires expanded mental life rather than a limit that diminishes the sense of possibility. At this point, a fictive assertion of belief may fully be made by the poem's speaker: "We say God and the imagination are one . . ." The traditional belief in a healing and consoling God has been replaced by Stevens with a belief, of equal credibility, in God as a metaphor for the imagination's transforming power. Stevens says in his essay "The Irrational Element in Poetry" that "the poet who wishes to contemplate the good in the midst of confusion is like the mystic who wishes to contemplate God in the midst of evil." Stevens's description here of the poet's wish is an unmistakable parallel to Frost's wish in "Directive" to be "whole again beyond confusion."

The candle that the muse has instructed her poet-lover to light at the poem's ceremonial opening has become the candle of the poet's imagination, and now it seems to light not only the room and his mind, but the whole night sky: "How high that highest candle lights the dark." This light, which has flared up in the dark "out of the central mind," the mind of all human wishing, the mind that acknowledges its need for solace, is able then to provide that solace. In meeting this fundamental human need, the fictive light is thus affirmed as real, and in this light the poet can make himself at home in the "dwelling" of his mind, just as Wordsworth, in "Tintern Abbey," had wished for his sister, who often serves as Wordsworth's muse, to rescue him in a time of despair:

> . . . Thy mind
> Shall be a mansion for all lovely forms,
> Thy memory be as a dwelling-place
> For all sweet sounds and harmonies.[4]

The memory of Stevens's mother, linked inseparably to the female aspect of his psyche, dwells in his mind in the form of the muse. His mother has been generalized and transformed to become his "Interior Paramour," a collective figure who represents all the women who have loved him and contributed to his sense of self-worth. If the world, through fictive belief, can be made interior, then Stevens can indeed feel his love for the earth as the earth's love for him—just as Frost's lovers for a moment feel that "earth returned their love"—all within his imagination. Although the poet is literally alone in his room, he has the feeling of "being there together," and that feeling is so powerful that the sense of limits and boundaries vanishes. Nothing further is desired beyond such harmony—it "is enough." Stevens's poem dramatizes the feeling of sufficiency, of being at one with the loved persons who literally are always outside oneself, yet here in the mind, in this moment in time, are made interior. The poem itself, a soliloquy, makes manifest the imagination's sense that speech can take on the effect of touch. Such consolation in the face of passing time, as many of Stevens's poems show, is not final, though it has the power to evoke a momentary illusion of finality, the transient feeling of consummation that achieves an abatement of desire—desire, as Stevens well knows, that inevitably must return.

In Stevens's poem specifically addressed to the muse, "To the One of Fictive music," the poet calls her "Sister and mother and diviner love," where no doubt he has in mind Milton's muse-mother with "Wisdom thy sister" in his epic *Paradise Lost,* whom Milton invokes midway in his poetic journey:

> More safe I sing with mortal voice, unchanged
> To hoarse or mute, though fall'n on evil days,
> On evil days though fall'n, and evil tongues;
> In darkness, and with dangers compassed round,
> And solitude; yet not alone, while thou
> Visit'st my slumbers nightly, or when morn
> Purples the east: still govern thou my song,
> Urania, and fit audience find, though few . . .[5]

The imaginative mind is capable of projecting an image of itself just as it is capable of projecting an image of its absence: "Yet the absence of imagination had itself to be imagined." The muse of consoling thought in the form of the mind aware of itself is expressed part comically by Stevens in "Saint John and the Back-Ache," where the Back-Ache declares: "The mind is the terriblest force in the world, father, / Because, in chief, it alone, can defend / Against itself." And in his late elegiac masterpiece, "The Auroras of Autumn," Stevens claims that the purpose of his poem is to conjure up the memory of his mother as his muse in his attempt through poetic imagining to find consolation in the face of annihilation and despair: "The mother's face, / The purpose of the poem, fills the room." In Stevens's world, however, where paradoxically only flux is permanent, no consolation can last. And in Stevens's unending dialectic between solace and despair, between the poem as the creation of purpose and value and the poem as the willed confrontation with absence and emptiness, despair and a sense of disassociation also must be given their voice. The confrontation with nothingness is typical as well of Frost's poetry in moments of intense isolation, as in "Desert Places" with the assertion: "And lonely as it is, that loneliness / Will be more lonely ere it will be less."

The muse as earth mother, negatively regarded as the bringer of death through inevitable change, is personified by Stevens in "Madame La Fleurie" as the phallic woman who destroys rather than nurtures and protects her children, a "bearded queen, wicked in her dead light." This image of the muse-mother turned murderous like Lady Macbeth will "feed on him," rather than him nurse on her, and thus this nightmare version of the muse evokes the desolation Stevens feels when he acknowledges the collapse of his fictive credences whose "purpose" is to console and celebrate. The limit of reality, seen as desolation, is "evil death," the opposite of the imagined "ultimate good." The imagination's effort is spent, and Stevens must cry out: "And yet what good were yesterday's devotions? / I affirm and then at midnight the great cat / Leaps quickly from the fireside and is gone." The "great cat," Stevens's symbol for the imagination's fictive effulgence—"the auroral creature musing in the mind"—must necessarily vanish just as Stevens's solacing affirmation must collapse, leaving him to again confront the midnight darkness. The warmth of the fireside does not suffice when Stevens feels abandoned and alone in his own mind. Confronting this desolation, the poet must begin again to make a new affirmation "in the imagination's new beginning, / In the yes of the realist spoken because he must / Say yes, spoken because under every no / Lay a passion for yes that had never been broken." The realist, then, is one who knows that all consolation and affirmation must in time fail and be renewed, just as Frost claims that "All metaphor breaks down somewhere." Stevens's realist knows that the imagination's need to create affirmation out of a "passion for yes" is also a human absolute, like the Darwinian instinct for survival. Poetry, Stevens believes, "has something to do with our self-preservation." The imagination, renewing itself out of desire and need, will again flourish in creating a fictionalized vision of the nurturing mother-muse: "As if the innocent mother sang in the dark / Of the room and on an accordion, half-heard, / Created the time and place in which we breathed . . ."

II

Stevens's poem "Autumn Refrain" begins with a sense of diminishment and loss. The poet, as literal realist, must describe the desolate scene as it is, a scene that at this moment mirrors a diminishment in his own mind. Keats's muse-bird, the nightingale, in this poem is superseded by Stevens's muse-bird, the grackle, the immanent bird of physical reality:

> *Autumn Refrain*
> The skreak and skritter of evening gone
> And grackles gone and sorrows of the sun,
> The sorrow of sun, too, gone . . . the moon and moon,
> The yellow moon of words about the nightingale
> In measureless measures, not a bird for me
> But the name of a bird and the name of a nameless air
> I have never—shall never hear. And yet beneath
> The stillness of everything gone, and being still,
> Being and sitting still, something resides,
> Some skreaking and skrittering residuum,
> And grates these evasions of the nightingale
> Though I have never—shall never hear that bird.
> And the stillness is in the key, all of it is,
> The stillness is all in the key of that desolate sound.
>
> (Stevens 160)

The poem is set, not in autumn, but at the end of autumn and at the end of evening. The sounds of summer have diminished to a "skreak and skritter," and now even these reduced sounds are gone except that they reside in the poet's memory as a "residuum." In fact, he is hearing what is there only as an aftermath, a "refrain" in his mind, just as Frost's brook in "Hyla Brook" exists only in memory and, from the poem's immediate perspective, is now merely "a faded paper sheet / Of dead leaves." The late grackles are also gone, and so, too, are the sorrows associated with the season's ending—with all endings—which perhaps reminds the speaker of the continuity of what Wordsworth called "natural sorrow," another allusion to flux and transience.

The Stevensian speaker cannot "refrain" from thinking of sorrow, but just as the sun must go down, so, too, the moon must rise, and thus the hard *sk* and *g* sounds, suggesting sorrow, will be counterpointed with soothing *oo* and *ow* sounds, suggesting the consolations of the moon as the symbol of imagination. The sounds suggesting loss and bereavement evoke not only the past season and the completed day, but also the poetic past—Keats's mythic bird, and the past of religious belief that held to the idea of an immortal God. The appropriate commensurate song to celebrate a belief in immortality would have to be one of "measureless measures," like that of Keats's nightingale, but the atheist Stevens is compelled to declare that the symbolic nightingale is "not a bird for me." Stevens's own "measures," his poem as musical air or aria, must sing of limits and of disappearances, as Stevens made explicit in the credo of his essay "Two or Three Ideas":

To see the gods dispelled in mid-air and dissolve like clouds is one of the great human experiences. It is not as if they had gone over the horizon to disappear for a time; nor as if they had been overcome by other gods of greater power and profounder knowledge. It is simply that they came to nothing . . . It was their annihilation, not ours, and yet it left us feeling in a measure, we, too, had been annihilated. It left us feeling dispossessed and alone in a solitude, like children without parents, in a home that seemed deserted, in which the amical rooms and halls had taken on a look of hardness and emptiness. (Stevens, *Opus Posthumous*, 206–207)

The poet cannot deny his nostalgia for the lost belief in "measureless measures," for the idea of divinity, but he must now assert that such belief no longer is credible; it no longer falls within "the limits of reality" but in the category of Frost's "not to believe." The "nameless air" of the nightingale is an air he cannot breathe and a music he cannot sing. There is pain in the acknowledgment that he "shall never hear" immortal song, but that loss cannot be avoided. The "moon of words," the muse words of his imagination, returns him to the fact of nature's ephemerality by naming the nightingale as symbolizing the illusory wish for immortality. His imagination's first allegiance must be to the measuring of limits; the poet's primary muse thus is reality itself as he assumes that it exists beyond thought and is described elsewhere by Stevens as "the first idea." Thus the mortal grackle, not Keats's immortal nightingale, becomes Stevens's chosen bird. If, by the moon's light, consolation for transitory nature is to be found, solace must derive from the grackle's harsh sounds, which connote the vitality of what is real—the physical world. As Stevens says in Aesthetique du Mal," "The greatest poverty is not to live in a physical world."

With the statement of bereavement, "I have never—shall never hear," the poem comes to a heavy pause. Out of this pause, this silence, the poet (and reader) must draw a new breath and begin again to recreate himself as if from the "stillness of everything gone." His voice pours forth a powerful "and yet"—a sharp phrase that is counter in its energy to the exhaustion the poem's long first sentence has exacted. Stevens then shows the progression that "stillness" makes from the essence of absence to an encompassing presence: first, "the stillness of everything gone"; second, "being still"; third, "being and sitting still"; fourth, "the stillness is"; finally, "The stillness is all." As these phrases unfold, they take on personification and being, and finally become embodied fully in a musical "key."

The silence out of which the second half of the poem emerges is also the silence of the remembered residuum of sounds from the past autumn's "skreaking and skrittering." These sounds reside in the speaker's mind where he must again try to make himself at home, dwelling in thought. From these mere sounds, heard by the mind in silence, he must again compose "an alphabet / By which to spell out holy doom." What saves him from despair is the power of his memory to confront the collapse of the past and, from the ruins, to create a musical form, a refrain, that can console and affirm. Thus the muse of memory and the muse of the apperception of physical reality become a single mothering force in the poet's mind, personified by Stevens in "The Owl in the Sarcophagus" as "she that in the syllable between life / And death cries quickly, in a flash of voice, / Keep you, keep you, I am gone, oh keep you as / My memory, is the mother of us all."

The voice of memory "beneath / The stillness" speaks in the *gr* sound of the grackles, the actual bird of physical reality that has become the poet's source of inspiration, which "grates" in a rough music against the nightingale's "evasions," which represent the failure of the nightingale as a credible symbol. The concept of immortality must be replaced by the acceptance of the ultimate reality of loss and death as figured by the grackle. Although the note of nostalgia for the idea of immortality returns as another refrain in the poem, "I have never—shall never hear that bird [the nightingale]," this repeated phrase takes on a musical presence more powerful than what the words literally say. Again the poem comes to a pause and, with another energetic breath, the poet speaks from the stillness— taking stillness as this theme—creating himself anew in the very act of completing his poem. He has found "the key"; it is a musical key, and both he and the stillness come fully alive in the key word of being, the word "is"—"the stillness *is* in the key, all of it *is* / The stillness *is* all." The musical refrains of the poem indeed have emerged from "desolate sound," just as Frost's Oven Bird "knows in singing not to sing." Paradoxically, the

Stevensian speaker has not had to refrain himself; his muse has flourished. Confronting the "negations" of time and death, he has made music out of skreaks and skritters, out of the gutturals of grackles, and though this music, too, at the end of its season, will return to desolate sound and to silence. Thus, the poet has won a moment, as he says in his essay "The Noble Rider and the Sound of Words," of "ecstatic freedom":

For the sensitive poet, conscious of negations, nothing is more difficult than the affirmation of nobility and yet there is nothing that he requires of himself more persistently, since in them and in their kind, alone, are to be found those sanctions that are the reasons for his being and for that occasional ecstasy, or ecstatic freedom of the mind, which is his special privilege.[6]

III

If, like "the earliest single light in the evening sky," the poet "creates a fresh universe out of nothingness by adding [himself]," then reality, regarded by Stevens first as "nothingness," is the source of Stevens's need to create and fill the void. In this respect, "nothingness" for Stevens is a primary aspect of reality as it is for Frost when he speaks of the "universal cataract of death /That spends to nothingness." "Nothingness" is the starting point of a "necessary" process of creation for the artist, which can lead to a vision of physical nature that includes what is humanly imagined "Within what we permit, / Within the actual." This awareness of a necessity to be "Born / Again in the savagest severity, / Desiring fiercely," is inherent in Stevens's poem "The Plain Sense of Things," where reality is stripped down to its perceived minimum:

> *The Plain Sense of Things*
> After the leaves have fallen, we return
> To a plain sense of things. It is as if
> We had come to an end of the imagination,
> Inanimate in an inert savoir.
>
> It is difficult even to choose the adjective
> For this blank cold, this sadness without cause.
> The great structure has become a minor house.
> No turban walks across the lessened floors.
>
> The greenhouse never so badly needed paint.
> The chimney is fifty years old and slants to one side.
> A fantastic effort has failed, a repetition
> In a repetitiousness of men and flies.

Yet the absence of the imagination had
Itself to be imagined. The great pond,
The plain sense of it, without reflections, leaves,
Mud, water like dirty glass, expressing silence

Of a sort, silence of a rat come out to see,
The great pond and its waste of the lilies, all this
Had to be imagined as an inevitable knowledge,
Required, as a necessity requires.

> (Stevens 502)

After the mind has negated its own metaphorical structures of thought in order to begin to create a new poetic design, the imagination confronts a void both in itself and in nature, so Stevens begins his poem, "After the leaves have fallen, we return / To a plain sense of things." The falling of the leaves, like the negations of thought, has left the landscape as a projection of his mind diminished and virtually empty, and the poem's speaker must regard this emptiness to see what he can make of it in a new effort of creation. He seems to have "come to an end of the imagination" and arrived at a point of ultimate desolation much like Frost's "Word I was in my life alone," in "Bereft." Stevens's seemingly negative proposition of having come to an ending surprisingly has the effect, however, of a beginning and a renewal. The speaker cannot regard the plain sense of things plainly; rather, he makes an imaginative hypothesis from the crucial phrase "as if"—a phrase that recurs throughout both Frost's and Stevens's poetry. The speaker feels "Inanimate in an inert savoir," since he has not yet found a use for the knowledge of things as fallen, and yet his imagination has indeed begun to define this fallen condition as a prerequisite to the revitalization of itself.

The speaker says that "It is difficult even to choose the adjective / For this blank cold," but the phrase belies its statement: he has, in fact, chosen the adjective "blank." The choice, in a time of diminished energy, which has been described as "difficult," is seen by the reader as having been made, although the still inert speaker has not yet added his own cause—his need for a new structure in the mind—to nature's seasonal pattern of change. Not only has summer come to an end, but also the imagination's fictive creations have become a "minor house" in which the speaker now dwells, a house without the exotic flourishing of images or thought: "No turban walks across the lessened floors." The speaker must continue to examine his own desolate mind even as his mind is preparing to gather up new energy to reassert the belief that "poetry is part of the structure of reality."

The "greenhouse" is an effective image to convey the unity of natural growth with human design; it, too, is a structure that requires human care. The greenhouse's need for paint corresponds to the speaker's need to refreshen a worn structure, a need that is rooted in human nature. In the image of the slanting chimney we again see a structure that is both enduring and needing to be repaired. The past summer's blossoming and the past structures of the imagination have failed, since everything is transient and must be renewed or replaced. What was once a "fantastic effort," in the sense that it was a great effort, is now seen as "fantastic" in the sense of fantasy—no longer can it be given credence, no longer can it compel belief. The cycle of flourishing and collapse is seen as a mere "repetitiousness of men and flies," as if men have no more cause in the world than flies do. The speaker has not yet been able to make his "savoir" (his knowledge) animate; he has not yet been able to transform repetition into a musical structure that will express his own humanity and thus enhance and redeem the plain sense of things, nature merely as the laws of physical reality. At this point in the poem, the speaker cannot "think of resemblances and the repetitions of resemblances as a source of the ideal."

As in "Autumn Refrain," the word "Yet" marks a sudden release of energy and a leap of the imagination that had been prepared for earlier by the speaker's tentative "as if." The speaker now realizes that his imagination, seemingly inert, has begun its own recovery by confronting its own failure and its own blankness. The experience of inanimateness and nothingness, nevertheless, is both a necessary and a real experience, and reality, so perceived, itself becomes Stevens's muse. One must measure what one *is* against the backdrop of nothingness or "absence," and so the speaker can propose succinctly that "the absence of imagination had / Itself to be imagined." Affirming this paradoxical necessity, the speaker is then able to look at the "great pond," physical reality not yet "rescued from nature" by human thought, and see it as both "great" and "plain" at the same time. It is great in that it can contain and reflect many things, yet the speaker imagines its plainness, "without reflections," as if it can be seen apart from his own reflecting thoughts, his cognitive reflections. His mind has indeed added itself to the scene even as the scene is imagined as an abstraction existing independently of his mind as the "first idea." In this sense, the scene is not merely silence itself, since, through the mediation of the poet, the scene is capable of "expressing silence," and expressed silence, of course, must be made of words. The poet has created a fictive voice so that the silence may speak and articulate the universal human need for making connections, for resemblances, and thus personalizing the physical world.

Seeing—perception before it becomes apperception—begins as plain, ignorant, animal seeing, "of a rat come out to see," yet there is a potent energy in this animal instinct to respond to the environment. The wish to confront literal reality is the basis of the need for humanized seeing that results from having looked "with the sight / Of simple seeing, without re-flection." Through the eye of the poet seeking objectivity as a starting point in which the physical world is acknowledged in its independence from human perception, the great pond of reality first is seen as contain-ing only "its waste of the lilies." But what the poet also sees upon further contemplation is the necessity of viewing this waste and transforming it into a new structure of belief that weds him to his environment. Achiev-ing this unification is the necessity felt by the needful imagination as it confronts the "mud" of the pond, the world not yet humanized by the poet's metaphorical designs. The unhumanized world of physical fact and law is most needful of a transfiguring muse. The repetition of the phrase "Had to be imagined" is then no longer experienced as a "repetitiousness of men and flies," but as a musical form that celebrates a required "inevi-table knowledge." The necessity of obeying physical laws, including the transience that leads to human death, ceases to be experienced as a pain-ful limit, for the knowledge of such necessity is not wasted, and the poet, summoning his muse, whom Stevens elsewhere calls the "angel of real-ity," may again seek out the "possible for its possibleness." As Stevens's Professor Eucalyptus puts it: "The search / For reality is as momentous as / The search for God." The "possibleness" of the actual is inherent in what the mind can make of what it sees, so Stevens says. "The mind turns to its own creations and examines them, not alone from the aesthetic point of view, but for what they reveal, for what they validate and invali-date, for the support that they give."

In the face of a world that is always vanishing, Stevens's mind has the power to create its own solace through his musical fictions. Stevens re-sembles Wordsworth speaking to Coleridge at the end of *The Prelude* when Wordsworth says, "we shall still / Find solace—knowing . . . how the mind of man becomes / A thousand times more beautiful than the earth / On which he dwells." And so, too, Stevens's sense of "absence" and "possibleness" closely resembles Frost's sense of absence, depicted in "Desert Places" as "A blanker whiteness of benighted snow / With no ex-pression, nothing to express." This blankness evokes in Frost the need to "scare himself," into asserting some form of human meaning against nothingness and the existential void.

IV

Stevens begins his poem "The Woman in Sunshine" with a tentative sim-ile comparing the "warmth and movement" of the sun, which his senses perceive, with those same qualities in an imagined woman:

The Woman in Sunshine
It is only that this warmth and movement are like
The warmth and movement of a woman.

It is not that there is any image in the air
Nor the beginning nor end of a form:

It is empty. But a woman in threadless gold
Burns us with brushings of her dress

And a dissociated abundance of being,
More definite for what she is—

Because she is disembodied,
Bearing the odors of the summer fields,

Confessing the taciturn and yet indifferent,
Invisibly clear, the only love.

(Stevens 445)

Stevens's potentially solacing muse, the woman of the mind, is first considered to be "only that," as if she may easily be dismissed as a fantasy. The speaker must acknowledge the fact that there is no "image in the air" and that his sense of a woman's presence has emerged out of the *air*—out of nothing. In the literal sky there is neither "the beginning nor end of a form." There is nothing in nature itself that necessarily leads the speaker to conjure up an image of a woman. The air "is empty." The embodied image emerges only because there is something in the speaker, responding to the sunshine, that desires an image, and the woman's form is thus "visible to the eye that needs." The mind's leap from simile to vision is made in the stressed word "but," in which the human need to imprint human desire on the world is enacted: "*But* a woman in threadless gold / Burns us." Her image is not a "sleek ensolacing" because the undeceived speaker knows that she does not exist literally in nature; rather, she is a necessary creation because of the human need for meaning, which requires that "the poem makes meanings of the rock." Human nature requires such creations if we are to survive, and aiding in our survival is indeed the extreme claim Stevens makes for the imagination that "helps us to live our lives."

Beholding what is not there, the speaker apprehends the form of the woman delicately between "It is" and "It is not," and yet the form "burns" and illuminates like the sun. As his mind continues to assert its own presence in the scene, the speaker both sees a visible image, the "brushing of her dress," and, at the same time, apprehends the woman as an abstraction—a "dissociated abundance of being." The form of the woman does not exist as a necessary association with the image of the sun, but as an overflow from the speaker's need for abundance and the expression of the largess of his own being. Although the woman does not exist as a physical body, she can be seen through the poet's fiction, both as image and as idea, and thus "More definite for what she is" as a combination of image and idea. As a figure created out of the poet's need for unification with the world he inhabits, the image/idea of the woman is a "pure principle [whose] nature is its end." To apprehend the woman as "disembodied" is thus to apprehend the mind's power of embodiment—the power to create a solacing fiction from a sense of absence.

The mind, however, does not create wholly out of nothingness. Though it begins each new cycle of invention by confronting its own blankness and therefore discovers its own need to fill that emptiness, the mind also, through the senses, confronts a physical world. There is no limit to the possibilities of poetic invention, yet the poet's fictions always must adhere to physical reality: "In the poet's desire for resemblance [the poem] touches the sense of reality, it enhances the sense of reality, heightens it, intensifies it." There *is* a resemblance between the woman and the sun—they both give warmth—which is rooted in physical actuality and which the speaker may extend. So, the woman, though disembodied (since she is a fiction), may be embodied fictively in the poem as representing the essence of summer fruition, which includes the idealization of the nurturing mother, "Bearing the odors of the summer fields," as a mother bears a child.

"Bearing" implies both *making apparent* and *giving birth*. The image of the woman evokes and reveals the memory of summer fragrance in the reader's mind (who may be perusing this poem in winter), and in this sense the odors of summer emerge from the poem itself. Guiding the reader, the poet has turned to his own creation for the "support it gives." Though summer is evoked through sight and smell, the speaker must confess—through his image of the woman—that the sunshine is "taciturn," for it resembles a woman only by virtue of the poet's willed act of imagination. Still, physical reality remains "indifferent" to the poet's creation. The woman is both there and not there; she is to be seen and not to be seen; she is "Invisibly clear." As a "fiction that results from feeling," she exists as "the only love," the imagination's love for the real, a reality that must include the projections and identifications of the imagination. Thus the woman in sunshine becomes another example of a Stevensian "interior paramour," and the tentative "only" of the poem's opening becomes an affirmative "only" at the poem's conclusion.

If it is true, as Stevens says, that "A poet looks at the world as a man looks at a woman," then what the poet adds to what he sees is value, his own feeling of the preciousness of love. In the strictest physical sense, that love is not out there in nature, yet it does exist by virtue of the fiction, the "as if" belief that the poet propounds from his need for purpose and value: "If the imagination is the faculty by which we import the unreal into what is real, its value is the value of the way of thinking by which we project the idea of God into the idea of man." Such ideas must be sufficient, Stevens passionately believes, to provide meaning and consolation against the backdrop of nothingness and the flux of physical reality through humankind's own inventions. Although belief begins in the unreal, what we most need, Stevens continues to propound, is belief in the power of belief. As Stevens says in his poem addressed directly to the "One of Fictive Music," the muse: "Unreal, give back to us what once you gave, / The imagination which we spurned and crave."

In his poem "Note on Moonlight," Stevens again confronts the "mere objectiveness of things." He sees the "various universe" as if—again that crucial phrase—it had been created so that the poet might humanize it by adding his or her fictions to it. This "as if" assumption, so essential to both Stevens and Frost in defining how the imagination functions, is itself a fiction, yet the literal capacity of sight passes over naturally into the power of fictive envisioning. The poet cannot and need not separate knowledge of the universe's indifference from the imagination's sense of purpose: "the various universe, intended / So much just to be seen—a purpose, empty / Perhaps, absurd perhaps, but at least a purpose." And so the poet/speaker/musician composes another musical "note" of certitude—like Frost's "as if" certitude—that the speaker "know(s) to be a fiction," even an absurdity, and he is renewed and given solace by its being "Certain and ever more fresh. Ah! Certain for sure. . ."

"Sure" as this note may be, nevertheless it dissolves in the air. Ending with three dots, the poem provides an image of the note's vanishing, as the last word, "sure," dwindles away in the reader's ear. The muse of reality as transience both gives and takes away. So, too, the poet, knowing the limits of what is real and thus ephemeral must "unname" the very creations to which he has given fictive form "until this named thing nameless is / And is destroyed." The act of "unnaming" marks the acknowledgment of the transience of the "named" thing. For the affirming poet, it must be sufficient to know that solace cannot be permanently solacing; he must be able to feel that the desire for the solacing muse—like desire for an actual woman—is not "too difficult to tell from despair." The need to create anew, as a principle of both energy and entropy, and a source of human striving, necessarily leads to loss and defeat, yet the awareness of defeat quickens the "passion for yes" in the poet's wintry mind. This "inevitable knowledge," this equivocal blessing, Stevens chooses to see as sufficient to enable him to persevere, and thus he can "forego / Lament." The modern poet, Stevens says, "has to find what will suffice." Stevens's muse teaches him that there is no conclusion to this search for connection and meaning, but the muse-instructed poet knows, too, that the search itself, paradoxically, can be seen as an ultimate good, ultimate in the sense that it is always present as an effulgence of human desire. Stevens's fictive music is founded on the "rock" of the world whose "barrenness becomes a thousand things," and thus it takes the place of belief in "empty heaven," that obsolete credence, and enables Stevens to bear himself within the limits of reality as an "adventurer / In humanity."

V

A primary function of the muse, in her various incarnations in Frost's poetry, is to provide some kind of relative permanence, a hiatus, within the context of transience and natural flux. In "Never Again Would Bird's Song Be the Same," for example, the effect of Eve's voice as it mingled with the calls of birds in the garden of Eden, "Had now persisted in the woods so long / That probably it never would be lost." The figure of Eve serves first as Adam's muse, his inspiration to "believe," to create a fiction that unites Eve with the garden around her and, thus, in Adam's mind, enhances the beauty of the song of the birds: "He [Adam] would declare and could himself believe" is Frost's opening line, indicating subtly through the word "could" that belief is a matter of choice. What Adam, therefore, chooses to believe, inspired by Eve as his muse with her attendant birds, is clearly a fiction: "That the birds there in all the garden round / From having heard the daylong voice of Eve / Had added to their own an oversound, / Her tone of meaning but without the words." This fiction, in the spirit of "laughter," is what enables love as an idea to become embodied in emotional reality, to be made incarnate. Without this fictionalizing of nature, the world would be barren, just as Stevens depicts an unfictionalized world, so that when belief is added to the awareness of existential nothingness, the "barrenness becomes a thousand things."

Like Stevens, Frost also is challenged by barrenness, the failure of the transfiguring imagination in a time of negation. In such a depleted moment, the figure of the muse is depicted not as an inspiring lover, but as frigid and rejecting, and the mother is presented as a source of defensiveness and rationalized repression. In "The Subverted Flower," the grim poem that follows "Never Again Would Bird's Song Be the Same," in *The Poetry of Robert Frost,* Frost dramatizes the fall in its negative aspect as a scene of sexual repression and sexual rejection. A young man, sitting in a field, is holding a phallic flower (or his penis) in his hand. Frost is deliberate in leaving the distinction between the symbolic and the literal penis uncertain to emphasize the equal reality of what is symbolic and what is literal. The young woman beside him does not respond to his gesture of romantic invitation, "He smiled for her to smile, / But she was either blind / Or willfully unkind," and his response to her response turns his friendly smile into a frightening, animal grimace, "another sort of smile / Caught up like finger tips / The corners of his lips / And cracked his ragged muzzle." The image of the young woman "standing to the waist / In goldenrod and brake, / Her shining hair displaced," depicts her as a cultivated human being from the waist up, and of raw nature from the waist down with the image of the thicket or "brake" suggesting her pubic hair. The young man makes another attempt to reach out to her, "To touch her neck and hair," but again her response is one of disgust and fear as she readies herself to run away from what she now takes to be a situation of physical danger or rape.

At this moment the allegorical aspect of the poem becomes more explicit with "her mother's call / From inside the garden wall." The image of the "garden round" from "Never Again Would Bird's Song Be the Same" has become the "garden wall" in "The Subverted Flower." The young woman, Eve's inheritor, is now outside the garden in a fallen, sexualized world in which she feels she needs her mother's protection. But when she now looks at the young man, her would-be suitor, she sees in him her disgust transformed into his sense of "shame." In effect, he has become what she sees him to be; her projection has become his reality. And this reality of sexual desire as dangerous and corrupt, as fallen, is the sum of what she perceives: "A girl could only see / That a flower had marred a man." Frost, however, offers his reader another perspective of this sexual encounter in the voice of his narrator who, with attempted objectivity, remarks: "But what she could not see / Was that the flower might be / Other than base and fetid." Even so, the narrator does not know how to judge the young woman. Earlier in the poem, the narrator had made the conjecture that "she was either blind / Or willfully unkind," uncertain—as making moral judgments usually is in Frost—as to whether she was victim of her own blindness or morally culpable of a deliberate act of unkindness. Now the narrator can only report what the girl "could not see," as if her blindness were indeed the determining factor in her unnatural response to desire, though the narrator's own inclination to blame her returns with his description of her "too meager heart."

With the rejection derived from sexual disgust complete, the girl "looked and saw the worst," which in her eyes is the transformation of the young man into a beast, "the dog or what it was, / Obeying bestial laws." Seeing himself as she sees him, as a dog who "barks outright," the young man runs away as if trying to escape this degraded image of himself. The narrator's response to the girl's horror, which has caused the young man's downward metamorphosis, is a remarkable touch in Frost's poem. Unable to resolve his own ambivalence between blaming her or exonerating her (perhaps as the victim of her mother's disapproving morality) the narrator simply cries out in empathetic response to the girl's seemingly self-created suffering: "And, oh, for one so young / The bitter words she spit." And thus does the narrator express his own apparently inescapable uncertainty when it comes to interpreting another human being's motivation.

The girl tries to disown her speech as she tried to disown her body in her attempt to remove her words from her lips. Frost uses the loaded word "plucked" in describing this—"She plucked her lips for it"—as her mouth also becomes a "subverted flower." She cannot, however, separate herself from her own nature, her sexual body: "And still the horror clung." At this point, her mother emerges from the garden to rescue her from the animal self into which she also has metamorphosed as she "wiped the foam / From her chin." The girl has become defined by the same animal image she has projected onto the young man in perceiving him as degraded in a state of sexual excitement. Most significant for the symbolism of the poem is the fact that her mother "drew her backward home" into a garden that no longer can be regarded as Edenic or innocent. This retrogression is the overt manifestation of her failure to grow up and become a sexual adult, and it creates in her what W. H. Auden wittily called "the distortions of ingrown virginity." The "comb" that her mother uses to neaten her displaced hair is now a symbol of the repressive force of civilization or parental morality, Emily Dickinson's "town," and as such, the mother becomes the negative muse of denial and neurosis.

The muse as a figure of the beloved or the mother, degraded into the muse of disapproving morality, is always there to be recovered by the imagination in need of affirmation. The poet has the design-making power to create new form by uniting the need for fictive belief with some pattern of images in the physical world. The adding of a celebratory attitude to perception is essentially the work of metaphor, and, as Frost claimed in his essay, "The Constant Symbol," "Every poem is a new metaphor inside or it is nothing." A successful metaphor can unite a perceived object with the subjective feelings of the observer, and through metaphor the separation between outer and inner, between other and self, can be brought into a unity. Frost described metaphor as "the philosophical attempt to say matter in terms of spirit, or spirit in terms of matter, to make the final unity." Metaphor is language that extends touching beyond physical touch and makes it possible for words, whenever necessary, to enhance or take the place of body, since through metaphor—the muse's greatest gift—the alienating gulf between human beings, seeking meaning, and ephemeral nature with its impersonal Darwinian laws may be bridged.

VI

Frost opens his sonnet "The Silken Tent" with a crucial distinction between metaphorical thinking and the use of simile that is merely a comparison: "She is as in a field a silken tent / At midday." The difficult but significant phrase here is "as in." Frost does not say that she is *like* a silken tent, since the metaphor of the tent does not merely describe the "she" of the poem but rather the relationship between the speaker and the woman observed. The tent, as a complex metaphor that develops throughout the poem, conveys the speaker's feelings about the lady and his sense of the significance of their bond. Fastened to the ground yet extending upward, the tent evokes an image of the two of them together, both female and male, in their shared desire for earthly physical pleasure and, at the same time, the "heavenward" wish for transcendence that expresses the longing of their souls:

> *The Silken Tent*
> She is as in a field a silken tent
> At midday when a sunny summer breeze
> Has dried the dew and all its ropes relent,
> So that in guys it gently sways at ease,
> And its supporting central cedar pole,
> That is its pinnacle to heavenward
> And signifies the sureness of the soul,
> Seems to owe naught to any single cord,
> But strictly held by none, is loosely bound
> By countless silken ties of love and thought
> To everything on earth the compass round,
> And only by one's going slightly taut
> In the capriciousness of summer air
> Is of the slightest bondage made aware.[7]

The "she" of the poem may be an actual woman sitting in a field whom the speaker loves, a woman remembered, or both. She is as much an apparition as she is literal, and thus, as the figure who inspires his imagination, she must be regarded as the speaker's muse as well as his lover.

Frost's poem insists on her double reality, to which is added the speaker's subjective response to that reality.

The metaphorical unity of Frost's poem may be seen and felt in several ways. Structurally, the poem is composed as a single-sentence—as if the synthesis of movement and stillness when the tent "sways at ease" can be contained within a single breath, a single moment of thought. The apparent antithesis of earth and heaven is resolved in the image of the tent as both tied to the ground and aspiring upward in its "cedar pole / That is its pinnacle to heavenward." Likewise, the antinomies of man and woman, body and soul, emotion and thought, are seen as unified in the poem's insistence on centrality: it is "midday," the pole is located as "central," and the lovers feel themselves to be at a mysterious spiritual center, measuring "everything on earth the compass round" by their own passion for unity. The recurring (four times) crucial verb of the poem, "is," which introduces the poem's first and last lines, insists that this is a moment of physically existential being that, nevertheless, is infused with a sense of the immanence of the immortal soul contained within a mortal body. The contributing presence of the poem's speaker, at one with the woman he watches, is made clear in his subjective interjection that the cedar pole "signifies the sureness of the soul." To observe and to respond interpretively through signification are a single action reflected in the speaker's mind.

Frost's poem evokes a muse/woman, not as fatally unattainable like Keats's "La Belle Dame Sans Merci" or as a devouring mother who would "feed on him" as in Stevens's "Madame La Fleurie," but as there to be touched and loved. The poem's central paradox puts forth the belief that the feeling of freedom can result from the willed constraint imposed on the chooser by his own choice. If, as in the ballads of such poets as Wordsworth, Keats, Hardy, and Yeats, the mind is sometimes represented as a scene of separation between the lover and his desired beloved, with the implication that the beloved has unsuccessfully replaced the lost mother, then Frost's poem represents the mind as a scene of union in which the soul's longing for immortality—a longing that exacerbates the sense of transience—is, for the duration of a breath, at least momentarily assuaged. With passionate serenity, human longing ceases for a moment and achieves its temporary reward of rest and completion.

Frost's tent "is loosely bound / By countless silken ties of love and thought," so that even the fact of bondage cannot be exactly located. Bondage so diffused is barely experienced as a constraint; the lover does not wander from the choice of his beloved. And when the wind of chance or temptation blows, as blow it must "In the capriciousness of summer air," the lover experiences only the most delicate self-consciousness of having made a limiting commitment. At this moment, the speaker is mainly defined by what he feels, evoked subliminally by all the "silken" sibilants that thread through the poem, and yet his mind is not devoid of self-awareness. In this state of felt self-awareness, he "Is of the slightest bondage made aware," so that thought, too, is experienced as sensuality. In this sense, Frost has realized Keats's deepest wish: "O for a life of Sensations rather than of Thoughts!" by making thought an extension of sensation. Choice for the speaker has become indistinguishable from the fictive act of belief out of which the will to choose has emerged. Frost's vision of the momentary fulfillment of human love, and therefore also of human thought, suggests a hopeful alternative to thought as necessarily dichotomous and burdensome, the antithesis of sensation, as in Keats's "Where but to think is to be full of sorrow and leaden-eyed despairs." In a moment of amorous connection and happiness, thought almost dissolves in pleasure—*almost* dissolves, for if we should lose thought altogether, how could we savor the knowledge that such passion is a choice of limitation, accepting the necessity of the "bondage" of nature as what Stevens called "a vital boundary"? In order to be truly free, Frost implies here, one must know that one is free. Freedom, as Frost's poem celebrates its triumph, is the consummate gift of the muse, who in his mind the beloved has become. She is at once real and at the same time the metaphorical woman in the field who signifies a possibility inherent in nature, in whose service bondage means moving at "ease" in its chosen ties, touched by the mind's delicate spice of airy "awareness."

The poem achieves its signification of the "sureness of the soul" against the backdrop of the implied uncertainty of the soul's unsureness or even the uncertainty of whether the soul exists. The Frostian speaker conjures up the muse/woman in the field, just as Wordsworth calls on his sister-muse, Dorothy, in Book Eleven of *The Prelude* to rescue him from disbelief and uncertainty in which he "lost / All feeling of conviction, and, in fine, / Sick, wearied out with contrarieties, / Yielded up moral questions in despair." In this moment of both moral and artistic crisis, Wordsworth's sister appears as a gift of God (the meaning of Dorothy's name) in his mind:

> Then it was—
> Thanks to the bounteous Giver of all good!—
> That the beloved Sister in whose sight
> Those days were passed, now speaking in a voice
> Of sudden admonition—like a brook
> That did but *cross* a lonely road and now
> Is seen, heard, felt, and caught at every turn,
> Companion never lost through many a league—

Maintained for me a saving intercourse
With my true self; for, though bedimmed and changed
Much, as it seemed, I was no further changed
Than as a clouded and a waning moon:
She whispered still that brightness would return,
She, in the midst of all, preserved me still
A Poet, made me seek beneath that name,
And that alone, my office upon earth.
                                        (Wordsworth 337, book XI, lines 333–49)

It is nature's indifference, against which Frost, like Stevens—whose "Interior Paramour" is derived from Wordsworth's "saving intercourse with my true self"—seeks to preserve himself. Seen as an inexorable process epitomized in Frost's image of an abandoned wood pile's "slow smokeless burning of decay," natural decay without a direction or goal, can be countered by the human capacity for deliberate signification. The creation of fictive or metaphorical belief, by means of which "the sureness of the soul" is evoked and given credence, is one of Frost's many examples of making "a stay against confusion." Frost's sense of uncertainty, the "capriciousness of summer air," or of ongoing decay, does not duplicate Wordsworth's vision when crossing the alps of the "immeasurable height of woods decaying, never to be decayed" as a "symbol of eternity," but Frost's often vexed spirits are not entirely thwarted by the larger Darwinian spectacle of ephemerality and loss. Perhaps Frost's vision of decay, which calls forth the need for a countering muse capable of fabricating literary form, is closer to Darwin's cheerful contemplation of the lowly worm, seen by Darwin as a kind of partner with human beings in the cultivation and renewal of the earth in his late work, *The Formation of Vegetable Mould, through the Action of Worms, with Observations of their Habits.*

The plough is one of the most ancient and most valuable of man's inventions; but long before he existed the land was in fact regularly ploughed, and continues to be thus ploughed by earthworms. It may be doubted whether there are many other animals which have played so important a part in the history of the world.[8]

From a spectacle of a woman in a field to the study of the behavior and function of worms, the muse may inspire a poet (or scientist) to promulgate forms of his own according to the capacity of what Darwin calls "man's inventions" and what Frost calls a "gathering metaphor." And so, in one of his lighter moods, Frost, in "A Considerable Speck," seeing "a living mite / With inclinations it could call its own" on a sheet of paper on which the poet is writing, concludes in the spirit of celebration of the human capacity to create form out of fictive belief: "No one can know how glad I am to find / On any sheet the least display of mind."

Chapter 6

Enigmatical Reserve: Robert Frost as Teacher and Preacher

I proposed to give one [course] in philosophy on judgments in history, Literature, and Religion—how they are made and how they stand, and I was taken on by the department [at Amherst] like odds of a thousand to one. Well the debacle has begun. Here begins what probably won't end till you see me in the pulpit. —ROBERT FROST[1]

I

In describing one of his own poems, Robert Frost claimed that it has the "proper enigmatical reserve." Frost believed that the surface of a poem, like speech, should be simple and immediate, yet that, upon further scrutiny, the poem should reveal itself, paradoxically, as elusive. After all, life does not readily yield up its meaning or purpose—indeed, if life has intrinsic values. The poet must be accurate in describing his limited sense of the mysteries of nature and of God, and he must be true to his own "confusion"—to use one of Frost's favorite words. What the poem contains is not merely private knowledge but the poet's own "uncertainty" about such questions as how humans are to be judged by God or what if anything about divinity is revealed through nature, and the order the poem imposes on this uncertainty functions to dramatize, not simplify or dismiss, what it is that puzzles him. Frost said, "I don't like obscurity or obfuscation, but I do like dark sayings I must leave the clearing of to time." If Frost as poet is also to be thought of as teacher and preacher, then we, as readers, often must regard his poems as if they are parables. His poems speak most profoundly when they speak by indirection; they are indeed "dark sayings," engagingly "enigmatical," and the best of them maintain Frost's characteristic "reserve." The dark qualities of a Frost poem, however, do not necessarily determine that the poem will be without humor. There is often an element of playfulness even in Frost's most serious poems. The play of the poem—the poet's power to create a design—is what Frost summons to contend with nature's random destructiveness and his own confusion in the face of cosmic mystery. Poetic design thus may have some aspect of playfulness or even laughter. Frost takes delight in the resistance to uncertainty and disorder that humor can provide. About "The Road Not Taken," Frost was once overheard to say, "it's a tricky poem, very tricky." Frost had his own game to play with the game life seemed to be playing on him:

> Forgive, O Lord, my little jokes on Thee
> And I'll forgive Thy great big one on me.
> (Frost 428)

Frost's poems, then, are "tricky" out of a mischievous sense of delight in the intricacies of tone and image that a poem can organize, and "tricky," too, in that they themselves resemble the dangerous and uncertain paths toward possible salvation, whether divine or psychological, that people must choose to follow in the course of their days. The image of the road appears in many of Frost's poems, but it is always uncertain what revelation the road leads to, even when the destination or place is as specific as the "frozen wood" in "The Wood Pile" or the old couple's new home in "In the Home Stretch."

Frost begins "the Oven Bird" with a playful and strategic lie: "There is a singer everyone has heard." A reader, unaccustomed to Frostian trickery, will simply accept this line for what it states, but Frost knows perfectly well that not every reader has heard the call of an oven bird. And surely no one has heard an oven bird that says "leaves are old" or that "the early petal-fall is past" as the talkative bird does in this poem:

> *The Oven Bird*
> There is a singer everyone has heard,
> Loud, a mid-summer and a mid-wood bird,
> Who makes the solid tree trunks sound again.
> He says that leaves are old and that for flowers
> Mid-summer is to spring as one to ten.
> He says the early petal-fall is past
> When pear and cherry bloom went down in showers
> On sunny days a moment overcast;
> And comes that other fall we name the fall.
> He says the highway dust is over all.
> The bird would cease and be as other birds
> But that he knows in singing not to sing.
> The question that he frames in all but words
> Is what to make of a diminished thing.
> (Frost 119)

Frost is playing a game with the reader's credulity, for the question of what we can believe on the basis of the little that we know is precisely the problem Frost is exploring here. What Frost is leading the reader toward is the contemplation of the design of the poem itself. Although the literal sound the bird makes is described merely as "loud" and is, in this sense, distracting, Frost invites the reader with him to "make" of this sound some speech that is humanly useful. Nature only speaks when the poet makes nature speak. What the poet believes, beyond what he hears and sees, is necessarily of his own invention.

The oven bird's milieu is "mid-summer" and "mid-wood," yet the bird speaks of the "highway dust." Both poet and bird, as it were, are midway in the journey of their lives, and though this road inevitably leads to dust and death, what matters most is the kind of song the poet freely chooses to sing along the way. As Emerson says, "In popular experience everything good is on the highway." (Frost commented about Emerson, "I owe more to Emerson than anyone else for troubled thoughts about freedom.") The poet, fictionalizing his way hopefully toward some metaphorical truth, tells us that the bird "makes the solid tree trunks sound again." This new sound becomes the sound of the poet's voice incorporating and extending the literal call of the oven bird, just as Frost describes Eve in the garden of Eden listening to the birds: she "added to their own an oversound." This addition is the result of what Frost calls "making believe," the invention of metaphor. Metaphor is fabrication, something added to physical reality, actually a lie the poet constructs in the name of some more expansive truth, and thus it contains the reality of what the poet adds to what is there. Yet this making, enigmatic and uncertain, remains for Frost the essential source of human belief. Such making is what Frost also calls "real art . . . believing the thing into existence, saying as you go more than you even hoped you were going to be able to say."[2]

The season of fall is linked in "The Oven Bird" with the fall from the garden of Eden by the poetic act of naming: "And comes that other fall we name the fall." The poet has merged his voice with the oven bird's by both speaking for him and describing him, just as Adam, in the Book of Genesis, names the animals, projecting an aspect of his verbal self upon them. So, too, the linking of literal meanings, speech, with poetic meanings, song, accomplishes the construction of a design by which the total poem exists in its own form and its own right. The poem as both sung prose and spoken song enables Frost—as an oven bird—to know "in singing not to sing," so that speech can become song, and song can incorporate speech (as it does in this poem). Frost here represents factuality with speech and subjective responsiveness with metaphor, and it is these all sonnets diminished is this a 15 line sonnet?

linkings that constitute poetic design, which contends with the uncertainty of what to make, for example, of both mortality and flux in nature as well as the myth of the fall.

Belief for Frost is always grounded in the questions out of which belief emerges. As the maker of belief, Frost teaches through the medium of metaphor, which in this poem is bird's questioning song: "The question that he [both Frost and the oven bird] frames in all but words." The question of "what to make of a diminished thing" is framed, just as the form of the sonnet constitutes a structural frame, and thus the question *implies* more than the words themselves literally can ask. The question, which probes more deeply than just meaning, as song extends speech into emotion, embodies the *feeling* of the enigma of what man can make of himself and of his world. The "sentence sound often says more than the words," Frost once asserted. It is only because (like the bird's song) the poem is framed, because it is a made thing, that the question it asks, and the answer of exploratory belief that it implies, can remain dynamically in tension. The poem, though grounded in part in the natural fact of how oven birds sound, remains open to the reader's own scrutiny. Such is the style of Frostian teaching.

The question asked by the oven bird is "what to make of a diminished thing." It comes at the end of the poem and thus it throws us back to the beginning, so that the poem makes a kind of circle. But the question, though specific enough, is also enigmatic: What "diminished thing?" Summer is a diminishing from spring, as the oven bird says, "as one to ten." Fall is a diminishing from summer. The fall from the garden of Eden is a mythical diminishing. Death, the highway "dust,' represents the diminishment of life. (What meaning might one make of death in speculating about the myth of the fall?) The poem is a diminishing of the oven bird's loud call and its *possible* meanings. (All poetic form is made by choice and selection and is thus a diminishing of nature's plenitude as well as a verbal augmentation.) Aging on the highway, Frost, too, is a diminished thing. The poem itself, however, is the poet's only answer to these questions, for it is, indeed, what the poet has made; it is an order, a design, to set against uncertainty, to set against "the fall" and against death. Thus Frost takes some measure of consolation in the fabricating power of art: "When in doubt there is always form for us to go on with." And so the reader is left with the enigma of what to make of the poem, a thing "diminished" into shape from the chaos and confusion of life. Frost offers us a man-made form, and it is for the reader to be strengthened by it as such, to find in its own framed coherence what Frost himself believed to be there, "a momentary stay against confusion." And those readers who actually have heard the call of an oven bird (or have looked it up in Roger Tory Peterson's *A Field Guide to the Birds*) will know that what the oven bird says is: "Teacher! Teacher!"

II

If the role of the poet-teacher is to make nature speak with a human voice, the role of the poet-preacher is to dramatize for the reader the mystery of divinity in the face of which the poem, as fictive design, must be given shape. In this role, too, one finds the characteristic Frostian reserve:

> There may be much or little beyond the grave,
> But the strong are saying nothing until they see.
> (Frost 299)

Or, in a lighter mood:

> And I may return
> If dissatisfied
> With what I've learned
> From having died.
> (Frost 413)

But Frost must speak—he must bear witness to the enigma of God in nature and offer his readers the story of that confrontation.

Frost describes a solitary man (perhaps Adam before the creation of Eve) in his poem "The Most of It," a man who walks out to a "boulder-broken beach," repeatedly, it seems, to wake a voice that would answer to his cry.

> ### The Most of It
> He thought he kept the universe alone;
> For all the voice in answer he could wake
> Was but the mocking echo of his own
> From some tree-hidden cliff across the lake.
> Some morning from the boulder-broken beach
> He would cry out on life, that what it wants
> Is not its own love back in copy speech,
> But counter-love, original response.
> And nothing ever came of what he cried
> Unless it was the embodiment that crashed
> In the cliff's talus on the other side,
> And then in the far distant water splashed,
> But after a time allowed for it to swim,
> Instead of proving human when it neared

And someone else additional to him,
As a great buck it powerfully appeared,
Pushing the crumpled water up ahead,
And landed pouring like a waterfall,
And stumbled through the rock with horny tread,
And forced the underbrush—and that was all.

(Frost 338)

The solitary man in the poem cries out as if to a god, unheeding or asleep, who might respond to the man's call if properly summoned. In his naive wish, he is like the boy of Winnander in Wordsworth's *The Prelude*,[3] who, "both hands / Pressed closely palm to palm," as if in unconscious prayer, "Blew mimic hootings to the silent owls, / That they might answer him." But, unlike Frost's man, Wordsworth's boy does receive a certain answer, and he does hear a voice speaking in the silence: the owls "shout again / Responsive to his call." What Frost's man receives is merely the "mocking echo of his own" voice, and so the narrator tells us that "He thought he kept the universe alone." The man is literally alone, like Adam without a female companion, and alone in the deeper sense that he is without a god who functions as the keeper, the protector, of the universe, a god in whom the man can believe. A man may believe in himself as someone who "has promises to keep," social obligations that he can choose to realize, but the universe is more than a man alone can keep or protect, more than he can keep watch over.

What the man cries out for, like Adam before the creation of Eve, is "counter-love, original response." He wishes for God's love, counter to man's need, and God's original creative presence. Without God, man's world is only a "boulder-broken beach," and man's voice, calling out "on life," is a mockery of man's deepest desires. The narrator tells us that "nothing ever came of what he cried / Unless it was the embodiment that crashed / In the cliff's talus." The whole mystery of this poem hangs on the word "Unless," on what the man (and the reader) makes of that crashing embodiment. The poem's enigma is whether to regard that embodiment as a kind of incarnation or revelation, or merely as a physical phenomenon that has occurred "some morning" by chance. If it is seen as an incarnation of God's design, then it is, indeed, the "most of it," the most a man can wish for: it is revelation. If it is merely a physical event and not God's "voice in answer," it must then be seen as the limiting "most" man can receive from nature merely as a process of physical transformation. What might be conceived of as God's design of creation, in that case, would be no more than the blind design, according to the principles of Darwinian evolution, of nature as indifferent to human hopes and aspirations.

The narrator describes the effect of the crashing embodiment literally, yet the impression the reader receives is uncertain and mysterious. There is a series of echoes: first, we hear the crash of loosening and tumbling stone; then we hear the boulders splashing in the water. But what follows is a strange gap after which the boulders in the water *seem* to turn into a "great buck."

The narrator says that this happens "after a time," as if it might be evolutionary time, as if the man has witnessed divine causality unfolding in a visionary instant. The narrator's difficult syntax suggests that it was the embodiment that allowed this transformation to take place. But even as the buck appears, it does not fulfill the man's expectation or hope. The buck is not seen as "original response," as "someone else additional to him." Like Adam naming the animals before the creation of Eve, the man senses that something is still missing in his world, companionship or human conversation, that has not yet been revealed. Described by the increasingly elusive word "it," the buck is not regarded as the "most of it," although its natural power, like that of a waterfall, is awesome. The question still remains: has the man witnessed more than a display of nature's chance permutations and indifferent power?

What are the man, the narrator, the reader, to believe? The buck, with bountiful energy, "Pushing the crumpled water up ahead," seems to know at some level of awareness what it is doing there, to have instinctual direction. But is this nature's random energy and force that "stumbled through the rocks," or is there the suggestion of a design that is to be read symbolically, as if life is to be seen here emerging from chaos and inorganic matter, pushing, landing, stumbling, forcing? The way the buck "forced the underbrush" resembles the way the image of the buck emerges in the mind of the man who is watching. That a powerful image is perceived is certain, but what can the mind make of that image, uniting rational thought with unconscious symbolic implications? It is as if the buck gets born in the mind of its perceiver. The narrator draws no conclusions, makes no assertions, and says flatly, "that was all." Just as the title of the poem is firmly ambiguous, in that "most" might mean everything the man hopes for, revelation, or merely the limit of what nature offers, so, too, is the last word, "all," ambiguous and reverberant as an antithetical counterpointing of the word "most." The phrase "that was all," therefore, with Frostian tonal irony, may imply disappointment, in that the man, hoping for a "voice in answer," sees only a buck, or "that was all" may suggest the man's jubilation in witnessing a feature of divine revelation—all, everything. The buck, though not what the man expected, may be regarded as an embodiment of God's presence in nature—an embodiment that at least for Adam might have anticipated the creation of

Eve. The poem keeps these alternative possibilities of interpretation clearly and absolutely in balance. Frost's readers, like the man in the poem, are left to believe, if they will, one or the other, or perhaps, more accurately, they are left, knowing the extremes of possibility—belief or disbelief—unable to choose, confirmed only in their uncertainty.

III

Can one become "whole again beyond confusion" as Frost speculates in "Directive?" We see Frost again and again in his poems walking out, journeying, into the darkness or venturing into an equivalent interior darkness, "To scare myself with my own desert places." Frost's skeptical heroism lies in his refusal to avoid such confrontation or to retreat into comforting dogma. In his sonnet "Acquainted with the Night," written in Dantean terza rima, Frost is in his own circle of hell, locked into an obsessive "I" of self-consciousness:

> *Acquainted with the Night*
> I have been one acquainted with the night.
> I have walked out in rain—and back in rain.
> I have outwalked the furthest city light.
>
> I have looked down the saddest city lane.
> I have passed by the watchman on his beat
> And dropped my eyes, unwilling to explain.
>
> I have stood still and stopped the sound of feet
> When far away an interrupted cry
> Came over houses from another street.
>
> But not to call me back or say good-by;
> And further still at an unearthly height
> One luminary clock against the sky
>
> Proclaimed the time was neither wrong nor right.
> I have been one acquainted with the night.
> (Frost 255)

The poem returns at the end to the line with which it begins, for there seems to be no way out of this hellish circle. The speaker's movements outward in body and inward in thought both lead to the same darkness, the same "night." The "city light," and later the moon, the "luminary clock," paradoxically illuminate only this essential darkness, this absence of meaningful self-identity. We see the isolated speaker as if he were trying to walk beyond life itself to confront death, the ultimate isolation. In doing so, he detaches himself from the sorrow of human affairs as he looks back at the "saddest city lane" and feels a pang of guilt as he passes "the watchman on his beat" for the extreme alienation he has perversely chosen. And so he drops his eyes, "unwilling to explain," even if he could, for he knows that the watchman is there to guard human lives and protect against the darkness, while he has elected to submerge himself in this dark night of the soul.

How much death, how much isolation, can one experience and still return to tell of it? When the speaker says, "I have stood still and stopped the sound of feet," the reader may feel that the speaker's heart has virtually stopped, or worse, that his spirit has died within his stilled body. That this is indeed spiritual death is suggested by the speaker's reaction to the anonymous "cry" that comes from the city of human suffering: the cry, he feels, has nothing to do with him, it does "not call me back or say good-by." Having "outwalked the furthest city light," the speaker, in his imagination, journeys "further still," even beyond the world, to an "unearthly height," and envisions the moon as a clock. But time, the cosmos itself, is regarded as being without moral content and thus without meaning: it is "neither wrong nor right." In another sense, he is out of time altogether, since in ordinary life there is always some obligation to be kept. To feel so totally alienated from other people and from time, in effect, is to be in some kind of psychological or spiritual hell. Such is the dark night that Frost confronts and finds within himself.

But the speaker does return, just as the poem returns to its first line. As close to death as he has come, he has not died and experienced the ultimate isolation, nor has he wrung from death its mystery. He says, having said it before, "I have been one acquainted with the night," and the reader knows that he has been, is, and will continue to be so acquainted. He will go on. He will, for a time, outwalk the death within him. He is "one"—he feels himself to be alone—but such confining isolation is not equal to death itself. He has not passed over the border of the land from which "no traveler returns." He still does not *know* death, for he is merely "*acquainted* with the night." This is what he circles back to tell us. As far as we may journey into darkness, Frost implies, we can never know the final darkness or discover what ultimately it may reveal. All we can know, so Frost insists, is that we are lost or confused. With this paradoxical knowledge, we may begin our journey again, and if we are "lost enough to find [ourselves]," as Frost speculates in "Directive," we will go on trying to assert form—such as the circle this sonnet strategically makes in its confrontation with both night's literal obscuring darkness and the symbolic darkness of having lost one's spiritual direction.

What every Frostian engagement with nature teaches is that God's ways and His purpose for men are obscure, and the poet-preacher, must lead the reader to the intellectual realization that we must not pray for the wrong thing so that we do not deny or sentimentalize the divine mystery. Frost's courage is to live within the circle of doubt and still try to approach God through prayer. But as he says with ironic humor, "People should be careful how they pray. I've seen about as much harm as good come from prayer. It is highly doubtful if man is equipped for judicious prayer."[4] The implication of the concept of "judicious prayer" is that it is not the result of reason, but of belief, and belief, for Frost, is always an act of invention or making. Frost, in the voice of God speaking to Job, says in "A Masque of Reason," "There's no connection man can reason out / Between his just deserts and what he gets." Frost must be the inventor of prayer, guiding his reader, in the hope that the human drive toward making form and order corresponds to something like a divine command to do so. And yet human order, the poem, must always acknowledge that in nature itself God's meaning is not to be discerned. The poet-preacher must teach his readers to pray that they be able to pray; he must teach them the absolute humility—that man is not capable of judging his own works or his own worth. If there is a divine mercy, perhaps it is God's response to such humility, or as Frost says in "A Masque of Mercy":

> Our lives laid down in war and peace, may not
> Be found acceptable in Heaven's sight.
> And that they may be is the only prayer
> Worth praying.
>
> (Frost 520)

The "may not" and "may be" phrases here are decisive in their brave assertion of uncertainty—an uncertainty of which one, paradoxically, can be sure.

IV

In "The Draft Horse," an anonymous couple, like Adam and Eve envisioned late in the world's history, are seen on a typically unspecified journey:

> *The Draft Horse*
> With a lantern that wouldn't burn
> In too frail a buggy we drove
> Behind too heavy a horse
> Through a pitch-dark limitless grove.

And a man came out of the trees
And took our horse by the head
And reaching back to his ribs
Deliberately stabbed him dead.

The ponderous beast went down
With a crack of a broken shaft.
And the night drew through the trees
In one long invidious draft.

The most unquestioning pair
That ever accepted fate
And the least disposed to ascribe
Any more than we had to to hate,

We assumed that the man himself
Or someone he had to obey
Wanted us to get down
And walk the rest of the way.

(Frost 443)

We do not know whether this couple are leaving home or returning home. They are in "too frail a buggy," suggesting the frailty of their bodies, and their lantern, suggesting their reason, sheds no light. It is "pitch dark," nothing can be seen. The narrative of the poem is enacted in this total darkness, so that, in effect, everything that takes place is imagined as in a nightmare vision. The grove through which the couple move is "limitless." It would seem that there can be no end to their journey, no destination that might reveal the purpose and meaning of their travel's effort. The thought of infinitude is itself a tormenting part of their dilemma. Suddenly, a figure, described blankly as "a man," comes out of the woods and stabs their horse dead. His action is assumed to be deliberate, but for what intent or purpose, we do not know. Since the act occurs in absolute darkness, the reader can only assume that the speaker of the poem *assumes* that it is a man, though it might as well be an angel or a devil or the speaker's own perverse fantasy. And the assumption that this is a deliberate act is also enigmatic: has the horse-slaying man done this out of evil, merely to harm, or is there some purpose in the act, since it forces the couple to dismount and make their way through the dark entirely by the strength of their own spirits and determination? Can the man's destructive but challenging act be a metaphor for God's inscrutable will?

Having first been described as "too heavy a horse," the "beast" goes down "ponderous" with the weight of its own mortality. Everything weighs finally what death weighs. Death defines the measure of all things, and the "shaft," which seemingly gave the horse direction and purpose, is broken. If the "little horse" in "Stopping by Woods on a Snowy Evening" shows an instinct to return home, not to remain in the dangerously enticing woods, the heavy horse in this poem reveals only that this basic wish to dwell in the familiar may be defeated. And just as the mysterious man has come "out of the trees," so, too, does the night move "through the trees" as if the man and the night were the same or were directed by the same force. The night moves in an "invidious draft," enwrapping and destroying the "draft horse"; their names merge, agent and victim become one, and all is reduced to a wind. The work of the draft horse has been completed, but nothing that the poem's speaker can understand through reason has been accomplished.

Can anything be made of this apparently meaningless and random event? The speaker describes himself and his companion as an "unquestioning pair." They are not, however, unthinking; they seem to know that knowledge has its limits in this "limitless grove," and, quite simply, they must accept this. They accept "fate" as a necessity, knowing that their freedom—if freedom has any reality at all—exists only in the attitude they take toward their fate, and thus the speaker says that they are "the least disposed to ascribe / Any more than we had to to hate." In their reluctance to respond to this event as the design of a malevolent force—a "design of darkness to appall" as Frost calls it in his poem "Design"—they begin to define their own humanity. They will have to make something positive from this seemingly rebuking event—something that derives from their own humanity, though they will never be certain that they are right to attribute this generosity to anything other than themselves. They will have only the fragile certainty of what belief provides. Yet the believer may speculate that this is precisely what God wants, precisely what His design demands: that we must respond to nature, and thus to God, out of our own believing, not God's revelation. Therein perhaps lies our freedom. In this sense, it is the meaning that we make out of unmeaning that reveals us in our greatest humanity, as God says to Job in "A Masque of Reason":

> Too long I've owed you this apology
> For the apparently unmeaning sorrow
> You were afflicted with in those old days.
> But it was of the essence of the trial
> You shouldn't understand it at the time.
> It had to seem unmeaning to have meaning.
>
> (Frost 475)

The ability to make meaning of "apparently unmeaning sorrow" is synonymous, Frosts suggests here, with our ability to pray. We must not pray for something; rather, we must *make* something and hope the trial of that uncertain making will lead to our salvation—if not beyond the grave, at least within the measure of time, the journey of our lives.

And so, in "The Draft Horse," the couple make what may be called a creative *assumption.* They choose to accept the apparently causeless punishment of fate as having a positive aspect. They assume that nature and human events must "obey" the laws of fate and that there is intent behind this design that must remain obscure to them. The man—that mysterious agent—no less than themselves, obeys the author of this design. The grove, the night, the wind, the man, the journeying couple—all are part of the design. And the only free act that the couple can perform is to "assume," which is an act of believing, that there is meaning in this enigmatical design. The closest Frost comes to naming God in this poem is when he refers to "someone [the man] had to obey," yet an unknowable God is possibly there by implication. What this obscure, controlling force demands, or so the couple *choose* to assume, is only that they "get down / And walk the rest of the way." Why this "someone" wants this, they are not told, and they do not know. Just as the grove is limitless, so, too, are the possible explanations for what the couple have experienced and what the reader has been given to witness. Although reason cannot unravel the mystery of what is limitless, Frost's parable of uncertainty and confusion is rich with implications that he, as poet-preacher, has locked into the poem with firm intent. The poem itself resists the darkness that it confronts, both as a man-made order and as an assumption that the outer darkness, the cosmos, is also an order, and, as such, may be believed to contain a benevolent or purposeful intent. This is the inherent prayer the poem makes and invites the reader to participate in. And so to this darkness the poet-teacher must unceasingly turn, for it is the source of all that he is and all that he may become. As Frost said in his letter to "The Amherst Student":

The background [is] hugeness and confusion shading away from where we stand into black and utter chaos; and against the background any small man-made figure of order and concentration. What pleasanter than that this should be so? . . . This confusion . . . we like it, we were born to it, born used to it and have practical reasons for wanting it there. To me any little form I assert upon it is velvet, as the saying is, and to be considered for how much more it is than nothing.[5]

Perhaps, then, Frost's readers may assume that there is indeed good in the couple's having to "walk the rest of the way," without revelation or resolution, entirely on their own. They are compelled to make of the "way" what they can and what they will, just as the poet has made the finite form of his poem out of unlimited darkness. Where the "way" will lead, the poem does not tell us, but as Frost says, "The one inalienable right is to go to destruction in your own way. What's worth living for is worth dying for." What lies beyond the grave the stoically strong do not venture to guess at. There may be nothing, and that puzzle remains as part of the darkness in which we live. But if Frost as teacher, preacher, and poet, "acquainted with the night," is to keep going along the "way," and if he is to be true to the God of a frightening transient world whom he speculatively believes in but is certain that he does not know, he must imitate his enigmatical creator and maintain his own "proper enigmatical reserve" in the making of his poems.

Chapter 7

Robert Frost's "As If" Belief

I

> *Never Again Would Bird's Song Be the Same*
> He would declare and could himself believe
> That the birds there in all the garden round
> From having heard the daylong voice of Eve
> Had added to their own an oversound,
> Her tone of meaning but without the words.
> Admittedly an eloquence so soft
> Could only have had an influence on birds
> When call or laughter carried it aloft.
> Be that as may be, she was in their song.
> Moreover her voice upon their voices crossed
> Had now persisted in the wood so long
> That probably it never would be lost.
> Never again would bird song be the same.
> And to do that to birds was why she came.[1]
>
> (Frost 338)

As a great believer in the power of belief, Frost nevertheless held that belief was achieved through an act of choice, not through passive acceptance of traditional religious doctrine. In his essay "Education by Poetry," Frost claimed that "The person who gets close enough to poetry, he is going to know more about the word *belief* than anybody else knows, even in religion nowadays. . . . Every time a poem is written . . . it is written not by cunning but by belief." Frost's view that reality includes, at least in part, how we see it, how we interpret it, and what we say about it, can be traced back to Wordsworth's lines from "Tintern Abbey" where he describes "the mighty world / Of eye, and ear,—both what they half create, / And what perceive." Belief, contending against "uncertainty," was for Frost a made rather than a found thing; it was grounded in assertion, and always it possessed some spirit of play, as in "making believe," the imagination's realm of conjecture, of speculation, of "As if."

The speaker in "Never Again Would Bird's Song Be the Same" begins his benign version of the Fall by entering the mind of Adam and making a fine distinction between what Adam says to Eve in praising her, what he would "declare," and what he thinks in flirtatiously addressing her. The crucial word here is "could." Adam *could* himself believe that the birds in the garden have begun to imitate Eve's tone of voice so that their song takes on a new eloquence, but it is left open to the reader to speculate whether or not Adam does choose to believe what he is capable of imagining, and thus declaring. If Adam is choosing to believe that bird song is indeed influenced by Eve's presence, in what sense, literal or metaphorical, is such believing to be understood? When a man flatters a woman, his Darwinian motive may be to deceive and exploit for the purpose of perpetuating his genetic inheritance, or to entertain and woo, in which case the spirit of wooing appropriately invites hyperbole of expression. The romancer's linguistic hyperbole, as a matter of fact, may correspond quite accurately to an emotional reality as in the spirit of Shakespeare's sonnet expressing genuine affection which begins "When my love swears that she is made of truth, / I do believe her though I know she lies." In this way fiction can enhance reality without betraying it or violating its limits; the fictional "as if" can merge with the factual reality.

Frost sets the first nine lines of his poem in Edenic time within the "garden round," the image of roundness suggesting completeness and security. So, too, Eve's voice is associated with daylight and the spirit of "laughter." And yet Frost evokes the sense that creation is ongoing, meaning is being added to sound, and the crossing of voices—Adam's, Eve's, the speaker's, and the bird's—increases the sense of the complexity and richness of the physical world. The speaker's lyricism reveals his bemusement in colloquial phrases, such as "admittedly" and "Be that as may be." These phrases can be read as a cipher for the poem as a whole: being and speculation, physical fact and making believe, are inseparable aspects of existence when consciousness and speech and, above all, art's "as if" have entered the world. *art over natural song*

The oversound that Eve's singing adds to the singing of the birds is extended through the "Moreover" of the speaker's commentary as crossings augment earlier crossings over evolutionary time. Quite suddenly the scene of the poem shifts from the garden into the woods; prelapsarian time has passed, and we are now in the present. What has taken place, as if it were barely worth noticing, is the Fall and the expulsion from the garden. Although Edenic innocence may have been lost, something more important, according to this particular poem of laughter and make-believe,

[handwritten: creatively new]

[handwritten: Paradise]

has not been lost. What has not been lost is the fiction of Eve's effect on the birds, and, by extension, the effect that human presence has had upon nature. Bird song would never be the same because it has been enhanced through Eve's presence; her voice's "oversound" becomes metaphor as human meaning is expressed in song. What Eve has brought into the world, according to this speaker in his own fictional act of believing, is the human capacity for art. Eve in Frost's upbeat representation here did not come into the world to bring death and grief to all creatures, including Adam, but, rather, to bring art and the capacity for celebration, though the phrase "probably it never would be lost" sounds the one tentative and perhaps ominous note in the poem. The final line begins with three unstressed syllables, giving special emphasis to the first stressed word, "that," inviting the reader to discover the proper interpretive antecedent. "And to do that to birds" makes a round with its own refrain, imitating the garden round, and so the metrically stressed word "that" can only refer to Eve's great gift to nature and to Adam—the gift of enhancement through belief, the gift of metaphor, the gift of "laughter," the gift of art.

[handwritten: not all but add.]

II

Hyla Brook

By June our brook's run out of song and speed.
Sought for much after that, it will be found
Either to have gone groping underground
(And taken with it all the Hyla breed
That shouted in the mist a month ago,
Like ghost of sleigh-bells in a ghost of snow)—
Or flourished and come up in jewelweed,
Weak foliage that is blown upon and bent,
Even against the way its waters went.
Its bed is left a faded paper sheet
Of dead leaves stuck together by the heat—
A brook to none but who remember long.
This as it will be seen is other far
Than with brooks taken otherwise in song.
We love the things we love for what they are.

(Frost 119)

In "Hyla Brook" the reader is instructed to listen to a brook that has dried up and lost its song, and thus, in effect, the poem is a response to and a celebration of the brook's silence. The poem opens with the implication that there is a specific listener for this poem, since the speaker refers to "our brook"; the intimate "our" suggests the auditor may be his wife. By the end of the poem it has become clear that this is indeed a poem about the strengthening of the bond of love through the mutual metaphorical viewing of an object in nature, just as the woman says in "West-Running Brook": "As you and I are married to each other, / We'll both be married to the brook. We'll build / Our bridge across it, and the bridge shall be / Our arm thrown over it asleep beside it." "Hyla Brook" possesses two qualities that are named as "song" and "speed." But while the brook's speed is literal, a material quality, the quality of song is not inherent in the brook itself and thus necessarily implies a subjective beholder who imagines that the brook is singing. Without this metaphorical belief, the brook cannot become a symbol for the bond this couple will cherish and sustain.

The poem moves backward in time, for it is a poem, after all, about seeing the past, the signs of which have physically vanished, so that a present absence gives way to a past presence. Paradoxically, the brook's absence is seen and heard again in the poem as if it were once again early spring when the Hyla frogs were there, and, even further back, to winter, with its "ghost of sleigh-bells in a ghost of snow." The brook moves one way and the weeds move another, just as the speaker's mind both remembers and looks ahead. Again, as in "West-Running Brook," love is defined as having the power to embody and affirm contraries, male and female, past and present: "It must be the brook / Can trust itself to go by contraries / The way I can with you—and you with me."

All the speaker actually sees in "Hyla Brook," from June on, is a bed of dry leaves, so that someone not familiar with this landscape would not see a brook at all and would not know the Hyla frogs ever lived there. Only by virtue of memory, by cherishing what has been there before, can the mind bring to the eye what is now gone and thus give body to absence: "A brook to none but who remember long." Filling the silence, seeing into the past are then projected into the future as a bond of understanding between the speaker and his wife. Frost gives the reader a lesson on how to surpass literal sight as he assures us: "This as it will be seen is other far / Than with brooks taken otherwise in song." The bond between the man and the woman in this poem requires that the past be contained even in the radically changed present and continued into the future. This is precisely what ongoing love must believe in order to accomplish its mission of renewal against the entropic flow of time. Frost is teasing his reader with a subtle boast, saying in effect, that any other poet would write a poem about a brook that is truly a brook, but for someone like himself, someone who knows the landscape well enough to remember that a brook once was there, a poem can be written, as it were, by heart, about a brook that is no longer there.

To love a brook that is no longer a brook, the speaker must incorporate the past, as if it still existed, into the way he now sees "dead leaves stuck together by the heat," so that the absent brook can become a metaphor for the continuity of love despite ephemerality and flux. The poem's final line, "We love the things we love for what they are," which at first reading seems so solidly committed to a literal and factual things-as-they-are reality, can now be seen as reverberant with innuendo and implication. For the brook is both what it once was, a brook, and what it is now, merely dead leaves stuck together. To love things for what they *are* must include loving them as well for what they once were, and also for what they still may be. Reality will not be fixed in a simple, declarative "they are." What things are for Frost is what the mind can make of them through belief, *as if* this sonnet-song itself were written on a "faded paper sheet." Frost transforms his brook—which is no longer to be seen literally—into a metaphorical brook that continues to flow in the speaker's memory, the mind's underground, so that the poem's last line reads as a promise to continue loving, a promise flowing even into the silence of an as yet unarticulated future, creating a unity that Frost describes in his essay "Education by Poetry" as a "relationship of two that is going to be believed into fulfillment . . . the belief of love."

III

The Need of Being Versed in Country Things
The house had gone to bring again
To the midnight sky a sunset glow.
Now the chimney was all of the house that stood,
Like a pistil after the petals go.

The barn opposed across the way,
That would have joined the house in flame
Had it been the will of the wind, was left
To bear forsaken the place's name.

No more it opened with all one end
For teams that came by the stony road
To drum on the floor with scurrying hoofs
And brush the mow with the summer load.

The birds that came to it through the air
At broken windows flew out and in,
Their murmur more like the sigh we sigh
From too much dwelling on what has been.

> Yet for them the lilac renewed its leaf,
> And the aged elm, though touched with fire;
> And the dry pump flung up an awkward arm;
> And the fence post carried a strand of wire.
>
> For them there was really nothing sad.
> But though they rejoiced in the nest they kept,
> One had to be versed in country things
> Not to believe the phoebes wept.
>
> (Frost 241)

There are limits, however, to the fictions that Frost will grant speculative credibility. As Frost has claimed, "All metaphor breaks down somewhere," and because of Frost's stoical unwillingness to allow belief to become a sentimental form of wished-for consolation in the face of what he perceives as Darwinian nature's essential indifference, Frost has also adopted an antithetical attitude toward belief, even a skepticism about the human inclination to believe that benevolent meanings can be found in the known universe. In wondering hopefully, for example, what might follow death, Frost grimly asserts: "The strong are saying nothing until they see." To resist belief, or as "The Need of Being Versed In Country Things," puts it, "Not to believe," becomes essential to Frost's philosophic dialectic between belief and skeptical uncertainty.

One of Frost's favorite mischievous poetic strategies with which to resist the temptation to believe that one can find meaning in nature is to parody the pathetic fallacy, projecting human emotions and thoughts onto animals and objects. Frost does this in such a straightforward manner that the reader may be slow to notice Frost's irony and take it into account. The "Need of Being Versed in Country Things" opens with such a strategy. With mock romantic diction, Frost attributes to the house a competitive motive, as if the house were jealous of the sunset and had tried to emulate the glow of the sunset by bursting into flames. The zaniness of this idea is played down in the understatement in the next lines in which Frost reveals only that the house has burned down, "Now the chimney was all of the house that stood," and he offers the reader an attractive simile, "Like a pistil after the petals go," that distracts the reader from responding to the literal and painful fact that the house actually has been destroyed by fire.

Frost continues his game of assigning intentionality to inanimate things in the next stanza by introducing the barn as a character in this rural drama. The speaker suggests that the barn, in empathy for the house, also would have burst into flames, but was not allowed to do so because the wind, to which will and thus choice also are attributed, did not cooperate. And so the barn, it would seem, is left to endure the human emotion of feeling "forsaken." Frost has deliberately created the illusion that everything that has occurred in this scenario has some kind of meaning, purpose, or volition as a way of expressing his deeper skepticism about the human need to find meaning in nature and natural events.

The next stanza is more simply factual in describing the effects that the house's destruction have had on the barn, yet what, through apparent denial and repression, has not been overtly expressed here is that the family that worked the farm has moved away. The desolation of the barn is evoked indirectly, rather, by the narrator's account of the activities that no longer take place in the barn. In effect, the narrator here is describing the past, dwelling upon the activity of harvesting hay, which has ceased on this farm because of the fire. With the fourth stanza, however, the imagery of the abandoned barn, with birds flying in and out through broken windows, becomes more overt, yet this realistic effect is counter-balanced by the humanized depiction of the birds as the speaker compares their sound to a "sigh."

With these two pivotal lines, "Their murmur more like the sigh we sigh / From too much dwelling on what has been," the speaker subtly offers his critique of his own narration, for he himself has been dwelling too much on what has been, and the poem, his sigh, has so far failed to confront fully the farm's destruction, the fact of meaningless and purposeless loss. The pun on the word "dwelling" is especially significant here since no one can dwell in a house that has burned down; one can only dwell in thought, in a negative sense, on what has been lost beyond retrieval.

The implications of the speaker's self-critique become more overt in the next two stanzas when the distinction between the birds' response and the human reaction to the burned house is emphasized through rhetorical repetition in the phrase "Yet for them." For the birds nothing significant to their survival really has changed: the renewal of spring when the lilacs rebud carries with it no sense of loss; the dry pump and the fence post wire remain objects without connotations of human activity. With this recognition the narrator can now distance himself from the birds whose lives have not been affected by the fire with the explicit statement: "For them there was really nothing sad." The speaker then can locate the birds in their own proper dwelling place, the nest, which is to be distinguished from the human dwelling place, not merely the farm, but the mind as well with its capacity for memory and remorse.

The double meaning of the word "versed," as suggested in the title, now becomes manifest in the penultimate line, "One had to be versed in country things." A poem has to be grounded in the belief of the expressive power of metaphor, even a metaphor evoking the pathetic fallacy, yet it must, dialectically, also call such belief into doubt since all metaphor breaks down somewhere. One must understand the indifference of nature and country things, and be versed in nature's separateness to write (in verse) a believable nature poem. The poem's final paradox, then, is revealed in the phrase "Not to believe." One must resist the need to believe that nature is empathetic or that nature mirrors human sorrow with the impassioned intellect's counter ability "Not to believe," which enables the poet to hold to the skepticism that allows him to be versed in the knowledge of unassuageable sorrow without false consolation. The writing of the poem—being versed in both senses of the word—helps the poet maintain the toughness of his commitment to this intractable truth about the apparent purposelessness of nature, so that his stoical ability, not to believe, offers its own reward: the poet, though tempted, will maintain his heroic dignity by not allowing himself to deceive himself through any sentimentalized vision of an empathetic or caring nature. Frost thus has found a way to affirm his belief in the mind's resistance to its own inclination to believe in consolations that reality will not confirm, and thus the poet's willful choice *not to believe*, like his commitment to philosophical uncertainty, takes its equal place in the workings of his imagination in which doubt and credulity contend with one another without any final resolution.

IV

"*Out, Out—*"

The buzz saw snarled and rattled in the yard
And made dust and dropped stove-length sticks of wood,
Sweet-scented stuff when the breeze drew across it.
And from there those that lifted eyes could count
Five mountain ranges one behind the other
Under the sunset far into Vermont.
And the saw snarled and rattled, snarled and rattled,
As it ran light, or had to bear a load.
And nothing happened: day was all but done.
Call it a day, I wish they might have said
To please the boy by giving him the half hour
That a boy counts so much when saved from work.
His sister stood beside them in her apron
To tell them 'Supper.' At the word, the saw,
As if to prove saws knew what supper meant,
Leaped out at the boys hand, or seemed to leap—

He must have given the hand. However it was,
Neither refused the meeting. But the hand!
The boys first outcry was a rueful laugh,
As he swung toward them holding up the hand
Half in appeal, but half as if to keep
The life from spilling. Then the boy saw all—
Since he was old enough to know, big boy
Doing a man's work, though a child at heart—
He saw all spoiled. Don't let him cut my hand off—
The doctor, when he comes. Don't let him, sister!
So. But the hand was gone already.
The doctor put him in the dark of ether.
He lay and puffed his lips out with his breath.
And then—the watcher at his pulse took fright.
No one believed. They listened at his heart.
Little—less—nothing!—and that ended it.
No more to build on there. And they, since they
Were not the one dead, turned to their affairs.

(Frost 136)

In "Out, Out—" we hear a narrator who is outside the story he is telling,
but who wishes to enter into the scene as one of the characters as if he
might be of some help. As narrator, however, he has only one role to
play—the role of witness. Essentially, what he witnesses is the absence of
divine meaning or purpose in nature and in human affairs. The phrase
"lifted eyes," with subtle irony, serves as a parody of Psalm 121, which
opens: "I will lift up mine eyes unto the hills from whence cometh my
help." No help will come from the hills or anywhere else in Frost's poem.
In the larger existential sense, not only the boy's loss of his hand and his
death, but also the indifference of nature cause the watchers to take
fright, and it is this reality which, at heart, "No one believed." The title of
the poem is an allusion to Macbeth's soliloquy that ends with the phrase
in which Macbeth sums up the tale of his life as "signifying nothing."
This poem, like many of Frost's poems, is a confrontation with such
nothingness—a nothingness in which the onlookers here will be com-
pelled to believe. Toward the end of the poem, the words "little—less—
nothing!" complete the echo on the theme of nothingness from Shake-
speare's play.

The confrontation with the meaninglessness of death is anticipated
early in the poem with the image of dust: "The buzz saw snarled and rat-
tled in the yard / And made dust." The poem's narrative arc is of dust re-
turning to "dusty death" (Shakespeare's phrase), although the narrator
and reader are at first misled by the sweet-scented odor of the cut wood in
the breeze. The narrator, along with those other would-be believers who

as if it were a day – but work makes it night + *finish* *but he's only a "helper" not a child god.*

have lifted eyes, appears to be enjoying a vision of great depth into nature itself—"the five mountain ranges one behind the other / Under the sunset, far into Vermont"—as if nature were beautiful and benign, a spectacle of Wordsworthian and biblical revelation. But the narrator subsequently will realize that he has had, rather, a vision of nature's beautiful indifference, which he can describe but cannot affect. He says, "day was all but done. / Call it a day, I wish they might have said." In his admission, "I wish," we hear the narrator seeking to intrude into the story, to become simultaneously both actor and narrator. Until now, we have seen him as the seemingly omniscient narrator, the removed narrator, but now he cannot control the world of the story; all he can do is tell the story and contain his own grief to the best of his ability as a witness. His "as if" statements—"the saw, / As if to prove saws knew what supper meant," and "the hand, / Half in appeal, but half as if to keep / The life from spilling,"—both fall into the category of wishing rather than fictive believing for they are clearly contrary to fact.

We hear the narrator's human voice intrude again in two other places. When he says "However it was," describing the meeting of the saw and the boy's hand, he expresses his reluctance to complete his story of the boy's needless death in that beautiful Vermont sunset. The narrator, however, is not the one who can cry out because he is not in the story. The boy gives voice directly to his terror, but the narrator can cry out only as a storyteller, by implication, in partial identification with the boy whose tale he is relating: "The boy's first outcry was a rueful laugh, / As he swung toward them holding up the hand." The boy's horrible laughing cry seems to bring him to a final vision that replaces the earlier vision of the five mountain ranges: "Then the boy saw all." But the boy does not see all. The most his terror can believe is that he is going to lose his hand; he is not able to take that terrible imagining to its finality of nothingness—"Don't let him cut my hand off— / The doctor, when he comes. Don't let him, sister!" The boys vision of *nothing* is not complete: the loss of his hand will become the loss of his life.

nothing but a saw

And so for the narrator, there will be, ironically, an increase of less, until less becomes nothing, and there is nothing he can do. For a moment, his narration is reduced to the impotent word "So," and in that minimal word all his restrained grief is held. In effect, Frost's poem contains exactly what the narrator cannot express. That strangled "So" is the narrator's cry of bearing witness to a story that finally must be believed for what it is—unredeemable loss—in a scene he cannot enter. He cannot rescue the boy: "the hand was gone already." Yet there is still more *nothing* to be perceived: "the watcher at his pulse took fright." In the poem's sense of human helplessness in an indifferent Darwinian universe where

but not his writing

but only as brutes

survival in part depends merely on chance circumstances, we are all potential watchers, and what we see is death without redemption, signifying nothing. So. So? So! How shall we read that enigmatic word? But the story is not over yet; the boy will die, and someone must tell of it: "And they, since they / Were not the one dead, turned to their affairs." There is a strange coldness in the characters of Frost's poem as they continue their lives in the spirit of necessity; there is still the work of brute survival for them to do. In the spirit of "Let the dead bury the dead," their instinctual commitment is to life and continuity. In a revealing letter, Frost wrote: "And I suppose I am a brute in that my nature refuses to carry sympathy to the point of going crazy just because someone else goes crazy, or of dying just because someone else dies."[2] All the narrator, holding to his sanity, can do as he attempts to contain his personal grief, is express his sorrow through the telling of the tale that confirms a belief he dreads but must acknowledge, and that tale, which his commitment to the truth demands that he relate, becomes an extension of his own empathizing identity, his capacity to believe in the suffering of others. Beyond the uncertain "So" of his own voice, he has become imaginatively one with the characters to whose lives he has borne witness, but whose sorrows he cannot ameliorate. In this poem, the wish for some kind of "as if" consolation meets head-on Frost's "Not to believe" skepticism, which, nevertheless, does not exclude the story-telling narrator's imaginative compassion. In his confrontation with "nothing," the narrator has only the design of his story to cling to.

no

V

After Apple Picking

My long two-pointed ladder's sticking through a tree
Toward heaven still,
And there's a barrel that I didn't fill
Beside it, and there may be two or three
Apples I didn't pick upon some bough.
But I am done with apple-picking now.
Essence of winter sleep is on the night,
The scent of apples: I am drowsing off.
I cannot rub the strangeness from my sight
I got from looking through a pane of glass
I skimmed this morning from the drinking trough
And held against the world of hoary grass.
It melted, and I let it fall and break.
But I was well

Upon my way to sleep before it fell,
And I could tell
What form my dreaming was about to take.
Magnified apples appear and disappear,
Stem end and blossom end,
And every fleck of russet showing clear.
My instep arch not only keeps the ache,
It keeps the pressure of the ladder-round.
I feel the ladder sway as the boughs bend.
And I keep hearing from the cellar bin
The rumbling sound
Of load on load of apples coming in.
For I have had too much
Of apple-picking: I am overtired
Of the great harvest I myself desired.
There were ten thousand thousand fruit to touch,
Cherish in hand, lift down, and not let fall,
For all
That struck the earth,
No matter if not bruised or spiked with stubble,
Went surely to the cider-apple heap
As of no worth.
One can see what will trouble
This sleep of mine, whatever sleep it is.
Were he not gone,
The woodchuck could say whether it's like his
Long sleep, as I describe its coming on,
Or just some human sleep.

(Frost 68)

The main themes of this elegiac poem, written in the flowing form of varying line lengths and intermittent rhymes Milton had used in "Lycidas," (his poem of death and rebirth), are longing and fear. The longing for heaven and the transcendence of earthly weariness and sorrow bring to mind Keats's "Ode to a Nightingale" and Dylan Thomas's "Poem in October," which opens with an allusion suggesting transcendent desire quite similar to Frost's: "It was my thirtieth year to heaven." The speaker of Frost's poem desires to take satisfaction in the harvest, which represents his completed life's work, and he wishes to give himself over to what he believes is a merited fatigue, as if his life's effort has earned him repose and peaceful sleep.

Although the speaker claims that he is done with apple picking, he is troubled by thoughts of his not having completed the harvest: "And there's a barrel that I didn't fill / Beside it, and there may be two or three /

an attitude that outlives the work itself but is an allusion

Apples I didn't pick upon some bough." The sense of satisfaction, of a consummation devoutly to be wished, eludes him. If the phrase "essence of winter sleep" suggests death, rather than just the cycling of the seasons, then the image of the world the speaker perceives through the pane of ice is a vision of an afterlife that lacks repose and continues the mental troubles and uncertainties of the life the speaker has lived. Frost's speaker's unease resembles (even with his echo of Shakespeare's word "rub") the undermining of Hamlet's wish to find a consummation in death in the fear that if death is like sleep, then death also might be troubled by bad dreams:

> To die: to sleep.
> To sleep? perchance to dream. Ay, there's the rub;
> For in that sleep of death what dreams may come,
> When we have shuffled off this mortal coil,
> Must give us pause.[3]
>
> (*Hamlet* III, I, 64–68)

The vision of the world seen through the pane of ice, as the ice falls from the speaker's hand, gives the speaker pause, and this vision leads directly, as a transition in which one image fades into another, into the speaker's prophetic depiction of the enlargement of life's frustrations his dreaming might take in death as he assumes it also will take in his oncoming sleep. The pane of ice acts like a magnifying glass so that the apples become intensified in their emotional and symbolic implications, particularly as the speaker is made aware of their disappearance. Thus, the image of the disappearing magnified apples expands into a more inclusive sense of imminent loss.

Poised on the ladder, the speaker is aware of the strain on his body from his efforts at harvesting. His arched foot on the ladder's rung, which keeps the ache, makes him feel as if he is to be eternalized in his own special torment—the torment that comes from his desire for the great harvest. The speaker's idealistic hope, his belief in the very purpose of his life, symbolized by the goodness of the apples, is tenderly expressed in the lines: "There were ten thousand thousand fruit to touch, / Cherish in hand, lift down, and not let fall," but this desire is defeated by the speaker's failure to prevent some of the apples from falling. The gentle tone, made of balanced phrases, associated with cherishing, is undercut by the speaker's fear of imperfection and failure: "For all / That struck the earth, / No matter if not bruised or spiked with stubble, / Went surely to the cider-apple heap / As of no worth." In this allegory of salvation, a principle, Darwinian in its emphasis on randomness, is introduced: even though these fallen apples are not flawed, not bruised or spiked, and their fate is caused by no inherent fault of their own, they are discarded "As of no worth." Fate here is the result of chance conditions even though the individual experiences the randomness of the discarded apples as if it constituted a judgment of himself. The inescapable implication here of the issue of human worthiness derives from the speaker's identification with the discarded apples. The speaker's anxiety in "After Apple Picking" is whether or not he, like the rejected apples, finally will be judged "as of no worth."

In "Directive," Frost expresses this identical anxiety as the journeyer in that poem seeks "A broken drinking goblet like the Grail," but fears the mystery of salvation, for perhaps the goblet is "Under a spell so the wrong ones can't find it, / So can't get saved as Saint Mark says they mustn't." Frost leaves the question unresolved in all these poems as to whether he can believe in such a view of salvation, but the possibility remains, unresolvable in its uncertainty, that he may ultimately be judged to be one of the apples of no worth or that he may prove to be one of the "wrong ones" who can't be saved.

The speaker goes on to identify this anxiety as what he fears will "trouble / This sleep of mine." The poem ends with a contrast between the guiltless mentality of animals, the long sleep of the woodchuck, which will last only through the remainder of the winter, and the human sleep, which expresses the unconscious depth of the mind. It is as if the speaker wishes that the woodchuck were there to console him or that he could return to a simpler form of animal life. The final, elusive phrase, "just some human sleep," rings with typical Frostian uncertainty: are human beings truly set off from the rest of creation by the nature of their dreaming and their thoughts about death and judgment? And is that human distinction just a human peculiarity? What, if anything, can one allow oneself to believe may come after apple picking? Frost insists on maintaining a skeptical stance in regard to questions of an afterlife. The poem's final phrase, "Or just some human sleep," is remarkable for its recalcitrance, how much it refuses to say, not even indicating whether human or animal sleep is to be preferred.

VI

Two Look at Two
Love and forgetting might have carried them
A little further up the mountainside
With night so near, but not much further up.
They must have halted soon in any case

With thoughts of the path back, how rough it was
With rock and washout, and unsafe in darkness;
When they were halted by a tumbled wall
With barbed-wire binding. They stood facing this,
Spending what onward impulse they still had
In one last look the way they must not go,
On up the failing path, where, if a stone
Or earthslide moved at night, it moved itself;
No footstep moved it. This is all, they sighed,
Good-night to woods. But not so; there was more.
A doe from round a spruce stood looking at them
Across the wall, as near the wall as they.
She saw them in their field, they her in hers.
The difficulty of seeing what stood still,
Like some up-ended boulder split in two,
Was in their clouded eyes: they saw no fear there.
She seemed to think that two thus they were safe.
Then, as if they were something that, though strange,
She could not trouble her mind with too long,
She sighed and passed unscared along the wall.
This, then, is all. What more is there to ask?
But no, not yet. A snort to bid them wait.
A buck from round the spruce stood looking at them
Across the wall, as near the wall as they.
This was an antlered buck of lusty nostril,
Not the same doe come back into her place.
He viewed them quizzically with jerks of head,
As if to ask, Why don't you make some motion?
Or give some sign of life? Because you can't.
I doubt if you're as living as you look.
Thus till he had them feeling almost dared
To stretch a proffering hand—and a spell-breaking.
Then he too passed unscared along the wall.
Two had seen two, whichever side you spoke from.
This *must* be all. It was all. Still they stood,
A great wave from it going over them,
As if the earth in one unlooked-for favor
Had made them certain earth returned their love.

(Frost 229)

As one of Frost's most affirmative poems, "Two Look at Two," a poem
blessed with an unusual moment of certitude, begins and ends with the
word "love." In behalf of the lovers who prepare to descend the mountain
with night so near, the speaker seeks to cast a spell of belief over the
harsh and challenging landscape by attempting to read into the landscape

a benevolent message from the earth. To make such an interpretation, a deliberate act of forgetting is necessary, like Coleridge's "willing suspension of disbelief." Since Frost chooses to leave the object of this evocative word, "forgetting," unspecified, the reader is invited to surmise that ordinary logic and rationality must temporarily be suspended for the casting of a love spell to take place as an assertion of playful imaginative belief. Frost overtly articulates the connection between belief and playfulness in his review of "King Jasper," by his fellow poet E. A. Robinson, when he exclaims, "The play's the thing. Play's the thing. All virtue in as if." Here Frost echoes Touchstone's remark in Shakespeare's *As You Like It:* "Your 'if' is the only peace-maker; much virtue in 'if.'"

The lovers climb up the mountain may be read as symbolic of their desire, their onward impulse, not merely for physical consummation but for some spiritual unity between them and the earth. There are limits, however, to what human aspiration can achieve, and these confines are represented by the "tumbled wall." At this point in the poem the lovers appear to accept these constrictions as absolute as they take "one last look the way they must not go, / On up the failing path." They will be proven wrong in their disappointment, in thinking that the only spell of enchantment lay in the road they could not take, an enchantment that perceived the landscape as possessing its own animation, "where, if a stone / Or earthslide moved at night, it moved itself; / No footsteps moved it." The lovers' regret, expressed by their sigh, "This is all," nevertheless leads to a new possibility as a doe appears in the landscape, and the central inner refrain of the poem, the rhyming antithetical words "wall" and "all," is established. Basically, the wall will connote the limits of imaginative belief, and "all" will connote the enlargement of imaginative speculation that places its trust in metaphorical and fictive expression, the realm of "as if."

By placing the doe "Across the wall, as near the wall as they," the narrator turns the wall into a kind of mirror in which the lovers project themselves into the bodies of animals, representing their own creaturely selves, and in this fiction the animals are given human thoughts. The poem, in its exploration of various perspectives and kinds of looking, creates a metaphor of the lovers regarding themselves by having them perceived by the animals. The thinking attributed to the animals is in actuality the projection of the lovers onto the animals, which is projected back onto the people. This is indeed a poem about looking at looking. Later in the poem, the narrator will say, "Two had seen two, whichever side you spoke from," and, of course, the poem in its representation of the lovers as interchangeable with the thinking animals has indisputably been spoken from both sides: human awareness and animal instinct.

Just as the words "wall" and "all" are woven through the poem, so, too, are variants of the words "stood" and "still." First, the lovers are depicted as "They stood facing the wall," stopped in their place even though they still had an "onward impulse." When the doe appears, it is similarly described; it stood looking at them. Furthermore, when the doe looks at the halted lovers, the speaker depicts what the doe perceives in this mysterious way: "The difficulty of seeing what stood still, / Like some upended boulder split in two." The words "stood" and "still" come together here to make a heavily significant stop, a momentary cessation of movement suggesting that the lovers have projected onto the deer their own apprehension that in some sense they lack sufficient inner animation and that, therefore, they resemble stones. Again, we must emphasize that such an attitude reflects the existential fear the lovers have about themselves, which has been attributed to the doe through the lovers' projection of their fears onto the animals. This fear that essentially there is nothing unique in being human must be overcome if love is to flourish.

Seen in yet another way from the doe's perspective—a simplified aspect of the lover's looking at themselves—there is nothing to be frightened about. The doe's sigh, "She sighed and passed unscared along the wall," further links the doe to the lovers in their earlier sigh, "This is all." The triumph over this basic fear of natural conditions enlarges the first "all" into this more inclusive second all: "*This,* then, is all. What more is there to ask?" The overcoming of physical fear, however, does leave more to ask. The security to be found in the love between a man and woman and between the two of them and the landscape has not yet satisfied the implicit hope of the "onward impulse" for some fully satisfying consummation of their love, both sexual and spiritual. Beyond their doubt that such a consummation was possible, they had nevertheless implicitly assumed it, as they continued their journey, even when they met the barrier of the wall with its barbed-wire binding.

With the appearance of the buck, the symmetry of the wall as a mirror is completed, as is made clear by the repeated phrase "Across the wall as near the wall as they." The phrase "stood looking" returns to reinforce the connection between the lovers and the doe and the buck, their animal counterparts. A dialogue between the body and soul of the lovers is, in effect, being conducted through the metaphor of the lovers observing themselves by looking at themselves through the eyes of the doe and buck. The reminder that the lovers' onward impulse contains an element of sexual desire is reinforced in the synecdoche of the buck's "lusty nostril." But then the theme of how the lovers perceive themselves in their quest for fulfillment is restated, again through projection, in the narrator's description of the buck's response to the lovers:

He viewed them quizzically with jerks of head,
As if to ask, "Why don't you make some motion?
Or give some sign of life? Because you can't.
I doubt if you're as living as you look."

(Frost 229–30)

The essence of life, from the animal or bodily point of view, appears to
lie in the ability to move, so for the moment the humans, in their stillness,
seem to possess only the semblance, the look of being alive. The lovers'
doubts about themselves are again projected onto the buck who is look-
ing at them, and thus they are tempted to reach out across the wall and to
enter into direct communication with their animal counterparts, with na-
ture itself. But for humans, nature cannot be approached in merely a
physical way; nature only can be apprehended through the spell of belief
cast by the metaphorical imagination, and so, as Frost's poem insists, the
lovers must resist the temptation to literally stretch a "proffering hand."
This standoff implies that human beings cannot reach each other merely
through touch to bring love to its completion and fulfillment; language
also is required, the particular language of belief made possible by meta-
phorical structures, such as this poem that cannily encircles itself with the
word "love.">
When the buck, the representation of physical and sexual power,
passes "unscared along the wall," the reader realizes that the lovers have
overcome not only physical fear but, as another projection of themselves
onto the buck reveals, the peculiar fear of nonentity or nothingness ex-
pressed in the taunt, "I doubt if you're as living as you look." In looking
at nature and in looking at themselves, the human lovers, finally, have
achieved an "all" that is commensurate with the hope inherent in their
initial onward impulse. They have reached a limit that, paradoxically,
does not feel like a limit: "This *must* be all. It was all." At this instant of
completeness, when boundaries have both been extended and affirmed,
the thematic words "stood" and "still" come together in a new and revel-
atory configuration: "Still they stood." The paradoxical structure of this
phrase makes use of two senses of the word "still," evoking both its aural
sense of stillness and its physical sense of ongoingness. The phrase con-
tains motion within stillness, continuity within stasis, so it functions as a
metaphorical refutation of the idea that the lovers are not fully alive
when they are not in motion. This significant and powerful paradox will
be found again in Frost's wedding poem to his daughter, "The Master
Speed," in which he says: "But in the rush of everything to waste, / That
you may have the power of standing still." The master speed is a meta-
phor for the stillness of the inner life to believe in the reality of love.

At this moment of triumph over physical fear and spiritual doubt, the narrator describes the feelings of the lovers with an unusual metaphorical figure, surprising because it does not derive from the mountain landscape that has thus far provided all the imagery for the poem. The image of "A great wave," either as an ocean wave or the wave of a gesturing hand, is entirely metaphorical since it belongs only to the interior experience of the lovers and the possibilities of what language can add to the physical universe. The "wave" can represent the lovers' heightened sense of consciousness of each other and of their relationship to the landscape. Frost suggested in a letter: "Life as a whole . . . will appear as a wave which rises . . . this rising wave is consciousness."[4] In a poem about looking, the culminating reward and surprise comes unanticipated as something unlooked-for, the one "unlooked-for favor." This is true linguistically of the unanticipated and unlooked-for figure of the wave, and it is even more significantly true of the exalted feelings that the lovers have experienced as they prepare to descend the mountainside. The way down, not the way up, will provide the lovers with their most triumphant moment of belief, which is expressed as a playful fiction posited in an "As if" construction—"As if the earth in one unlooked-for favor / Had made them certain earth returned their love." The certitude, grounded paradoxically in skepticism and forgetting, is as powerful or as fragile as the lovers' willingness to live within the spell cast by the *as if* play of imagination, its capacity for make-believe, for making believe, for making belief.

✐ Chapter 8

Self-Deception, Lying, and Fictive Truthfulness

I

The Old Testament's mythic narrative suggests that human history begins with language used either to create and accurately delineate or to deceive and misrepresent. The creative use of language is made manifest in the Lord's commanding Adam to name the animals, which Adam proceeds to do: "whatever the human called a living creature, that was its name." Adam's initiatory act of naming is both creative and descriptive without evasion or falsification. The origin of lying, on the other hand, can be found in the serpent's temptation of Eve to disobey the Lord's commandment not to eat of the fruit of the tree in the midst of the garden, when he claims that "You shall not be doomed to die. For God knows that on the day you eat of it your eyes will be opened and you will become as gods knowing good and evil." This is a complex lie, worthy of the serpent's cunning," in that it mixes a false claim—that Adam and Eve will indeed die—with the truth that their eyes will be opened, a truth whose irony they are not prepared to comprehend until too late, *after* they have come to distinguish good and evil.

The serpent's lying to Eve spreads like poison through the bloodstream: it leads to Adam's lying to the Lord, and subsequently takes the form of blame so that forever after in human history lying will retain the attribute of breeding upon itself, generating further lying to maintain the illusion of truthfulness. Adam's rejoinder to the Lord in response to his new and troubled recognition of the condition of his nakedness puts the blame on Eve, "she gave me from the tree," but also hints that maybe this is all God's fault since God was the one who gave Eve to Adam: "the woman who you gave by me" (Gen. 3:12, trans. Robert Alter, *Genesis* [New York: Norton, 1996]). Adam's evasion here reveals the kind of deception that facilitates betrayal, for Adam has already, in effect, broken his bond with Eve so that equality between them (as suggested in the first account by their both being created in God's image) is lost as a result of hoarded information. As a punishment for monopolizing what he knows, Adam is made to rule over Eve to their mutual sorrow. The excuse Eve makes to the Lord that "The serpent beguiled me and I ate" is also a partial truth masquerading as a whole truth since it denies Eve's fatal wish to become like a god herself. Eve is deceiving herself even as she is lying to the Lord: lying to someone else and self-deception are hopelessly intermixed.

Robert Trivers is the author of the theory of "reciprocal altruism," which significantly enhances Darwinian thinking in its explanation of how cooperative behavior can be adaptive. In his introduction to Richard Dawkins's book, *The Selfish Gene,* which propounds the basic tenets of modern Darwinism, Trivers expounds the following insight into the nature of deception:

If [as Dawkins argues] deceit is fundamental to animal communication, then there must be strong selection to spot deception and this ought, in turn, to select for a degree of self-deception, rendering some facts and motives unconscious so as not to betray—by the public signs of self-knowledge—the deception being practiced.[1]

The implications of this insight for human beings, particularly in respect to the relationship between men and women, is enormous. Given the fact "that the sex cells or 'gametes' of males are much smaller and more numerous than the gametes of females,"[2] it inevitably follows that the optimal strategy of males in getting their genes into the gene pool is to mate with as many females as possible. Males of all species do this by persuading females of their own fitness or status, and they do it by false advertising or deception whenever necessary. Females, in response, inevitably evolve the ability to detect such deception for the good of their own genetic offspring; then, or course, males have to get better at lying and females better at detecting lying, and thus an ongoing battle of the sexes forevermore characterizes one significant aspect of the relationship between men and women.

The complexity of mendacity, as articulated by Dawkins and Trivers, is doubly grim in its social implications, in that the male deception of females is made satanically more effective by the male's lying to himself in order to appear sincere and thus be more persuasive. Thus, if a man convinces himself that he is indeed in love with a woman, he is more likely to convince her as well in the articulation of his vows that he will be faithful to her and a good provider and father for her children. As Trivers makes clear, the repression of doubts, reservations, and ambivalences into the unconscious part of the mind creates a split in the psyche in which one part of the self is hidden from the other. Such a split helps define a central aspect of Freudian thought and its depiction of the mind as an arena of conflict. Janet Malcolm, in describing Freud's concept of "transference" as his "most original and radical discovery," makes a similar point about the inevitability of self-deception and its relationship to the deception of others:

The most precious and inviolate entity—personal relationships—is actually a messy jangle of misapprehensions, at best an uneasy truce between powerful fantasy systems. . . . The concept of transference at once destroys faith in personal relationships and explains why they are tragic: we cannot know each other.[3]

Lying in the form of deception and camouflage often evolves in nature without requiring conscious intent, even when it appears as if deception were deliberate. For example, the philosopher Daniel Dennett improvises a scenario in which a bird plans out a step by step strategy for deceiving a fox by leading him away from her nest of eggs by pretending to have a broken wing and thus appearing to become an easy prey for the fox:

I'm a low-nesting bird, whose chicks are not protectable against a predator who discovers them. This approaching predator can be *expected* soon to discover them unless I distract it; it could be distracted by its *desire* to catch and eat me, but only if it *thought* there was a *reasonable* chance of its actually catching me (it's no dummy); it would contract just that *belief* if I *gave it evidence* that I couldn't fly anymore; I could do that by feigning a broken wing.[4]

Dennett's delightfully parodic point is that a strategy for deception need not be grounded in consciousness.

A further example of programmed unconsciousness, on the human level, can be seen in our species having evolved concealed female ovulation, replacing estrus, the overt display of fertility. As Jared Diamond points out: "It's especially paradoxical that in *Homo sapiens,* the species unique in its self-consciousness, females should be unconscious of their own ovulation."[5] The effect of this bodily transformation, no doubt, was to encourage mates to stick around and help with parenting and be rewarded with regular sexual pleasure. It was not necessary, of course, for ovulation to be concealed from the woman as well as the man. The function of a woman's not knowing when she was fertile (unlike chimpanzees with their dramatic ovulation display) was that she could enter into sexual relations at any time without having to fake enthusiasm and involvement. Deliberate faking would be necessary if she knew that she was not fertile at the time of intercourse, and such dissembling would run the risk of being less than convincing. One might say, with comic irony in this reductionist account of female sexuality, that women have to fake themselves out so that they don't have to fake it, since otherwise their minds would be on procreation rather than recreation. And thus, armed with self-unawareness, a woman could enter the realm of sex whose purpose is pleasure—sex designed to keep a man at home and hearth. Such nondeliberate female self-deception, awareness repressed into the unconscious mind, is parallel to a man's falling in love, believing in his amorous state, in order to be persuasive in wooing a woman and subsequently being rewarded with sexual enjoyment and the improved chance of getting his genes into the gene-pool. Such is Shakespeare's bitter diagnosis of lust in sonnet 129 where he concludes: "All this the world well knows, yet none knows well / To shun the heaven that leads men to this hell."

With the evolutionary advent of consciousness, however, the possibilities for deception become greatly enlarged. This is well explained by what cognitive scientists call "Theory of Mind": the ability to imagine that someone else's mind can hold beliefs that differ from one's own. Chimpanzees have this capacity for deception and can use it to mislead others in the troop about where a food source can be found so that later, when they are alone, they can hoard the food for themselves. Franz de Waal, a leading primatologist, says that a "sign of higher cognition in chimpanzees is their deceptive nature," which he defines as the "deliberate projection, to one's own advantage, of a false image of past behavior, knowledge or intention." De Waal goes on to describe his observation that "these apes con each other. I saw them wipe undesirable expressions off their face, and hide compromising body parts behind their hands."[6]

Human children, at about the age of four, seemingly spontaneously, learn to distinguish their minds from others, and they do so with the realization that "other individuals can have beliefs and desires that are false." Robin Dunbar asserts that "they . . . can lie with the skill and persuasion of an expert."[7] The dark aspect of this capacity to imagine another individual as separate from yourself, as an independent entity, with whom you will have to compete for resources, is that it forms the basis for complex and sophisticated lying—lying that is tied to the struggle for survival and, especially, to the competition for finding a suitable mate and perpetuating one's genes into the next generation.

But personal lying or aggression in the competition for sexual success is not the worst manifestation of what we have come to think of as evil. War and even genocide are also grounded in both the deception of others and in self-deception. In Sigmund Freud's great essay "Thoughts for the Times on War and Death," written at the outbreak of World War I, he says: "The warring state permits every such act of violence. . . . It practices not only the accepted stratagems, but also deliberate lying and deception against the enemy."[8] And then, more hopefully, Freud says:

"But a little more truthfulness and upright dealing on all sides, both in the personal relations of men to one another and between them and those who govern them, should also do something towards smoothing the way to alter this regrettable state of affairs."[9] Lying and deception, it seems, work both for and against our species.

Freud goes on in his essay to deepen and enlarge what he means by "truthfulness" in extending it to include self-awareness, particularly the awareness that we repress the knowledge of our own personal death. "At bottom no one believes in his own death," says Freud, and this denial, activated in the unconscious, he further argues, projects itself onto others in the form of aggression: "Would it not be better to give death the place in actuality and in our thoughts which properly belongs to it, and to yield a little more prominence to that unconscious attitude towards death which we have hitherto so carefully suppressed?"[10]

Not long ago it was commonly believed that war was a peculiarly human activity, the result of the corrupting influence of civilization. The secret consolation hidden within this belief is that if war is judged to be the result of civilization, then, theoretically, war could be prevented by an alternative civilization. The choice would seem to be in human hands. But we now know, through the field research of Jane Goodall and others, that warlike behavior is to be found even among marauding bands of chimpanzees. "Chimpanzee-like violence preceded and paved the way for human war, making modern humans the dazed survivors of a continuous, 5-million-year habit of lethal aggression," says Richard Wrangham[11]; and Jared Diamond reminds us that "genocide has been part of our human and prehuman heritage for millions of years."[12] Current theory proposes that Cro-Magnon man, the predecessor of *Homo sapiens,* exterminated Neanderthals in the struggle for succession. The roots of violent behavior are more endemic to our nature than we had dared to imagine.

Such compelling and troubling new information reveals how deep in our genetic inheritance the proclivity toward violence lies, and that the moral project of civilization is more complex than merely reforming its own societal mistakes. The will toward achieving a moral and just society, not just within a group but across all cultural differences, based on the capacity for empathy, requires nothing less than our ability to reinvent ourselves. In the words of the poet William Butler Yeats: "I must remake myself." Such remaking, a form of self-mastery, requires that we improve in learning to tell the truth about ourselves: our evolutionary and biological inheritance, our selfishness, our willingness to deceive, our cruelty and murderousness. In "Three Essays on the Theory of Sexuality"

Freud warns us that "Cruelty in general comes easily to the childish nature, since the obstacle that brings the instinct for mastery to a halt at another person's pain—namely a capacity for pity—is developed relatively late."[13] In other words: It is hard to grow up.

In his essay "Politics and the English Language," George Orwell makes his appeal for truthfulness, that we employ language to communicate rather than to obfuscate and deny. "In our time," says Orwell, "political speech and writing are largely the defense of the indefensible."[14] Orwell is making the same point as Freud in that lying to others most likely has a component of lying to oneself as in schizophrenia: "All issues are political issues, and politics itself is a mass of lies, evasions, folly, hatred and schizophrenia," Orwell claims. And just as Freud based his measured hopefulness on a "little more truthfulness," so, too, Orwell, making his appeal that "language [be used] as an instrument for expressing and not concealing thought,"[15] articulates his hopefulness in a reformed attitude to language itself: "One ought to recognize that the present political chaos is connected with the decay of language, and that one can probably bring about some improvement by starting at the verbal end."[16]

If the struggle to achieve empathetic morality over the obstacle of instinctual selfishness simply pitted willed rationality and the concept of justice over emotional impulse, then morality would have no chance of prevailing. But what we possess as a part of our genetic inheritance—and just as deeply genetically rooted—is the capacity for sympathy, which, through culture, makes possible the extension of empathy into fictive art. This enlargement of the realm of empathy is the other side of the evolutionary story of cheating, deception, aggression, war, and genocide. Imagining what another individual is thinking, with the further awareness of what feelings must be associated with any particular thought, though providing an opportunity for deception and manipulation, also makes possible the identification with others. In other words—and this is of extreme importance for the evolution of morality and love—the origin of the capacity to lie, with the attendant temptation to lie, is exactly the same as the origin of the capacity for compassion. Darwin himself, in his late book, *The Descent of Man,* claimed that "any animal whatever, endowed with well-marked social instincts, would inevitably acquire a moral sense or conscience, as soon as its intellectual powers had become well developed." Darwin gives great emphasis to the human capacity for "sympathy," and he conjectures further, perhaps somewhat wishfully, that "sympathy . . . seems now to have evolved into an instinct."[17]

The new Darwinian paradigm, significantly updated on the basis of what we now know about genetics thanks to the work of Gregor Mendel, includes two basic ideas that explain why cooperation and altruism are likely to evolve on the human and cultural levels even though they are grounded in the "selfish" behavior of genes. William Hamilton's theory, called "kin selection," demonstrated that a successful survival strategy can derive from one individual's investment in the welfare of the genes of those to whom one is most closely related. For example, if one brother (who shares 50 percent of his sibling's genetic endowment) drowns while saving, say, two other brothers from drowning, the genetic arithmetic is still in favor of the survival of his genes, despite his personal death. Hamilton argued that the instinct to bond with others for one's own genetic benefit is thereby built into the dynamic of evolutionary law.

In 1971, Robert Trivers, in an essay entitled "The Evolution of Reciprocal Altruism," extended Hamilton's ideas in showing that instinctive cooperation, often overriding selfishness, could emerge through natural selection. Kin selection could get mutual altruism started, so that a "gene that repaid kindness with kindness could have spread through an extended [human] family."[18] The discoveries of Hamilton and Trivers are fully in accord with Darwin's basic insight into "sympathy" evolving in social animals, with the further development, aided by the emergence of language and the capacity for abstract thought, of sympathy as a moral principle, affirmed and celebrated in religion, philosophy, law, and art.

Shakespearean morality, whose crown virtue is the gift for forgiveness, is concordant with Darwin's concept of sympathy, based, as it is, on the Theory of Mind capacity for both seeing someone else as other and at the same time identifying with that other person rather than seeking to deceive or exploit him or her. To give two examples from Shakespeare's plays: Having shown competitive rage against Laertes at Ophelia's grave-site, claiming his greater love yet aware that Laertes is in a state of grief because of the death of his own father, Hamlet says to his attending friend, Horatio:

> But I am very sorry, good Horatio,
> That to Laertes I forgot myself,
> For by the image of my cause I see
> The portraiture of his.
> (*Hamlet*, V, ii, 75–78)[19]

And in an even more universal claim, King Lear, aware of the suffering of all humankind, aware of our bodily vulnerability to the forces of nature, proclaims this universal imperative to his own moral consciousness:

> Poor naked wretches, wheresoe'er you are,
> That bide the pelting of this pitiless storm,
> How shall your houseless heads and unfed sides,
> Your loop'd and window's raggedness, defend you
> From seasons such as these? O! I have ta'en

> Too little care of this. Take physic, pomp;
> Expose thyself to feel what wretches feel,
> That thou may'st shake the superflux to them,
> And show the heavens more just.
> (Lear, III, iv, 28–36)[20]

Through his fictional portraits, as in the above quotation or in Glouce-ster's parallel remarks, Shakespeare proclaims:

> Let the superfluous and lust-dieted man,
> That slaves your ordinance, that will not see
> Because he does not feel, feel your power quickly.
> So distribution should undo excess,
> And each man have enough.
> (Lear, III, i, 67–71)

Thus the audience is given to observe that the capacity for sympathy and empathy, seen as an alternative to lying and deception, can transcend mendacity's devious inventiveness within the form of literary art. So, too, the universal male fear of being cuckolded, and the inclination to jealousy in both sexes, may be overcome through the making of vows, which are a fictive structure with the potential to become, in the words of Robert Frost, "believed into existence" and thus, through the summoning of conscious will, enacted into historical reality.

Given the dynamic logic of repression, however, self-awareness always will remain at least a step behind self-deception. But the very knowledge of this Darwinian/Freudian fact can help increase the power and efficacy of conscious choice—as is indeed the case with Hamlet whose fundamen-tal wisdom, paradoxically, consists of knowing that he cannot know. Hamlet proclaims, "I do not know / Why yet I live to say 'This thing's to do,'" in trying to search out and delineate his confused and ambivalent emotions associated with his presumed duty to kill the king. The wonder-ing reader might well speculate that the very meaning of "readiness" in Hamlet's oracular, "the readiness is all," lies in the acceptance of limited self-knowledge.

II

In Shakespeare's *As You Like It*,[21] an exchange between Audrey, a coun-try wench, and Touchstone, a clown, reads:

TOUCHSTONE: Truly, I would the gods had made thee poetical.
AUDREY: I do not know what "poetical" is. Is it honest in deed and
    word? Is it a true thing?

TOUCHSTONE: No, truly, for the truest poetry is the most feigning; and
  lovers are given to poetry, and what they swear in poetry
  may be said as lovers they do feign.

(III, iii, 17–24)

At the heart of Shakespeare's complex view of love, particularly in his
comedies, resides the insight that love, at least in part, must be regarded as
a fiction, an invention, an illusion, and yet, as in poetry, the contrived idea
of love adds meaning to reality. In *A Midsummer Night's Dream,* for ex-
ample, Theseus declares: "The lunatic, the lover, and the poet, / Are of
imagination all compact," and though they all deal in deception, including
self-deception, they also have the power to give such palpable embodi-
ment to their lying that the lies, transfigured as art, take on a truth of their
own. Theseus goes on to describe the poet's imagination, which "bodies
forth / The forms of things unknown . . . and gives to airy nothing / A local
habitation and a name." Likewise, Wallace Stevens, an exemplary modern
celebrator of things fictive, asserts the human need for such "lying" when
he cries out: "Unreal, give back to us what once you gave, / The imagina-
tion which we spurned and crave." William Butler Yeats, in an extreme
formulation, insists on the imagination's power to create fictions and the
human capacity to love, beyond genetic selfishness, when he says that
"love itself would be no more than an animal hunger but for the poet." As
lovers and poets, by the lunatic light of our nocturnal minds, we dream
ourselves back into wakefulness, back into a reality that has the power,
through will and imagination, to transcend our evolutionary hungers.

Lying for the sake of love or for the sake of poetry assumes that lying
can have a benevolent effect as an expression of the capacity for empathy.
The belief in the "white lie" places the human need for consolation or the
assertion of moral ideals, such as commitment and faithfulness, above the
literalness of reality—reality seen reductively as unmitigated fact. Even
Plato, who in *The Republic* attributed the highest virtue to the primacy of
direct truthfulness and thus would exile the imitative arts from his repub-
lic, relents in behalf of fictive pleasures when he says that "she [the hon-
eyed muse] shall be allowed to return from exile, but on this condition
only—that she make a defense of herself in lyrical or some other meter."[22]
So, too, in the writings of Sigmund Freud, nobility is to be found when
pleasure gives way through reasoning to the dictates of the "reality prin-
ciple" without denying the need for fantasy and dreams, which also are
undeniable constants in human nature.

In conflicting claims of the need for sensuous pleasure and its extended
realm of wishfulness, and the recognition of the often brutal and unflatter-
ing facts of reality, we can recognize the ground of human ambivalence.

Our particular ambivalence toward lying, even in its most benign forms, is characteristic of our psychology as exemplified, for example, in such words as *fabricate,* which means both to make, to create, and to make up or deceive; or *fabulous,* which means both legendary, pertaining to a fable, and barely credible, straining belief. The origin of our word *poetry* is the Greek *poiein,* meaning to make or construct, in which such making becomes part of the poetic imagination as in the act of making believe. We have designs on each other and all of us (no doubt poets in particular) design our beliefs.

In his essay "The Lie Detector," the biologist Lewis Thomas takes delight in the fact that human beings cannot lie without the lie's having an actual effect on our bodies. (Scientific detection has been upgraded with brain scans and we have been informed that "telling a lie produces telltale changes in the brain.")[23] Thomas expounds:

A human being cannot tell a lie, even a small one, without setting off a kind of smoke alarm somewhere deep inside a dark lobule of the brain, resulting in the sudden discharge of nerve impulses . . . Lying, then, is stressful, even when we do it for protection, or relief, or escape, or profit . . . We are a moral species by compulsion, at least in the limited sense that we are biologically designed to be truthful to each other.[24]

The inability to lie with psychological impunity, so Thomas reasons, demonstrates to him that we are not moral beings merely by social necessity or conditioning. Thomas's contention, though it makes its point, may be somewhat optimistic in the light of the findings of evolutionary psychology, as propounded by Trivers and Dawkins, who argue convincingly as to the deep inclination to cheat and deceive as a basic survival strategy. The distinguished linguist Steven Pinker claims that "Primates are sneaky boldfaced liars. They hide from rivals' eyes to flirt, cry wolf to attract or divert attention, even manipulate their lips into a poker face." And Pinker goes further in adopting the theory that "the human brain is the outcome of a cognitive arms race set in motion by the Machiavellian intelligence of our primate forebears."[25]

In reflecting on the counterclaims of artistic lying, making believe without the intent to manipulate or deceive, and the tough-minded adherence to the literal truth, I once considered performing an experiment on myself. When giving a poetry reading of my own work, I would have myself strapped to a lie detector so that I would then be able to find out what effect my own lying—for the sake, of course, of creating narrative episodes and seemingly autobiographical poetic fictions—had on my own body. Would my body respond as if I were guilty of some crime against instinctual morality, as Thomas might assume? Would the ghost of Plato rise from the audience and wave me off with a sweeping gesture of banishment? Or would some evolutionary instinct to succeed through any competitive strategy, justified here as art, override any vestige of moral sensibility?

I could, so I conjectured, recuse myself by pleading the Fifth Amendment or by claiming poetic license. The Examination Center I consulted informed me that the police do not give lie detector tests to heart patients or to pregnant women because such tests are dangerously stressful. Since I am sometimes able to fancy myself as pregnant with new poems, I ought to be exempt, and so the speculation alone of this experiment has sufficed. Furthermore, a bolder strategy, I think, would be to recite an hour-long nonsense poem—a poem of pure sounds with repetitions and variations like a musical composition. Nonsense, like music, can offer pleasure liberated from the criteria of truthfulness—like the lyric forms that Plato permits in his *Republic.* Or perhaps, also like music (which we have an innate aptitude to learn as we do with language), there is a possible evolutionary explanation in that the tones of the human voice, as in a lullaby, evoke the bonding experience of mother and child, about which Sandra Trehub speculates that "we are born with a musical brain because music provides a special communication channel between parent and child."[26]

And again like music, nonsense is free of intellectual content—except for the feeling of pitch and duration of its vowels and consonants and the rhythm of its unfolding—and such feeling cannot lie because it cannot be measured by anything other than itself. How it sounds is what it is, despite one wag's quip about Richard Wagner when he claimed that "there was less there than meets the ear." The introduction of "nonsense" effects into a literary context, like the interruption of logic or consistency, is often an essential aspect of humor. Thus nonsense, deliberately intentional as such, can embody the spirit of play in that it lives and moves by the rules of its own making. Nonsense defies what feels like the tyranny of reason and logic (including the awareness that one must struggle to survive and eventually die) by momentarily liberating thought from Freud's "reality principle." Nonsense expresses the triumphant anarchy of the mind, the lover's expansive sense of possibility; nonsense may be experienced as a holiday from the necessity of facing reality's painful truths.

And yet, though beyond the criteria of falsification and veracity, beyond issues of morality, my nonsense poem, I suspect, would leave me standing before the microphone rather lonely. If anyone in the audience remained after an hour of my declaiming pure and meaningless sounds, no matter how mellifluous, they would, I am sure, miss the basic pleasure of human communication—not just recognizable words and sentences, but human communication that strives toward accuracy and truthfulness. Human sharing is so precious that we easily forget that we cannot live without reaching out to touch each other through meaningful language—language that assumes some measure of objectivity and therefore ties us to the world of facts, conditions, and laws that constitute our commonality. Without this measure of objectivity everything is open to interpretation and "depends on what the meaning of 'is' is" in the unforgettable words of a great contemporary evader; without objectivity, the distinction between lying and truth telling breaks down.

The greatest liar in literature, Shakespeare's Iago, who defines himself as "I am not what I am," a deconstructive phrase that is irretrievably elusive, speaks in tautologies that mimic the sound of meaning but lack the content: "It is as sure as you are Roderigo, / Were I the Moor, I would not be Iago." This is nonsense used as a deceptive strategy. In the face of such obfuscation, science may provide us with our best model for seeking a common world whose laws are independent of our religious or political preferences. When measured and observed, photons *are* both particles and waves; Hubble's expanding universe *did* originate in a Big Bang explosion; Einstein's theory of relativity is not itself relative in defining the interdependent coexistence of space and time. The laws of gravitation and the numerical quantity of pi are not culturally constructed, as Alan Sokal had to remind the academic community in his famous hoax in which he submitted an article to the politically correct fashionable magazine, *Social Text,* stating that:

"physical reality," no less than social "reality," is at bottom a social and linguistic construct, and that the pi of Euclid and the G of Newton, formally thought to be constant and universal, are now perceived in their ineluctable historicity, and the putative observer becomes fatally de-centered, disconnected from any epistemic link to any space-time point that can no longer be defined by geometry alone.[27]

The editors of *Social Text,* in an act of almost incredible self-deception no doubt resulting from their political biases, could not perceive either the absurdity of the claims being made or the pretentious and jargon-ridden language in which the claims are couched. After the brouhaha that followed Sokal's exposure of his salubrious hoax, he wrote, "I'm a stodgy old scientist who believes, naively, that there exists an external world, that there exist external truths about that world, and that my job is to discover some of them."[28] There is deep satisfaction to be found in discovering impersonal truths, even, paradoxically, truths that are painful to confront, like the indifference of nature—"red in tooth and claw," as depicted by Tennyson—to human wishes, or the cruelty of natural selection, which the evolutionist George Williams described as follows: "Natural

selection really is as bad as it seems." Huxley goes on to maintain there-
fore that natural selection "should be neither run from nor emulated, but
rather combated."[29] These unflinching observations ring, in my ears, with
heroic nobility, as do the rousing words of Sigmund Freud that summon
us to existential stoicism: "As for the great necessities of Fate, against
which there is no help, we will learn to endure them with resignation."[30]
No lying permitted here!

III

There is no phrase more exuberantly happy than one that appears in
Lewis Carroll's poem "Jabberwocky."[31] After his son has slain the mon-
strous Jabberwock, the father cries out, "O frabjous day!" His jubilation
carries him virtually beyond the limits of language, which generally is bet-
ter at naming emotions than evoking them, not only in the round note of
the rush of breath in the vowel "O," but also in the invented adjective
'frabjous," which has its own stressed grab and grip and lipful juiciness.
And yet "frabjous" is not totally beyond meaning, for it suggests the
words *fabulous* and *joyous,* with an extra *r* thrown in for the pleasure of
rolling it up from the throat and over the teeth while the whole phrase
presses itself against the norm of iambic meter—a pleasure fabricated for
the love of its invention. Nonsense here, unlike Iago's obfuscations, is not
meant to avoid truthfulness or to mislead, but to enhance the expression
of jubilation.

Often closely related to nonsense, humor, too, can have an expressive
and liberating effect. In addition to the storytelling fictiveness of much
humor, jokes also have the power of suddenly revealing a hidden or re-
pressed truth. When, for example, Diane Keaton says to Woody Allen, in
Annie Hall, that "sex without love is a very hollow experience," Allen re-
plies, "yes, but of all the hollow experiences I know, sex is the best." The
pleasure of this joke lies in the fact that the truth of the primacy of sexual
need, sanctimoniously concealed by Keaton's high-minded remark, is re-
leased into the open, and its truthfulness is immediately recognized by the
liberated moviegoer.

When Polonius comes to Hamlet to deliver the simple message that his
mother, Gertrude, wants to speak to him, the following exchange takes
place:

POLONIUS: My lord, the queen would speak with you, and presently.
HAMLET: Do you see yonder cloud that's almost in shape of a camel?
POLONIUS: By the mass, and 'tis like a camel, indeed.

HAMLET: Methinks it is like a weasel.
POLONIUS: It is backed like a weasel.
HAMLET: Or like a whale.
POLONIUS: Very like a whale.
HAMLET: Then I will come to my mother by and by . . .
POLONIUS: I will say so.
HAMLET: By and by is easily said.

(Hamlet, III, ii, 380–90)

This passage illuminates the danger in communication from excessive subjectivity by making a (grim) joke of indulgently finding resemblances in something as amorphous as a cloud. There is no connection between seeing the cloud as a camel, a weasel, or a whale and Hamlet's agreeing to Polonius's request to come to see his mother, and this breakdown in logic is the source of Hamlet's aggressive humor. When Polonius, with forced politeness, replies, "I will say so," Hamlet completes the irony of this whole exchange by remarking how "easily" language can be manipulated for devious purposes. As he has said earlier to Rosencrantz and Guildenstern in response to their betrayal of him by spying for King Claudius, the abuse of trust "is as easy as lying." Humor and irony can have the brief power to free us from the tyranny of logic, momentarily replacing the "reality principle" by the "pleasure principle," to again use Freud's terminology, but the joke or the witty remark must carry within it, shared by the audience, the awareness that the departure from logic and connectedness can only be temporary, so that a return to ordinary, objective truthfulness appears necessary and inevitable.

Enjoyment in inventiveness and creation, the pleasure of giving names to things and in some sense thus appropriating or possessing them, whether it be Humpty Dumpty's "*my* name means the shape I am—and a good handsome shape it is too," or Adam's act of naming the animals, or Shakespeare's giving to "airy nothing a local habitation and a name," is the antithesis of lying. Inventive art, in all the genius of its fictive powers, includes the means to return us to reality, the commonality of the physical world and its universal laws. "The supreme virtue here is humility," says the poet Wallace Stevens, "for the humble are they that move about the world with the love of the real in their hearts."[32] The main distinction between dreaming and works of art, says Freud, is that literary art leads us back into reality from its realm of imagination, thanks to its capacity for communication. Philip Rieff pointedly makes this distinction when he describes Freud's view of art: "A work of art is a system of shareable meanings, as a dream or daydream is not; a dream is merely expressive."[33] Our highest morality, grounded in Darwinian sympathy and our knowledge of our genetic inheritance as cheaters and deceivers, demands that we bear witness to ourselves and our origins. Bearing true witness can be the achievement of literary art as well as science. Knowledge of our evolutionary origins, grounded in our biological studies as well as in the archaic structure of our dreams, however, does not seal our fate to repeat what we have been, but can provide us with the intellectual tools, and can heighten our motivation, to remake ourselves. As Richard Dawkins says hopefully at the conclusion of *The Selfish Gene:* "We have the power to defy the selfish genes of our birth."[34]

In his famous essay "Of Truth,"[35] in considering humankind's "natural though corrupt love of the lie itself," Francis Bacon leaves room for an act of willful choice in whether or not to succumb to the innate temptation to lie when he makes the following distinction: "It is not the lie that passes through the mind, but the lie that sinketh in and settleth in it, that doth the hurt." The deliberate and active choice for truthfulness, Bacon goes on to assert, is the sovereign good of human nature, and this good is to be measured against the evil of deception and lying: "There is no vice that doth so cover a man with shame as to be found false and perfidious." Bacon then goes on to quote from Montaigne who wrote: "If it be well weighed, to say that a man lieth, is as much to say, as that he is brave toward God and a coward towards men," to which Bacon himself adds: "For a lie faces God and shrinks from man." The implication of the Montaigne/Bacon conceit is that the liar deceives himself by repressing his knowledge that God perceives his lie. In modern terms, the self-awareness that he is lying is denied and driven back into his unconscious mind where it will fester and return with even more egregious lying and with aggression toward others. As with Bacon's eloquent essay itself, human art, willed into fictive form, has the power to overcome the temptation to lie in its satanic aspect as deliberate deceit of others by first acknowledging the basic inclination toward self-deception. In according truthfulness its high status as a virtue, Bacon also celebrates the "belief of truth, which is the enjoying of it."

IV

As Frost's poems demonstrate, however, truth—whatever that word might convey—is difficult to enjoy, though the making of artistic designs and forms is surely a source of pleasure. Nevertheless, the restrictions and burdens imposed on us by reality evoke the temptations of avoidance and denial. Frostian concepts of Belief and Uncertainty are inseparable from his awareness of and dramatic depictions of the self-deceiving characters (narrators included) who populate his poems. His general skepticism about divine revelation or any kind of transcendent truth shows continuously throughout his poetry. Belief in Frost, particularly about God or meanings inherent in nature, is almost always presented equivocally or ironically. Although we hear Frost propound in his essay "Education by Poetry"[36] that "the self-belief, and the love-belief, and the art-belief, are all closely related to the God-belief," nevertheless any hint of the possible presence of God is more likely to be troubling or even terrifying, as in "Design" or "The Draft Horse." The bleak invocation of God's presence in a typical poem like "Bereft" hardly evokes the sense that God or God's Truth is adequate company or a cure for human loneliness.

> *Bereft*
> Where had I heard this wind before
> Change like this to a deeper roar?
> What would it take my standing there for,
> Holding open a restive door,
> Looking down hill to a frothy shore?
> Summer was past and day was past,
> Somber clouds in the west were massed.
> Out in the porch's sagging floor,
> Leaves got up in a coil and hissed,
> Blindly struck at my knee and missed.
> Something sinister in the tone
> Told me my secret must be known:
> Word I was in the house alone
> Somehow must have gotten abroad,
> Word I was in my life alone,
> Word I had no one left but God.
>
> (Frost 251)

Frost's conclusion that "Word I was in the house alone / Somehow must have gotten abroad, / Word I was in my life alone, / Word I had no one left but God," does not leave the reader with any sense of the revelatory word of God, only with the speaker's paranoid sense that others are aware of his loneliness and that their awareness exacerbates his own sense of isolation. The intensity of his isolation is the content of his somewhat guilty "secret." The "word" of this poem has nothing to do with what a committed believer might call the Truth in the mystical sense that "In the beginning was the Word, and the Word was with God, and the Word was God" as proclaimed by Saint John at the beginning of his gospel.

A distinction must be kept in mind when reading Frost between the idea of Truth as an abstraction and the idea of truthfulness, which pertains to a finite proposition. For example, in "For Once, Then, Something," in looking down into the bottom of a well to discern the identity of some object glittering there, Frost ironically speculates that it might be "Truth" or merely "A pebble of quartz." Frost's dismissal of the concept of truth as such is much like Stevens's parodic line, "Where was it one first heard of the truth? The the." In Stevens's outrageous concluding line in "The Man on the Dump," the word "truth" finally is replaced by the word "the," suggesting ironically that "the" is the more specific and useful word. For Frost, the abstract idea that there is something we might call the Truth goes beyond uncertainty into meaningless abstraction. Even when Frost uses "Truth" capitalized as a term as in "Birches," he does so to make the distinction between his fancy that the birch trees have been permanently bent down by a boy's swinging on them and the truthful "fact about the ice storm." In other words, truth here is known in its specificity, as a phenomenon of nature. His dismissal of Truth in its abstract grandiosity is part of Frost's anti-romantic strain, his worldliness, his suspicion of anything smacking of transcendence, as distinguished, say, from Keats's identification of Beauty and Truth in both his poetry and his letters. Let us remember, however, that an urn speaks the famous abstract equivalence, "Beauty is truth, truth beauty" (a silent urn at that), and that highly cerebral fiction, like the fiction of Frost's talking "Oven Bird," who says oratorically that "The highway dust is over all," might be a warning to the reader to take grand claims with a touch of skepticism.

Frost's "Neither Out Far Nor in Deep" is a little masterpiece of tonal ambiguity in which Frost's general attitude toward people who search for an all-abiding or transcendent truth is presented ironically yet not without a measure of sympathetic identification with the possible implication that Frost himself must be numbered among the "people" whom the poem satirizes:

> *Neither Out Far Nor In Deep*
> The people along the sand
> All turn and look one way.
> They turn their back on the land.
> They look at the sea all day.
>
> As long as it takes to pass
> A ship keeps raising its hull;
> The wetter ground like glass
> Reflects a standing gull.
>
> The land may vary more;
> But wherever the truth may be—
> The water comes ashore
> And the people look at the sea.

They cannot look out far.
They cannot look in deep.
But when was that ever a bar
To any watch they keep?

(Frost 301)

The depiction of the people, lumped together without distinction, all looking one way, indicates a kind of collective thoughtlessness, even stupidity. Although the "land" is where they spend their lives, they neglectfully turn their attention elsewhere, almost as if mesmerized by a compulsion to find meaning beyond themselves rather than within their own personal narratives. The ship that goes past them as they watch reveals nothing about its journey or destination, so that the detail of its "raising its hull" is a detail of nondisclosure, a fact without implication. "The wetter ground like glass" has the effect of a mirror that juxtaposes the image of the people with an image of the gull, thus suggesting (with an irresistible pun) that the people are gullible.

The tongue-in-cheek narrator, expressing a phony tentativeness in claiming that the "land may vary more" (of course it does), goes on to propound a vastly empty "truth" that can be reduced to what is tautologically obvious: "The water comes ashore, / And the people look at the sea." Wow! What a revelation! Yet, surprisingly, the narrator does not burst out into condescending laughter. Rather, there is a detectable hint of sympathy in his understated lines, "They cannot look out far. / They cannot look in deep," even as these lines also increase the reader's awareness of the absurdity of the people's searching for something that might be called "the truth." The final lines of the poem seem to me to be open to opposing meanings or implications, depending on how they are read tonally, and I suspect that Frost wanted his readers to hold both meanings in mind without trying to resolve their apparent contradiction. On the one hand, the lines can be read in tones of astonishment implying wonder at how dumb the people can be; on the other hand, the lines can be heard to suggest heroic perseverance and determination; the people will not be discouraged from believing in some kind of transcendent truth, like God, even though neither Truth nor God can be known. This second reading returns us to the overriding Frostian dialectic of belief and uncertainty.

"Provide, Provide!" is a poem that raises the question of what one can believe in old age to bring solace for one's decline and social abandonment. Its underlying irony is that the beautiful young woman, Abishag, who was given to King David to warm and console him in his old age ("And they sought out a beautiful young woman through all the territory of Israel, and they found Abishag," Kings 1:3) has now herself grown old (having been transported by Frost to Hollywood) and has become a model of all the aged who are in need of comforting as the poem's angry speaker makes clear to the unidentified person to whom the poem is addressed:

> *Provide, Provide!*
> The witch that came (the withered hag)
> To wash the steps with pail and rag,
> Was once the beauty Abishag,
>
> The picture pride of Hollywood.
> Too many fall from great and good
> For you to doubt the likelihood.
>
> Die early and avoid the fate,
> Or if predestined to die late,
> Make up your mind to die in state,
>
> Make the whole stock exchange your own!
> If need be occupy a throne,
> Where nobody can call *you* crone.
>
> Some have relied on what they knew;
> Others on being simply true.
> What worked for them might work for you.
>
> No memory of having starred
> Atones for later disregard,
> Or keeps the end from being hard.
>
> Better go down dignified
> With boughten friendship at your side
> Than none at all. Provide, provide!
>
> (Frost 307)[37]

It is difficult to account for the speaker's unmistakable bitterness, with its clubbing effect of rhyme repetitions in each stanza as the speaker's irony becomes increasingly acerbic in offering his impossible advice. The poem opens with its brutal and unsympathetic description of Abishag as a "witch" and a "withered hag," and further satirizes her and her culture, which takes false "pride" in beauty as if beauty had the power to last. The speaker then immediately assaults the poem's apparently doubting auditor as someone who resists the fact that it is likely that people's fortunes will decline. The poem thus becomes an implied disquisition on the general human proclivity toward self-deception, the inability to face reality.

As an assault against the auditor's defense of self-deception, the speaker offers absurd advice: "Die early and avoid the fate," and, even worse, he goes on to assume that human beings have no power to choose

at all, being "predestined." The speaker seemingly cannot control his out-
bursts of sardonic recommendations: "Make the whole stock exchange
your own! If need be occupy a throne," as he concludes with the contra-
diction, "Where nobody can call *you* crone," since he has already iden-
tified her with Abishag whom he called a "witch."

The speaker's tone softens just a little with the lines, "Some have
relied on what they knew; / Others on being simply true." But what the
"some" might have known is left entirely unspecified, and what "simply
true" refers to in this poem remains completely elusive so that the over-
all design of the poem suggests that there is no such thing as simple
truth, only speculation and uncertainty, grounded, as is highly likely, in
illusion. "What worked for them might work for you" is a line totally
without reference or meaningful consolation; empty as hypothesis, it
functions only as evasion.

And yet one might argue that the poem does, after all, offer something
that one might consider to be a "simple truth" spoken emphathetically in
the next straightforward lines: "No memory of having starred / Atones
for later disregard, / Or keeps the end from being hard." The word
"atones" is quite strange in this context since it implies some kind of
guilt, but how can one be guilty of growing old and losing one's beauty?
Unless, perhaps, the guilt here is that of evasion or denial of this very
truth—a truth that is, after all, recognizable: the truth of endings "being
hard." And if this is so, might the reader not speculate—with Frostian un-
certainty of course—that the recognition of this "simple truth" about
endings, not to be confused with any form of divine meaning or purpose,
does indeed confer some kind of dignity?

Painfully, the poem returns to its tone of bitter irony as the idea of rec-
ognition of defeat, "to go down dignified," does not seem to convey the
possibility of dignity free of illusion since it is achieved only through the
financial purchase of friendship. Can the speaker's bitterness be partially
explained by the fact that *his* friendship has been so purchased and that
much of the poem's irony is directed against himself in his identification
with his anonymous auditor? Who can be sure? The word "boughten,"
an obsolete form of bought, though perhaps still in colloquial use in Frost
country, nevertheless carries a sneer within it, and the irony of the final
words "Provide, provide!" denies the possibility that any true provision
in the face of endings is possible. This is as dark a truth as one will find
throughout Frost's poetry. Is there any dignity, then, to be found in the
poetry of disillusionment—in the poem's address to the reader, which is
not quite the same as the speaker's address to the poem's auditor, the si-
lent "*you.*" And might even the poetry of disillusionment with its fictive
truthfulness, its deliberate stanzas, qualify as an example of what Frost

meant when he wrote that "when in doubt there is always form for us to go on with"?

Wisdom, as we learn from Socrates, begins with the acknowledgment of ignorance, just as Frostian certitude resides in its awareness of uncertainty. Uncertainty, however, can be expressed and given its own luminosity, as Frost maintained, in poetic form. The purposefulness of human poetic design can be summoned to contend against the Darwinian version of nature as flux and struggle, which we see represented with particular intensity and irony in Frost's sonnet "Design." In Frost's poem the design of nature reveals an uncaring and even malevolent deity if indeed any intent is to be found in nature at all. Self-deception with its Darwinian inevitability and its Freudian location in the unconscious mind may be difficult to detect or uncover, but such uncovering is one of the main purposes of the poet, just as it is the work of the evolutionist and the psychoanalyst, whose discoveries are to be found in nature and not beyond.

Frost's "momentary stay against confusion" describes the contained awareness of confusion, not the banishment of confusion that is then replaced by the certitude of permanent belief. A poem only can be valid in its *momentariness*, as an act of mind whose consciousness almost, but never completely, closes the gap between what it knows and what it knows it does not know. The awareness of the inevitability of self-deception, and thus uncertitude, can keep the poet alert, just as form may function as a style of paying attention, concentrating, and therefore, as a "clarification of life."

In "Choose Something Like a Star," Frost, speaking inclusively in the voice of a collective "We," invokes a star as a deliberate symbol to represent the mind's power to make a "momentary stay" in the presence of uncertainty or confusion, signified by the image "some obscurity of cloud." The speaker asserts the presence of "some mystery," but does not ask the star (a projection of his own capability of thought) for some transcendent truth in the face of mystery. Rather, he makes a request for something "we can learn / By heart and when alone repeat." The speaker is insistent on this point: "Use language we can comprehend," he goes on to say. He compares his star to Keats's in his poem "Bright Star,"[38] which depicts the watching and observing star as a "sleepless Eremite," with the power to be "steadfast"—Keats's word, which Frost emphatically repeats. This steadfastness, which Frost in "The Master Speed" has called the "power of standing still," makes manifest the mind's ability to resist the temptation of self-deception, to think too well of oneself or too badly (the self-indulgence of guilt), "to carry praise or blame too far." Within the general context of nature's transience and the more personal context of uncertainty, Frost poses the possibility of a choice that offers a moment of stability, a kind of eternity within an instant of time, in which "We may choose something like a star / To stay our minds on and be staid."

The two poets who had the greatest influence on Frost, I would argue, are William Wordsworth and Robert Browning. What Frost mainly derives from the earlier poet is not Wordsworth's deepest and most modern psychological insight that childhood experience, going back even to infancy, forms the basis for adult personality, but, rather, Wordsworth's assumption about nature that it is to be regarded as if it were a book to be read and interpreted for what it reveals about God's purposes. Frost makes such attempts at interpretation to see if, like Wordsworth, he can find evidence for the existence of some kind of deity in the examination of nature in poems like "Design" and "Directive." Invariably, these attempts are stymied.

Browning's main influence on Frost is stylistic and technical as revealed in Frost's interest in dramatic and narrative poetry, including the monologue. But Frost, I believe, is also influenced by Browning's exploration of the psychology of self-deception, as in "My last Duchess" and "Porphyria's Lover," and by Browning's interest in Darwinian issues, particularly in his great poem "Caliban Upon Setebos."[39] In that virtuoso poem Browning, appropriating the figure of Caliban from Shakespeare's *The Tempest,* has the primitive Caliban attempt to theologize about his local god, Setebos, and also about a higher God called the "Quiet," in an attempt to understand God by examining God's apparent manifestation in nature and in human affairs.

In speculating that there might be "something over Setebos / That made Him," Caliban imagines a "Quiet" deity who makes "Himself feared through what He does," and Caliban attributes to him such qualities as unprovoked vindictiveness. This ironically named "Quiet" god would please the Satanic Accuser in the Book of Job as he is described when he "Next looks down here, and out of very spite / Makes this a bauble world to ape yon real." Caliban's Quiet deity of Darwinian indifference is, again like the God in the Book of Job, distinguished by his creative power: "all it hath a mind to do, doth, / Esteemeth stars the outposts of its couch, / But never spends much thought nor care that way." Yet Caliban's view of this all-powerful god is that he cannot be appealed to: "here are we, / And there is He, and nowhere help at all," although this plaintive remark is darkened with a touch of self-aggrandizing paranoia: "the best way to escape His ire / Is, not to seem too happy." This self-absorption of Caliban's thought is much like Frost's "scaring himself with his own desert places," though Frost, unlike the character Caliban, is fully and critically aware of his own self-absorption, and this very awareness deepens Frost's sense of his own isolation.

Frost's scaring himself also might be thought of as his attempt to take control of his fear, to become the agent rather than the victim of fear, but this is a strategy that cannot succeed, for there is a rational and objective component to fear that goes beyond self-absorption and self-deception in being "afraid of God." The biblical precedent, after all, describes a God who created nature and, having destroyed it once with a flood, remains a threat to destroy it again despite promises to the contrary. This is the fear that Frost expresses directly when, in "Once by the Pacific," he imagines an apocalyptic scenario in which God's first words, "Let there be light," become God's last words when "God's last *Put out the Light was spoken.*"

God's intentions and His final judgment are unknowable and are therefore an aspect of Frostian uncertainty, but so, too, are humans unknowable to themselves, making even self-judgment impossible. Not only are we unable to look into the mystery of the motivation of others, as with the family members in "Out, Out!" who turn back silently to their affairs when the boy dies from a buzz-saw accident, but also we fail when we try to evaluate the quality of our own lives. We cannot know if we are like one of the "apples" that "Went surely to the cider-apple heap / As of no worth."

This fear of the unknown, and its possibly eternal consequences, is the concluding focus of Frost's most theoretical and theological work, "The Masque of Mercy." Paul, a late-night customer, says to the keeper of a bookstore, "The fear that you're afraid with is the fear / Of God's decision lastly of your deeds." The Keeper, who does not literally believe in the possibility of punishment after death, nevertheless does not know how to view himself because he cannot imagine how God would or will view him: "But I'm too much afraid of God to claim / I have been fighting on the angels' side. / That is for Him and not for me to say." And the Keeper goes still further in regarding "the uncertainty / in which we act" as a kind of existential principle that ultimately only can be resolved by "God's mercy." Paul concurs with the keeper's statement about uncertainty when he says: "Yes, there you have it at the root of things. / We have to stay afraid deep in our souls." The Keeper's final speech poses "courage" as the virtue that will allow us all to live with the fear of uncertainty: "Courage is what it takes and takes the more of / Because the deeper fear is so eternal." And since this uncertainty is inescapable as an aspect of consciousness, Frostian "courage," what we have called heroic skepticism, is what is required to endure, to go on walking like the speaker in "Acquainted with the Night" or the couple in "The Draft Horse" who get down from their wagon and "walk the rest of the way."

Although for Frost "the deeper fear is so eternal," there is no Truth about the mind of God that can resolve the mystery of His ways, just as Job must finally put his hand over his mouth and say no more. The limited truth that Frost can know and can believe in is the truth of uncertainty, which includes uncertainty about the self, its unconscious depths, as well as about God. It is this limited truth, so Frost believes, that his poems must bear witness to. The poems themselves, with their willed and deliberated attempt at honesty, their resistance to false consolation, might, according to Frost's lifelong hope, achieve the "grace" of fictive truthfulness, beyond the personal failures of self-deception and moral weaknesses that are inevitable as one lives one's life within the contingencies of historical circumstance and Darwinian struggle.

Chapter 9

Reading the Landscape: Place and Nothingness

I

Some years ago, a literary critic, noted for his books about Romantic na-
ture poetry, was invited to teach at the Bread Loaf School of English in
Vermont. I arranged for him to be given one of the off-campus houses so
that he could enjoy the woodland setting that would seem to correspond
to his literary interests. After his first night in his rustic quarters, how-
ever, when I met him for breakfast, he complained that he had slept
poorly because his toilet had run all night. The campus caretaker re-
ported to me that the toilet was working properly, and in a flash I iden-
tified the problem. Having sought out the disoriented critic, I told him,
"What kept you awake last night was not the toilet but the stream that
runs outside your window." I had caught him in an act of unintentional
deconstruction, and, to his consternation, I urged him to reread Robert
Frost's poem, "The Need of Being Versed in Country Things."

Robert Frost asserted in a letter "that poetry is a fresh look and a fresh
listen." One cannot write a poem without being versed in the landscape
one would depict—the particular place. The responsive cadences implied
by the sequences of words on a page is what Frost meant when he said, "I
can't keep up any interest in sentences that don't SHAPE on some speaking
tone of voice." The willingness to listen to other voices—the voices in
which poems are spoken—constitutes part of the literary bond that can
hold writers together despite their proclivity toward competitive animos-
ity (of which Frost himself was sometimes guilty).

For many years Frost lectured and read his poems at the Bread Loaf
Writers' Conference and at the School of English on Bread Loaf Moun-
tain where Frost, through his poetry, shared his love for the names of
things. Animals, birds and plants—Frost is always accurate in referring
to them in his poems: the call of the oven bird, the way deer stop to look

back at you, the heal-all, usually blue in its aberrant white version, the fact that grape vines grow up birch trees. In August the fields and woods in Vermont brim with flowers in bloom: fireweed, black-eyed Susans, purple vetch, birds-foot, trefoil, tiger lilies, hawkweed, asters, chicory, thistle, purple loosestrife, daisy fleabane, small sun drops, joe-pye-weed, wood-sorrel, and jewelweed. The names themselves are a cornucopia of delights. And on Bread Loaf Mountain, following the constellations of the zodiac on a clear night, one can become inebriated with stars or transported with the first display of northern lights. The sense of awe, both wonder and dread, that comes from the feeling of human finitude in the presence of cosmic space, described by Frost as his own "desert places," ties us to our first ancestors and reminds us of our mere creaturehood, our vulnerability, and thus our need for language and for books in order to assert our momentary presence on this planetary stage. This world of lights and images, witnessed and named, of words spoken and listened to, constitutes the theatre in which we play out the obscure dramas of our lives. It was a theater that Frost knew well and that was dear to him. For those, as Wordsworth said, who "bend beneath our life's mysterious weight," the great poet of cure prescribed, "May books and Nature be their early joy," a prescription well heeded by his successor, Robert Frost.

II

In 1932, Sidney Cox, Frost's intimate friend, sent Frost his biography of him in which Cox took pains to relate what he knew about Frost's life to explain Frost's poetry. Cox's assumption was that a direct connection was to be found between Frost's historical experience and his art. With a severity that risked destroying their friendship, Frost wrote back to Cox: "To be too subjective with what an artist has managed to make objective is to come on him presumptuously and render ungraceful what he in pain of his life had faith he had made graceful."[1] The means by which grace may be achieved is through words—language employed faithfully and accurately, language made poetic because it is *versed* in country things.

No biographer can describe the leap an artist makes between his or her life and art, what Wordsworth called "the turnings intricate of verse." That particular transformation into fictive form is the very mystery of art. The ability to fabricate is, in part, a power the poet creates out of pure potentiality; one might say, out of nothingness. This power to create form from chaos or disorder derives from the cultivation of a discipline, the learning of a skill; its potential is inherent, but its realization must be earned. No aspect of craft is beneath the concern of the serious artist or the responsive teacher, and above all, the artist must know his or her place well enough to name the images that make up the particularity of that place. The commitment to achieve graceful form, to master a craft, and thus to be worthy of the Muse always has needed the reinforcement of a tradition that honors serious art and of a community that supports the process of learning. The love of words and patterns of words and the belief in the reality of the illusion that words can create constitutes the writer's essential bond with the reader, the teacher's bond with his or her students.

It is difficult to define exactly what Frost meant when he spoke of giving to words a form that possesses "grace." Perhaps grace comes when the mind holds onto something precious, when the distraction of Wordsworthian "getting and spending" or Darwinian struggle falls away and we achieve a clarification of what we value or what we love. Or perhaps grace comes when performance is in harmony with intention, and, paradoxically, we feel free of the limitation of being a singular individual bound by a single life. As artists, and as teachers of literary art, we become more than ourselves; we become what we have made and what we have celebrated through shared wonder in the face of literary accomplishment and its enlargement of our humanity. "All that is personal soon rots," Yeats said, knowing that the artist's inevitable argument against mutability is to preserve his or her words of shared caring, words cared into graceful form from what time would obliterate.

We do not invent language; we inherit it in the spirit of what Wordsworth called the "instinctive humbleness, / Maintained even by the very name and thought / Of printed books and authorship." Language has its own genius that recreates itself through our use of it. We are the means by which it grows and keeps itself alive. Like a god, it speaks through us and survives us. Our minds are created by language; our thinking is made possible by the innate structure it provides. And if we give ourselves wholeheartedly to the language, embracing it, cherishing its "intricate turnings," we may take on something of its grandeur and its majesty. I want to say with Frost that we receive its "grace," for we enter into the community of mind that crosses time and place, somehow containing them. Every true poem, by its very nature, is a celebration of its inheritance—the language that is never ours, though we, in our passing, partake of its ongoing grace. And surely Frost did have something like this concept of grace playfully in mind when he quipped, as if for the benefit of the critic who has been too long in the city pent, that "It takes all sorts of in and outdoor schooling / To get adapted to my kind of fooling."

For Frost the details and specificity of the physical world are often most effectively described against a background of absence or nothingness. In this respect Frost is particularly kindred to his contemporary Wallace Stevens, who proclaimed that "The greatest poverty is not to live in a physical world." Perhaps the grace that enables and inspires the artist to create form is most deeply understood in contrast to nothingness, its opposite, so that form, as Frost claimed, must be considered "for how much more it is than nothing."

III

The concept of nothingness or absence is present at the opening of the Book of Genesis: "In the beginning God created the heaven and the earth. And the earth was without form, and void; and darkness was upon the face of the deep." This concept of nothingness is equally important as an aspect of contemporary Big Bang theory in which the universe is described by Heinz Pagels "as a reexpression of sheer nothingness."[2] Edward Tyron speculated in 1973, reasoning that the total energy of the universe can be calculated as zero since there is a balance of positive and negative energy. "Our universe," Tyron reasoned, "could have appeared from nowhere without violating any conservation laws." In a more anecdotal mood, Tyron stated: "Our universe is simply one of those things which happen from time to time."[3] In the same spirit of cosmic playfulness, the mathematician Alan Guth remarked that "the universe may be the ultimate free lunch."[4]

We know that at the quantum level, where nature functions according to probabilities, not by Newtonian mechanical causal laws, "within one billionth of a trillionth of a second, an electron and its antimatter mate, the positron, can emerge out of nothingness without warning, come back together again, then vanish." Nothingness is a necessary idea, which Frost deeply believed, against which the idea of existence needs to be understood and defined. Although the opposite of creation may be thought of as destruction as in the relationship between order and entropy, it is equally meaningful to conceive of nothingness as the opposite of creation or as the womb of creation. Both the biblical account of God's creation of the world out of a void (or chaos as matter undifferentiated) and the Big Bang theory of the universe's origin can serve as suggestive models for artistic creation as well. Emily Dickinson intuitively asserted that "Nothing is the force / That animates the world."

IV

Attempting to hold the idea of creation and the idea of nothingness simultaneously in his mind, trying to unite the concept of presence and the concept of vanishing, Wallace Stevens's aged speaker, in "The Auroras of Autumn,"[5] beholding the spectacle of the Northern Lights, declares: "This is nothing until a single man contained / Nothing until this named thing nameless is and is destroyed." Poetic creation as an aspect of some worldly phenomenon, and the poet's mental annihilation of the named image, which renders it nameless again, is Stevens's way of seeing things simultaneously both in their presence and in their immanent vanishing. Naming the vanishing as well as the presence renders the image in flux nameless again and prepares the way for another act of naming. This imaginative power, as thus presented by Stevens, sees forms, possessed in their naming, collapsing back into loss, and sees loss generating new forms in an ongoing process of creative naming and unnaming in which absence becomes presence, and presence, absence.

If the idea of "nothing" is regarded, paradoxically, as the presence of absence, this concept can serve to objectify feelings associated with the intensified awareness of loss. The experience of loss, Stevens believes, is inseparable from the awareness of transience as an aspect of material reality, and thus nothingness becomes an essential concept for him—a concept that can be embodied in the metaphorical structure of a poem. In his poem "The Snow Man," for example, the image of the snow man represents the failure of the human mind when it responds to the physical landscape without projecting anything of itself onto the landscape. The imaginative poet must hear "misery in the sound of the wind," as if the wind were not only a physical fact, but also a symbolic entity that implied a corresponding human emotion such as "misery."

> *The Snow Man*
> One must have a mind of winter
> To regard the frost and the boughs
> Of the pine trees crusted with snow;
>
> And have been cold a long time
> To behold the junipers shagged with ice,
> The spruces rough in the distant glitter
>
> Of the January sun; and not to think
> Of any misery in the sound of the wind,
> In the sound of a few leaves,

Which is the sound of the land
Full of the same wind
That is blowing in the same bare place

For the listener, who listens in the snow,
And, nothing himself, beholds
Nothing that is not there and the nothing that is.
(Stevens 9)

Although this appears to be a poem about the imagination at its minimal level of activity, the poem in fact is about a new beginning and is thus appropriately set in the month of January. As Stevens says in "Aesthetique du Mal," describing the cycle of the seasons as an analogy to the cycle of the imagination as it moves from cold perception to warm perception, "After the final no there comes a yes, and on that yes the future world depends." The "no" of this poem expresses the failure of the mind to relate to the landscape, to personify it, and thus turn the landscape into a metaphor for human feeling, such as "misery." The emptiness of the landscape as "bare place," reflected in the poem as a rhetorical pattern of sameness, is transformed into its paradoxical opposite: the barrenness of the scene has its own kind of fullness, "full of the same wind," and is therefore capable of bringing forth new acts of mind or beholding in response to the challenged and energized imagination.

In arguing for the inseparability of physical fact and of human perception's affecting that fact, Stevens is following Heisenberg's principle of indeterminacy, which claims that at the quantum level any light that we use to see a particle affects the movement of that particle, so that the very act of observation changes the observed object. This powerful idea applies also to the imagining of nothingness, a nothingness as a present absence that, in Stevens's poem, represents the diminished reality of a physical world in which there is no human consciousness to contemplate it. Imagining absence, we project ourselves into that absence and thus create a new entity in the physical world. Hence, nothingness possesses a potential fertility out of which a poem, or even a universe, may be born. Stevens ends his poem by imagining a snow man who is "nothing himself" without Stevens's imagining of him, thus making a distinction between well imagined and poorly imagined nothingness: "nothing that is not there and the nothing that is." The nothing that is there is indeed the womb out of which the poem emerges, and, for the human mind to begin to fathom itself, the mind must contemplate its inner nothingness. Stevens succinctly formulates this idea again in "The Plain Sense of Things" where he says: "Yet the absence of the imagination had itself to be imagined." So absence becomes the idea of absence and is thereby given substance verbalized as an idea.

V

Antithetical to the idea of nothingness as a fruitful womb or as a principle of potentiality is nothingness perceived as the absence of meaning or of moral values. The theme of nothingness in *King Lear*[6] for example, is expressed first by his daughter Cordelia when she replies with the single word, "Nothing," to her father's public demand that she flatter him. Lear's angry response that, "Nothing will come of nothing" will prove paradoxically to be mistaken in the course of the play, in which a much deepened love between father and daughter will subsequently be born out of that very "nothing." Shakespeare shows us the truly negative aspect of nothingness in *The Winter's Tale*,[7] where the paranoid king, Leontes, is bitterly expressing suspicion and jealousy toward his faithful wife, Hermione:

> . . . is whispering nothing?
> Is leaning cheek to cheek? Is meeting noses?
> Kissing with inside lip? stopping the career
> Of laughter with a sigh? a note infallible
> Of breaking honesty,—horsing foot to foot?
> Skulking in corners? wishing clocks more swift?
> Hours, minutes? noon, midnight? and all eyes
> Blind with the pin and web but theirs, theirs only,
> That would unseen be wicked? is this nothing?
> Why, then the world and all that's in't is nothing;
> The covering sky is nothing; Bohemia is nothing;
> My wife is nothing; nor nothing have these nothings,
> If this be nothing.
> (*The Winter's Tale*, I, ii, 284–96)

In this speech, Shakespeare portrays the opposite of trusting love as negating jealousy and doubt. And since love is a human invention, an idea that transfigures animal desire into a complex passion that seeks to offer as well as to receive gratification, it follows that the doubting of this conception of love, born of the imagination, throws the world back into being a place without meaning, a place of moral chaos. In an emotional sense, Leontes has deconceived his own marriage, and, in doing so, he has given birth to a nothingness that he cannot imagine is capable of breeding anything but further nothingness. Thus is nothingness compounded on itself as in the dizzying conclusion to Leontes' speech: "nor nothing have these nothings, / If this be nothing," where the word "nothing" begets more of "nothing" until even sense and comprehensibility are emptied from Leontes' mind.

At the conclusion of the play, twenty years later, thinking that his wife has long been dead, and now deeply repentant and longing for her forgiveness, Leontes accepts an invitation to the house of his friend Paulina to see a statue of Queen Hermione unveiled. Paulina says: "prepare / To see the life as lively mock'd as ever / Still sleep mock'd death." Astounded by the statue's likeness to his wife, Leontes responds by observing: "The fixture of her eyes has motion in't. As we are mocked by art." If earlier it appeared that only nothing could come of nothing, here, to the contrary, satiric mockery—the painful reminder that a statue of stone, no matter how accurate the resemblance, cannot replace his wife— is transformed into the mockery of art, artistic imitation. This artistic imitation is so compelling to Leontes that, despite his skepticism, he moves toward the statue to kiss it: "What fine chisel / Could ever yet cut breath? Let no man mock me, / For I will kiss her."

Beyond Leontes' uttermost belief, but not beyond his secret hope, Hermione, however, truly is alive, though to the eyes of Leontes she has been miraculously reborn out of stone. In reality, this is a psychological miracle, love reborn out of long absence and contrition, that has been made possible by a restoration of faith on Leontes' part. Paulina expresses this deepest of Shakespearean beliefs in the power of faith and forgiveness in her line: "It is required / You do awake your faith." Embracing her at last, her love restored from stone, from death, from nothingness, Leontes cries: "O! she's warm. / If this be magic, let it be an art / Lawful as eating." And thus art as creation out of nothing, as imitation or magic, is returned to the realm of reality, the realm of "eating" and ordinary bodily survival.

VI

An intense awareness of nothingness as absence or darkness is often to be found in Frost's poetry. In "Out! Out!" for example, the boy who loses his hand in a buzz-saw accident, has his life slip away to "Little—less— nothing!" In "Desert Places" Frost scares himself with his own "empty spaces." And in "Acquainted with the Night," the night represents an inner psychological darkness as well as a physical outer darkness. These negatives are all aspects of a "background of confusion shading away from where we stand into black and utter chaos" where there is no reassuring sense of place and one is so totally lost that one may not even know what one is uncertain about. Such a landscape of lostness is described in "The Wood-Pile": "The view was all in lines / Straight up and down of tall slim trees / Too much alike to mark or name place by / So as to say for certain I was here / Or somewhere else."

The metaphor of a "desert place" is the Frostian equivalent of wilderness as represented in the Hebrew Bible and the New Testament, in which wilderness, as desert, does not carry with it the connotations of possible sublimity as it does for Romantic poets or for environmentalists such as Muir or Nash. In Exodus 32:5 "the desert land" is described as the "waste howling wilderness" and in Luke 4:1–2 Jesus is led into the "wilderness" where, "being forty days tempted of the devil . . . he did eat nothing." Biblical wilderness, like Darwinian nature, is seen in its adversarial aspect, its alien indifference to human needs, whose opposite is the garden of human cultivation. In this aspect of the fundamentally inhospitable, nature, seen as wilderness, is akin to chaos or nothingness since human order of any kind must confront and contend with primal disorder or chaos.

The coordinates, one might say, of "West-Running Brook," Frost's most extensive exploration of this backdrop of chaos, are place and nothingness. The unusual direction in which the brook flows invites the reader to reorient himself in both the physical and the psychological landscape just as the couple in the poem have to learn to "go by contraries" and at the same time locate themselves in relation to the "brook." The poem begins with the couple in dialogue about where they stand in the landscape: "Fred, where is north? / North? North is there, my love. / The brook runs west." And since this poem equates identifying oneself with some act of naming the place and location where one resides, the significant line that follows, spoken by the wife, is: "West-running brook then call it."

The theme of naming is continued in the voice of the narrator, whom we hear parenthetically—"(West-running Brook men call it to this day,)"—and whose comment sets the poem in a kind of indefinite and mythic past. For the wife, the named brook is seen as symbolic of her marriage and, more generally, as representative of how males and females can most beneficially interact on the basis of trust: "It must be the brook / Can trust itself to go by contraries / The way I can with you and you with me." And thus the narrator establishes a style of speech for the wife, a Frostian "sentence sound" that, in contrast to the husband's realism, combines fancy or metaphorical seeing with local description.

In response to her husband's rather flat description of their married identity, "what we are," his unimaginative "Young or new," the wife then enlarges her metaphorical naming of the brook so that the concept of marriage includes the specific place inhabited by the couple: "As you and I are married to each other, / We'll both be married to the brook." This is a concept beautifully paralleled in Wallace Stevens's line, "They married well because the marriage-place / Was what they loved." This metaphorical reading of the landscape is so intense for the wife, her fictionalizing so much a part of natural reality as she perceives it, that she chooses to imagine that the brook is communicating with her: "Look, look, its waving to us with a wave / To let us know it hears me."

Her personalizing of the brook, however, serves another playfully mischievous purpose that will emerge right after her husband's attempt at naturalistic description: "That wave's been standing off this jut of shore," his corrective to his wife's flight of fancy. And yet he resorts to a simile of a bird with "white feathers" to depict what he sees, and he has to catch himself from becoming even more fanciful by refusing the temptation to claim that rivers "were made in heaven." So his speech ends with his attempt at factual realism in contrast to his wife's personalizing of the brook as waving to her. "It wasn't waved to us," he asserts in his version of a Darwinian view of nature's indifference to human wishes, thereby giving the reader both a psychological and a stylistic example of the couple going by "contraries."

The wife's counter to her husband, reasserting her own way of seeing the wave, "It wasn't yet it was. If not to you / It was to me in an annunciation," makes manifest by suggestion what the wife has been hinting at to her husband—that she is pregnant. When earlier the wife had included the brook as part of their marriage, her provocative words had already provided a clue to what she has in mind to announce to him: "We've said we two. Let's change that to we three." But he does not yet divine what she is telling him and, perhaps sensing that she is gently taunting him, he expresses his annoyance with "It is your brook! I have no more to say," a rejoinder that deepens the drama of contraries behind which lies the crucial issue of trust. The long evolutionary history involving the loss of estrus whereby the human female does not reveal when she is fertile, combined with the lately evolved condition of concealed pregnancy in mammals, makes it difficult for the male to know if he is indeed the parent, and so under these conditions the issue of trust for a human couple becomes of paramount importance, as Shakespeare's plays are tireless in showing us.

Despite the husband's irritation at feeling somehow excluded, the wife, nevertheless, will not allow him to withdraw in a sulk, and urges him to go on talking. Thus newly enfranchised, her young husband delivers his longest and most impassioned speech. Now realizing that his wife is playing a game of contraries, he picks up on this theme, although he tries to do so by describing the brook in visual and (for him) believable terms.

Although his intent is to regard the brook in physical terms, almost inadvertently, as if swayed by her influence, he turns the brook into a symbol of evolutionary origins and, in doing so, he enlarges its emblematic implications into an even more comprehensive symbol of contraries: "Speaking of contraries, see how the brook / In that white wave runs counter to itself." Seen this way, the brook-wave represents a fundamental dialectic in nature: the universal movement toward entropy versus the capacity of matter, under special conditions (in which energy is borrowed from the sun), to organize itself into complex and living forms.

The husband continues his meditation in this mode of evolutionary speculation: "It is from that in water we were from / Long, long before we were from any creature," as he tries to imagine the "beginning of beginnings." In his mind, however, the sense of loss and of endings is simultaneous with his sense of origins, and he rejects the idea that existence is a static eternal dance; rather, he asserts that the stream of time "runs away, / It seriously, sadly, runs away / To fill the abyss' void with emptiness." This is indeed the background of nothingness against which all human meaning, everything precious to us, must be played out—an idea he states succinctly: "This is the universal cataract of death / That spends to nothingness." The wife's truth that they will be married to the brook has its counterpart in her husband's version of the brook as a force of division and disunity: "It flows between us / To separate us for a panic moment." Because there is something in nature and in ourselves that differentiates and divides, trust—an embodied form of grace—is needed to hold the married lovers together.

It is important to emphasize that the capacity for trust is not to be seen simply as an act of human will, the ability to make a vow and stick to it. Rather, it is built into human nature as an "instinct" for sympathy deriving from an evolutionary inevitability. Darwin, in *The Descent of Man*, proposed that

The moral sense follows, firstly, from the enduring and ever present nature of the social instincts . . . [and that] sympathy, though gained as an instinct, . . . has been rendered more tender and widely diffused through the effects of habit, example, instruction, and reflection.[8]

This is what the reflecting husband basically has in mind when he proclaims that the movement toward entropy and death is countered in the very image of the "stream of everything"—"by some strange resistance in itself." He becomes as subjective and impressionistic as his wife had been when, in a typically Frostian "as if" speculation, he says, "As if regret were in it and were sacred." In this terse statement he projects his own feelings and values into the landscape so that place and person become virtually inseparable.

One might consider regret and sacredness to be antithetical and mutually exclusive, but what they constitute in combination is another example of contraries, what Wordsworth described as the "reconciliation of discordant opposites." Perhaps we can say further that Frost is offering us his own version of human life as tragic in the Shakespearean sense in which the inevitability of loss can be perceived as offering life the possibility of achieving sanctity: "The brook runs down in sending up our life. / The sun runs down in sending up the brook." Creation and destruction, order and entropy, are absolutely linked in a kind of marriage, as reconciled opposites, as contraries. This universal pattern therefore serves as a model, according to her now impassioned husband, for the couple's relationship both to each other and to their place in nature.

The husband is now ready to make another try at identifying "what we are" within their new bond with his claim that "It is from this in nature we are from. / It is most us." The wife is quick to affirm his new definition, and though she is not yet ready to disclose the secret of her pregnancy (some tension between men and women probably never can be fully resolved) her pledge of agreement takes the form of another preparatory form of annunciation. The husband fully understands the spirit of celebrating what is sacred through an act of naming and immediately repeats her words with his own augmentation, "No, today will be the day / You said the brook was called West-running Brook," in which his "No" really functions as a "Yes," a succinct linguistic version of contraries as resolved opposites.

One can only speculate as to why the wife is not yet ready to disclose her pregnancy openly to her husband, but perhaps she wishes for him to surmise it for himself in order for him to make the discovery his own, his part in the contrary that binds them together. In any case, the final line of the poem, "Today will be the day of what we both said," can be heard as spoken by the wife or by the two of them together in a kind of duet. Their statement in the spirit of mutuality, implying trust, may be seen as a gift of grace, their affirmation of love against the backdrop of nothingness. This entire dialogue, as the narrator's earlier interjection makes clear, has taken place in the past and given the brook its name, and so the resolving phrase, "Today will be the day," establishes the poem in a kind of eternalized time that includes both past and present and thus seems to transcend the ordinary linkage of time and entropy as expressed by the husband in his earlier line, "Our life runs down in sending up the clock." And so, for these married lovers, "nothingness" becomes the very medium of the creation of belief—belief in mutual trust—which has the power to override uncertainty and suspicion by virtue of the imagination's ability to conceive of contraries, just as Shakespeare had claimed in defining the imagination's genius as the ability to "give to airy nothing / A local habitation and a name."

Chapter 10

Parenthood and Perspective

I

Having been children themselves, parents are experientially empowered to perceive their own children from a double perspective: from the eyes of a child and from their own eyes as adults. A father is a composite psychological being; he is both father and son together, a son-father and a father-son. This double perspective also can be expressed in terms of a multiple sense of time in which past and present become simultaneous: the son anticipating the future and the father remembering the past or, with further Wordsworthian ("The child is the father of the man") complexity, the father aware of the way he was fathered, which determined the kind of son he was, which determined the kind of father he has become, which determines the way he now views his son. In Freudian terms this would mean that Laius's murderous aims toward his son, Oedipus, are inseparable from Oedipus's wish to murder his father; neither can be given priority over the other. The father complex and the son complex have existed together immemorially. In the language of positive emotions, such as empathy and the sense of worthiness, the father's love for the son is inseparable from the son's capacity to accept and approve of himself, so that the grown son, as parent, becomes an approving father to his own son. Thus are the generations bound together in love or enmity both in the overt relationship of father and son and within the single mind of the father.

This double perspective which through self-awareness doubles back upon itself into a kind of infinite regress of the father perceiving the son perceiving the father perceiving the son . . . and so on, also can become manifest as a form of narrative technique within the range of effects open to lyric poetry. Much of Wordsworth's poetry employs this technique of *double narration,* the intertwining of past and present in one perspective, and this technique also can be found among exemplary post-Wordsworthians like Dylan Thomas, Theodore Roethke, and Robert Frost.

II

In Theodore Roethke's poem "My Papa's Waltz,"[1] for example, we are presented with a double narrator: a child and a man combined. In the course of the poem we hear the intermingling of their two vocabularies, the sensually immediate images of the "pans" and the "buckle" and the abstract, allegorical representation of "death." At the outset, the title suggests that we are listening to the poem from the son's, the child's perspective. It would be a very different poem if the title were "My Father's Waltz."

> *My Papa's Waltz*
> The whiskey on your breath
> Could make a small boy dizzy;
> But I hung on like death:
> Such waltzing was not easy.
>
> We romped until the pans
> Slid from the kitchen shelf;
> My mother's countenance
> Could not unfrown itself.
>
> The hand that held my wrist
> Was battered on one knuckle;
> At every step you missed
> My right ear scraped a buckle.
>
> You beat time on my head
> With a palm caked hard with dirt,
> Then waltzed me off to bed
> Still clinging to your shirt.
>
> (Roethke 45)

We enter the poem through the son's comic memory of his drunken father dancing with him, but as we move deeper into the poem it becomes clear that the perspective is that of the child having grown up, remembering this occasion long after his father has died. The phrase "But I hung on like death" is not spoken in a child's voice—it is, rather, the voice of the child having grown into an adult, capable of abstraction, now looking back and trying to reenter the scene when he danced with his father. The waltz in this poem, from the narrator's and the reader's perspective, thus becomes both a dance of life and a dance of death, whose complex doubleness only can be understood through the adult's perspective looking back, not from the child's perspective alone, since the child is totally contained within the scene. All that the child understands at the time is that he feels both danger and excitement. "We romped until the pans / Slid from the kitchen shelf," expresses the child's sensibility through verbs of action, but the phrase "My mother's countenance" clearly belongs to another vocabulary—that of the grown poet who is capable of assuming an ironically humorous tone.

The frowning mother is an outsider to the bond between father and son as the son experiences the passion of being roughly wooed by his father at the moment when their love seems complete even though it contains ambivalent feelings. The element of fear enhances rather than undermines the son's sense of pleasure. With the phrase, "The hand that held my wrist / Was battered on one knuckle," a growing sense of danger and of possible damage, is reinforced by actual pain: "At every step you missed / My right ear scraped a buckle." From the child's perspective, this is a moment of intense happiness even though it contains pain, but it is pain that the child willingly endures because it brings him closer to his father. "You beat time on my head / With a palm caked hard by dirt" continues the near violence of the drunken dance, and the image of "dirt" returns the reader to the earlier simile, "like death," making a kind of covenant between father and son through the reminder that we are all created out of dust and in time return to the waiting earth.

The father, in retrospect, has become an emblem of death for the grown son, the poet; he is now seen as being of the earth, of the dust to which he has in fact returned. The father has waltzed his son off to sleep and has, himself, been waltzed off to death. Looking back, the adult son remembers resisting being put to bed, and this moment epitomizes his resistance to the sorrow he feels in confronting the memory of his father's death, a resistance that has become manifest in the poem's insistence on emphasizing the comic elements of the memory. At the poem's end, the adult narrator is clinging to his memory of his father in the waltz. The narrating voice that speaks this poem is enriched by the merging of the child's voice and the adult's voice, and the two voices together become the voice, not just of the poet, but of his poem. Roethke's personal identity has been enlarged to include both his present and past self in the three-beat waltz of his poem, which gives new embodiment to the historical waltz of his childhood experience. Balanced between mourning and celebration, the poem is resolved on the side of comedy, which is to say that the son's memory is more a source of pleasure than of pain. It is as if the poet's dead father has returned to release him from grief and to relieve the burdensomeness of the body, weighted with mortality, with the lightness of the rhythm of the waltz.

III

Sigmund Freud in his late (1928) essay "Humor"[2] tells us that in humor the superego speaks "words of comfort to the intimidated ego." This is a remarkable statement since Freud usually portrays the superego, which "inherits the parental function," as severe, chastising, and constraining. In the case of humor, however, it is as if the father, the superego, allows the son, the ego, a moment of play exempt from the strictures of reality. Freud calls this holiday from the demands of the reality principle "a rare and precious gift." He makes a distinction between the holiday from reality that humor makes possible in the momentary feeling of triumph that comes in laughter and the unreality of dreams or insanity. Humor carries within it knowledge of the path back to reality, the world in which the self is limited by the constrictions of nature. This gift of the father to the son, interiorized as a benevolent dynamic between the superego and the ego, is a form of inner grace—to use Frost's word—much like that interim when we allow ourselves to inhabit the timeless world of a poem. Although the superego, according to Freud, is a "stern master," its tough sense of reality paradoxically includes the knowledge that we cannot endure reality all the time; we require the respite of temporary illusion in the form of play or art. Given this tolerance, the superego can remain true to its disciplining function even though, as Freud says wryly, it may "wink at affording the ego a little gratification."

The forms that humor can take are manifold even in poems concerned with the most painful themes, such as the loss of a loved one through death, old age, the rapaciousness of nature, human aggression and war, or the absence of moral purpose in a godless universe. From outrageous punning to extravagant irony, the range of the poet's devices is designed to give readers the feeling that they also can confront whatever truths have to be faced through the power of laughter. In their capacity to laugh, poets allow themselves temporary illusions of being in control, but these illusions fabricate their own truths by virtue of the fact that they acknowledge themselves as illusions or as artistic structures that function as the adult equivalent of the play of children. Laughter of this psychological magnitude may also be seen as a form of reconciliation between parent and child within the familial space of the mind, between the determination to see the world as it is and the acceptance of our vulnerability as creatures who cannot relinquish the need for pleasure and the momentary experience of emotional control.

A laughing father, such as Roethke's in his boisterous dance, may seem less remote, less an embodiment of intractable and repressive social or cultural forces if the son is able to partake of the father's spirit of humor, to join him in a comic dance, a binding of the generations as in the tradition of literary art, received by younger writers as their inheritance and blessing.

IV

In the stealing the boat passage from Wordsworth's *The Prelude*,[3] for example, the mature narrator describes a boyhood experience that both evokes the experience as it took place in the past in concrete physical terms and at the same time offers an interpretive perspective of that experience in abstract and conceptual terms:

> One summer evening (led by her) I found
> A little boat tied to a willow tree
> Within a rocky cave, its usual home.
> Straight I unloosed her chain, and stepping in
> Pushed from the shore. It was an act of stealth
> And troubled pleasure, nor without the voice
> Of mountain-echoes did my boat move on;
> Leaving behind her still, on either side,
> Small circles glittering idly in the moon,
> Until they melted all into one track
> Of sparkling light. But now, like one who rows,
> Proud of his skill, to reach a chosen point
> With an unswerving line, I fixed my view
> Upon the summit of the craggy ridge,
> The horizon's utmost boundary; far above
> Was nothing by the stars and the grey sky.
> She was an elfin pinnace; lustily
> I dipped my oars into the silent lake,
> And, as I rose upon the stroke, my boat
> Went heaving through the water like a swan;
> When, from behind that craggy steep till then
> The horizon's bound, a huge peak, black and huge,
> As with involuntary power instinct,
> Upreared its head. I struck and struck again,
> And growing still in stature the grim shape
> Towered up between me and the stars, and still,

For so it seemed, with purpose of its own
And measured motion like a living thing,
Strode after me. With trembling oars I turned,
And through the silent water stole my way
Back to the covert of the willow tree;
There in her mooring place I left my bark,—
And through the meadows homeward went, in grave
And serious mood; but after I had seen
That spectacle, for many days, my brain
Worked with a dim and undetermined sense
Of unknown modes of being; o'er my thoughts
There hung a darkness, call it solitude
Or blank desertion. No familiar shapes
Remained, no pleasant images of trees,
Of sea or sky, no colors of green fields;
But huge and mighty forms, that do not live
Like living men, moved slowly through the mind
By day, and were a trouble to my dreams.

(Book 1, 357–400)

The images of the "little boat," the "willow tree," the "rocky cave," and the "chain," could have been perceived exactly as such by the boy at the time he stole the boat, and though the boy must have *felt* anxiety, he would not have conceptualized his feelings as "troubled pleasure" as the adult narrator does in retrospect. The reader is aware of this duality of perspective throughout the passage, so that on the one hand we are given instances of direct perception and sensation such as "I dipped my oars into the silent lake," but only an adult would offer an evaluative qualifier of that action with a word like "lustily." And the conclusion of this boat-stealing is filled with conceptual terms such as "blank desertion" and "mighty forms." The sensibility of the boy, however, is retained within the philosophical and narrative mentality of the adult, whom the reader therefore conceives as the son within the father.

In what sense, then, does the son leave an inheritance for the father he will become, and in what further correlative sense does the adult poet become a kind of father to the reader? Another way of formulating these questions would be to ask what is the essence of growth that leads to and defines adult maturity? The whole passage has the aura of a mythic journey beginning with a departure from the "cave," as a womb-like representation of home, progressing through a sexual experience, the lusty boat ride, which brings forth a sense of guilt in the apprehension of the seemingly chastising "huge peak," and concluding with a deepened sense of the mind that includes an awareness of its unconscious depths in the form of troubled "dreams."

As the boy heads out across the lake, he is attuned to nature as a guiding presence, "the voice / Of mountain echoes," but the "circles" in which he at first seems protected and contained give way to a linear sense of direction, "one track / Of sparkling light." As if now directed toward a specific goal, defined by the "horizon's utmost boundary," the boy nevertheless perceives the sky in frighteningly neutral terms that pivot around the word "nothing." The boat is described in a strained and bizarre phrase as an "elfin pinnace," which makes it seem both ethereal and particular at the same time, and the secondary meaning of the term, pinnace as mistress or prostitute (see O.E.D.), is functional at the symbolic or unconscious level of the passage: for the boy the stealing of the boat, rowing "lustily," carries with it the implication of forbidden desire—Oedipal desire for the mother, the first forbidden object. The line "my boat / Went heaving through the water like a swan" emphasizes the sexuality of the experience, and perhaps carries with it as well a Zeusian allusion.

The intensified sensuality of the highly rhythmic act of rowing seems to be the direct cause of the boy's feverish apprehension of the "huge peak, black and huge" as a threatening apparition that, seen anthropomorphically, "Upreared its head," even as the adult in retrospect describes it abstractly and conjecturally: "As if with voluntary power instinct." To the sensibility of the boy, who has earlier heard nature in its mountainous form as a "voice," this huge peak is further characterized personally as a "grim shape," with a "purpose of its own." This purpose is unmistakably one of admonishment and disapproval of the boy's insurgent sexuality associated with the pinnace as forbidden incestuous desire.

Since the pinnace is associated with forbidden desire, the huge peak must necessarily be a representation of the restricting father (as superego in Freudian terms) projected onto the landscape. In an earlier version of this passage, Wordsworth was more explicit about where the boy was going in his stolen boat. The revised lines read: "By chance in travel to my father's house, / I from the village inn had wandered forth." The repressed allusion to the father returns (as repressed material always does) in the image of the mountain seen by the boy as threatening: the mountain "Strode after me." Shaking with fear, the boy's emotion is projected into the "trembling oars," and his feelings of guilt are expressed manifestly in the verbal phrase "stole my way," and by innuendo in the pun on the word "covert." The return "homeward" will leave the boy permanently changed, and the adult narrator's description of his state of mind, "in grave / And serious mood," offers the clue that the boy has experienced some connection between sexuality and death. The pun on the word "grave" might well be considered to be a slip of the tongue on the part of the narrator who, though an adult, has not yet achieved the full self-awareness of the poet himself.

What follows for the remainder of the passage is entirely in the vocabulary of the adult narrator, speculating on the boy's experience and how that experience has remained within him as part of his changed and deepened self. What the narrator now knows—though he does not know exactly how to name or describe it as the alternative "solitude / Or blank desertion" suggests—is that the boy has had his first inkling of some mental principle of absence or negation, anticipated earlier by the word "nothing." The rhetorical mode of the concluding lines begins with the word "no"—"no familiar shapes, no pleasant images of trees, no colors of green fields"—and resolves into the negative phrase "that do not live / Like living men," in describing the "huge peak" that has now been abstracted into one of the "huge and mighty forms."

The adult narrator has learned that the forms of thought that constitute the mind have become a "trouble to my dreams," so that confronting itself by recalling the stealing of the boat experience, the broadened mind is now aware of its own unconscious depths. The whole passage, one might say, is about the discovery of the unconscious mind, which is both the self and alien to the self at the same time. This guilty experience, fraught with Freudian symbolism, is itself the very stuff of dreams. The division between father and son remains as a permanent part of the unconscious even as a connection is made between the adult narrator and the earlier version of himself as son. The super-ego here has not offered the ego a respite from disapproval through the mediating power of humor as in Roethke's poem or, even more grandly, in Frost's great retrospective poem "Maple."

V

Before I turn to Frost's comic masterpiece, so daring and unusual in the laughter it brings to its subject of the initiation into adulthood, I will examine Dylan Thomas's most Wordsworthian poem, 'Fern Hill,"[4] as another example of such initiation, which depicts the emergence of guilt as synonymous with the onset of adolescent sexuality. In this poem, Thomas overtly employs the Wordsworthian technique of merging the adult narrator's voice with the immediate sensibility of the child so that adulthood seems less like a transcendence of childhood than the inevitable outcome of childhood experience.

Thomas begins "Fern Hill" with a phrase that announces his narrative technique, "Now as I was," so that throughout the unfolding of the poem "now" and "was" are inextricably merged in presenting recollection and past innocence about what the future will bring. Or when Thomas says of the boy he once was, in "Poem in October," that "his tears burned my cheeks and his heart moved in mine," he is offering his reader a metaphor for the boy-son self contained within the adult-father self that evokes their simultaneity in one composite body.

Fern Hill

Now as I was young and easy under the apple boughs
About the lilting house and happy as the grass was green,
    The night above the dingle starry,
      Time let me hail and climb
    Golden in the heydays of his eyes,
And honored among wagons I was prince of the apple towns
And once below a time I lordly had the trees and leaves
      Trail with daisies and barley
    Down the rivers of the windfall light.

And as I was green and carefree, famous among the barns
About the happy yard and singing as the farm was home,
    In the sun that is young once only,
      Time let me play and be
    Golden in the mercy of his means,
And green and golden I was huntsman and herdsman, the calves
Sang to my horn, the foxes on the hills barked clear and cold,
      And the sabbath rang slowly,
    In the pebbles of the holy streams.

All the sun long it was running, it was lovely, the hay-
Fields high as the house, the tunes from the chimneys, it was air
And playing, lovely and watery,
      And fire green as grass.
    And nightly under the simple stars
As I rode to sleep the owls were bearing the farm away,
All the moon long I heard, blessed among stables, the night-jars
    Flying with the ricks, and the horses
      Flashing into the dark.

And then to awake, and the farm like a wanderer white
With the dew, come back, the cock on his shoulder, it was all
    Shining, it was Adam and maiden,
      The sky gathered again
    And the sun grew round that very day.
So it must have been after the birth of the simple light
In the first, spinning place, the spellbound horses walking warm
    Out of the whinnying green stable
      On to the fields of praise

And honored among foxes and pheasants by the gay house
Under the new made clouds and happy as the heart was long,
    In the sun born over and over,
        I ran my heedless ways,
    My wishes raced through the house-high hay
And nothing I cared, at my sky blue trades, that time allows
In all his tuneful turning so few and such morning songs
    Before the children green and golden
        Follow him out of grace,

Nothing I cared, in the lamb white days, that time would take me
Up to the swallow thronged loft by the shadow of my hand,
    In the moon that is always rising,
        Nor that riding to sleep
    I should hear him fly with the high fields
And wake to the farm forever fled from the childless land.
Oh as I was young and easy in the mercy of his means,
    Time held me green and dying
    Though I sang in my chains like the sea.

                                   (Thomas 178)

    Thomas locates his boyhood self in both a literal and a mythic land-scape "under the apple boughs," and immediately the biblical connotation of the Fall is hinted at even as the imagery of "house" and "grass" and "dingle" evoke the physical reality of the scene from the boy's perspective. The line that follows, however, "Time let me hail and climb," introduces adult retrospection with the abstract conception of "time" and anticipates the poem's fated conclusion of tormented self-consciousness. The phrase "time let me" will in the last stanza become "time held me" and the single word "climb," not yet located in a particular scene, will later be given specificity when the boy will climb "Up to the swallow thronged loft."

    On this literal farm, which Thomas nevertheless equates with the garden of Eden, the boy feels like royalty as "prince of the apple towns," potent and in control, living a fairy tale world of make believe—as suggested by the phrase, "And once below a time," which plays off the familiar "once upon a time" but also suggests that the boy has not yet entered into the adult realm of time that brings with it the awareness of mortality. Before the poem ends, the boy will indeed "climb" up into the realm of time and the consciousness of bodily guilt and of death. But before the Fall occurs with the onset of sexuality, the boy experiences himself as if he were Adam who had been created in the image of the Lord whose first commandment was "Let there be light!" The rivers that run through the boy's home landscape nevertheless will eventually run into the sea at the poem's conclusion, and the "windfall light," suggesting good luck, will darken with the word "fall," which the phrase contains in its several senses.

The second stanza continues to evoke the ecstatic past, repeating the word "happy" and now linking it to the word "singing." The crucial theme of celebration, represented by the activity of singing, will paradoxically be enlarged to include the music of grieving. The linking of the "farm" and "home" provides the poem with its geography of making a journey across a border or threshold into adulthood, the land of exile, just as Wordsworth's boat-stealing passage describes a departure from home in the image of the cave. Once again the boy's instinctive celebration of the beauty of the landscape is interrupted by adult consciousness with the line "Time let me play and be," reiterating the phrase "let me," which reminds the reader that we are granted childhood as a kind of temporary holiday. In this realm of "once below a time," playing and singing are equated, though later playing will be replaced by work and labor as "sky blue trades," and unconstrained singing will become restricted within "chains." The boy's identification with Adam deepens and becomes more specific in its biblical reference when he is placed among the animals, as their namer, before Eve becomes part of his world. All nature is experienced by the boy as a time of holiday in the gorgeous lines "And the sabbath rang slowly / In the pebbles of the holy streams."

Just as the poem moves from a timeless realm, "below a time," into the awareness of ephemerality, the consciousness of mortality, so, too, it shifts from being suffused with sunlight to being dominated by moonlight. The phrase "All the sun long" suggests the belief that youth (sunson time) will last forever and that the stream of life as well as the stream that runs through the farmland, like Eden, will flow forever without reaching the confining sea. The aura of home is suffused with the feeling that all activity has the quality of "playing" and is everywhere accompanied by an ambient music, "the tunes from the chimneys."

With the oncoming of night and the need for sleep, however, the boy feels a new kind of bodily agitation, like Wordsworth's boy "lustily" rowing the boat. His inevitable fall into time and sexual guiltiness is anticipated in his dreams, just as in Adam's dream when Eve is taken from his rib in the biblical account. "The owls were bearing the farm away" is a typical Freudian dream reversal that reveals the boy's anxiety, his ironic wisdom, about the inevitability of having to leave home. As the phrase "All the sun long" gives way to the phrase "All the moon long," the same Wordsworthian darkness that "was a trouble to my dreams" exposes the mind's unconscious depths. Although "still blessed among stables," a new sexual energy, symbolized by "the horses / Flashing into the dark," stirs in the boy's blood.

In stanza 4, the boy wakes from his dream of impending sexuality, seemingly back into his Edednic innocence, with "the farm, like a wanderer white / With the dew, come back." Although the farm returns, it is now filled with sexual potential, the dew suggesting semen, and the image of "the cock on his shoulder" an implicit pun deriving from a surrealistic or dreamlike displacement of a body part. Sexual potential is given representation, yes, but it is not yet fallen or guilty sexuality, and so Thomas's invocation of "Adam and maiden" extends the narrative of biblical allusion from Adam among the animals to Adam with Eve, who is nevertheless still perceived as an innocent "maiden."

And so it seems that the boy can reawaken from a troubled dream of losing the farm as if he were reborn to a condition of permanently renewable happiness "In the sun born over and over," but again the voice of the adult narrator offers his retrospective commentary: "I ran my heedless ways." Heedless of time's passing, as if unaware of the harvesting sickle of father time and able to remain a "son" forever in sunlight, the boy is now depicted as running and thus as part of the running out of time, in stark contrast to the controlled and stately "walking" horses from the previous stanza. The reader is given a further hint that the farm is losing its Edenic quality when the narrator speaks of the boy's "wishes," since there can be no wishes in Eden where complete contentment reigns, where all desires are fulfilled. For another moment the permissiveness of time, the time that "let me hail" and "let me play," continues as it "allows" more music to suffuse the landscape, but almost imperceptibly that music shifts from a major to a minor key in its "tuneful turning."

With that turning, the narrator's voice, heavy with adult comprehension, now comes to dominate the poem with the full realization of limits and knowledge that "morning songs" will soon be heard as *mourning* songs, the latter meaning functioning as the unconscious counterpart of the former. The awareness that childhood is a time when the color green, as in the natural color of grass, also symbolically implies the greenness of inexperience, and that golden sunlight will give way to night is made explicit in the abstract language of adult conceptualization that relies on the theological word "grace," so meaningful to Frost. As in most of Thomas's poetry, philosophy's all-consuming issue resides in the question whether the grace given to mankind by God in the form of childhood innocence will be restored after death. But the immediate fact remains that the experience of growth into adulthood must necessarily be defined as an experience of loss.

The gathering tone of alienation is continued with the repetition of the phrase "Nothing I cared," which begins the final stanza—a phrase emphatically in contrast with the earlier description of the boy as being

In wait for her there. She read every word
Of the two pages it was pressed between,
As if it was her mother speaking to her.
But forgot to put the leaf back in closing
And lost the place never to read again.
She was sure, though, there had been nothing in it.
So she looked for herself, as everyone
Looks for himself, more or less outwardly.
And her self-seeking, fitful though it was,
May still have been what led her on to read,
And think a little, and get some city schooling.
She learned shorthand, whatever shorthand may
Have had to do with it—she sometimes wondered.
So, till she found herself in a strange place
For the name Maple to have brought her to,
Taking dictation on a paper pad
And, in the pauses when she raised her eyes,
Watching out of a nineteenth story window
An airship laboring with unshiplike motion
And a vague all-disturbing roar above the river
Beyond the highest city built with hands.
Someone was saying in such natural tones
She almost wrote the words down on her knee,
"Do you know you remind me of a tree—
A maple tree?

"Because my name is Maple?"

Isn't it Mabel? I thought it was Mabel."

No doubt you've heard the office call me Mabel.
I have to let them call me what they like."

They were both stirred that he should have divined
Without the name her personal mystery.
It made it seem as if there must be something
She must have missed herself. So they were married,
And took the fancy home with them to live by.

They went on pilgrimage once to her father's
(The house one story high in front, three stories
On the side it presented to the road)

To see if there was not some special tree
She might have overlooked. They could find none,
Not so much as a single tree for shade,
Let alone grove of trees for sugar orchard.
She told him of the bookmark maple leaf
In the big Bible, and all she remembered
Of the place marked with it—"Wave offering,
Something about wave offering, it said."

"You've never asked your father outright, have you?"

"I have, and been put off sometime, I think."
(This was her faded memory of the way
Once long ago her father had put himself off.)

"Because no telling but it may have been
Something between your father and your mother
Not meant for us at all."

                              "Not meant for me?
Where would the fairness be in giving me
A name to carry for life and never know
The secret of?"

                              "And then it may have been
Something a father couldn't tell a daughter
As well as could a mother. And again
It may have been their one lapse into fancy
'Twould be too bad to make him sorry for
By bringing it up to him when he was too old.
Your father feels us round him with our questing,
And holds us off unnecessarily,
As if he didn't know what little thing
Might lead us on to a discovery.
It was as personal as he could be
About the way he saw it was with you
To say your mother, had she lived, would be
As far again as from being born to bearing."

"Just one look more with what you say in mind,
And I give up"; which last look came to nothing.
But though they now gave up the search forever,

They clung to what one had seen in the other
By inspiration. It proved there was something.
They kept their thoughts away from when the maple
Stood uniform in buckets, and the steam
Of sap and snow rolled off the sugarhouse.
When they made her related to the maples,
It was the tree the autumn fire ran through
And swept of leathern leaves, but left the bark
Unscorched, unblackened, even, by any smoke
They always took their holidays in autumn.
Once they came on a maple in a glade,
Standing alone with smooth arms lifted up
And every leaf of foliage she'd worn
Laid scarlet and pale pink about her feet
But its age kept them from considering this one.
Twenty-five years ago at Maple's naming
It hardly could have been a two-leaved seedling
The next cow might have licked up out at pasture.
Could it have been another maple like it?
They hovered for a moment near discovery,
Figurative enough to see the symbol,
But lacking faith in anything to mean
The same at different times to different people.
Perhaps a filial diffidence partly kept them
From thinking it could be a thing so bridal.
And anyway it came too late for Maple.
She used her hands to cover up her eyes.
"We would not see the secret if we could now:
We are not looking for it any more."

Thus had a name with meaning, given in death,
Made a girl's marriage, and ruled in her life.
No matter that the meaning was not clear.
A name with meaning could bring up a child,
Taking the child out of the parents' hands.
Better a meaningless name, I should say,
As leaving more to nature and happy chance.
Name children some names and see what you do.

Notes

1. Taking Dominion over the Wilderness (pp. 1–32)

1. Charles Darwin, *The Origin of Species*, introduced and abridged by Philip Appleman (New York: Norton, 1975), p. 40.
2. Henry David Thoreau, "Walking," and Ralph Waldo Emerson, *Nature*, intro. John Elder (Boston: Beacon Press, 1991), p. 111.
3. Roderick Nash, *Wilderness and the American Mind* (New Haven: Yale University Press, 1967), p. 95.
4. Robert Frost, *The Poetry of Robert Frost* (New York: Henry Holt and Co., 1975).
5. *The Book of Job*, trans. with an intro. by Stephen Mitchell (San Francisco: North Point Press, 1987), p. 80.
6. Homer, *Odyssey*, trans. Robert Fitzgerald (New York: Doubleday Anchor, 1963), p. 2.
7. Leo Marx, *The Machine in the Garden* (New York: Oxford University Press, 1976), p. 72.
8. William Shakespeare, *The Tempest* (New Haven: Yale University Press, 1946).
9. William Blake, *The Poetry and Prose*, ed. David V. Erdman (New York: Doubleday, 1965).
10. William Wordsworth, *Selected Poems and Prefaces* (Boston: Houghton Mifflin, 1965).
11. Gerard Manley Hopkins, *A Hopkins Reader*, sel. John Pick (London: Oxford University Press, 1953), p. 13.
12. Dylan Thomas, *Collected Poems* (New York: New Directions, 1957), p. 146.
13. Ralph Waldo Emerson, *Nature*, and Henry David Thoreau, *Nature*, intro. John Elder (Boston: Beacon Press, 1991), p. 23.
14. John Muir, *The Mountains of California* (Berkeley: Ten Speed Press, 1991), p. 56.
15. Charles Darwin, "The Descent of Man," in *Darwin*, sel. by Philip Appleman (New York: Norton, 1979), p. 196.
16. Rachel Carson, *Silent Spring* (Boston: Houghton Mifflin, 1991).
17. David M. Raup, *Extinction* (New York: Norton, 1991).
18. Bill McKibben, *The End of Nature* (New York: Anchor Books, Doubleday, 1989).
19. William Butler Yeats, *Collected Poems* (New York: The MacMillan Company, 1959), p. 191.
20. Emily Dickinson, *The Complete Poems* (Boston: Little Brown and Company, 1960).
21. Walt Whitman, *Leaves of Grass* (New York: Norton, 1973).
22. Wallace Stevens, *The Collected Poems* (New York: Knopf, 1954).
23. William Carlos Williams, *Pictures from Brueghel* (New York: New Directions, 1962).

24. Sigmund Freud, *Civilization and Its Discontents* (New York: Norton, 1989), p. 112.

25. John Keats, *Selected Letters*, ed. Lionel Trilling (New York: Farrar, Straus, and Young, 1951), p. 92.

26. Darwin, *The Origin of Species*, p. 43.

2. Darwin, The Book of Job, and Frost's *A Masque of Reason* (pp. 33–60)

1. Charles Darwin, *The Origin of Species*, intro. Philip Appleman (New York: Norton, 1975), p. 41.

2. Charles Darwin, *The Descent of Man*, in *Darwin*, sel. by Philip Appleman (New York: Norton, 1979).

3. *The Book of Job*, trans. with an intro. by Stephen Mitchell (San Francisco: North Point Press, 1987).

4. Charles Darwin, *Notebooks 1836-1844* (Notebook B), ed. David Kohn (Ithaca, N.Y.: Cornell University Press, 1987), p. 195.

5. Ibid., Notebook D, p. 343.

6. Stephen Jay Gould, *Ever Since Darwin: Reflections in Natural History* (New York: Norton, 1977), pp. 26–27.

7. Richard Dawkins, *The Blind Watchmaker* (New York: Norton, 1987), p. 4.

3. Loss and Inheritance in Wordsworth's "Michael" and Frost's "Wild Grapes" (pp. 61–91)

1. Erik Erikson, *Identity, Youth, and Crisis* (New York: Norton, 1968), p. 141.

2. William Wordsworth, *Selected Poems and Prefaces* (Boston: Houghton Mifflin, 1965).

4. Mourning and Acceptance (pp. 92–111)

1. Alfred Lord Tennyson, *Tennyson's Poetry*, ed. Robert Hill (New York: Norton, 1999).

2. Sigmund Freud, *Collected Papers*, vol. 4, trans. Joan Riviere (New York: Basic Books, 1959).

3. William Wordsworth, *Selected Poems and Prefaces* (Boston, Houghton Mifflin, 1965).

4. *William Blake, The Poetry and Prose*, ed. David V. Erdman (New York: Doubleday, 1965).

5. Gerard Manley Hopkins, *A Hopkins Reader*, sel. John Pick (London: Oxford University Press, 1953).

6. Gerard Manley Hopkins, *The Letters of Gerard Manley Hopkins to Robert Bridges*, ed. Claude Colleer Abbott (London: Oxford University Press, 1935), p. 109.

7. Dylan Thomas, *Collected Poems* (New York: New Directions, 1957).

5. The Modern Muse: Stevens and Frost (pp. 112–135)

1. Wallace Stevens, *Opus Posthumous* (New York: Knopf, 1957), p. 163.
2. Wallace Stevens, *The Collected Poems* (New York: Knopf, 1954), p. 418.
3. Sigmund Freud, *Three Essays on the Theory of Sexuality,* trans. James Strachey (New York: Basic Books, 1975).
4. William Wordsworth, *Selected Poems and Prefaces* (Boston: Houghton Mifflin, 1965), p. 111.
5. John Milton, *Paradise Lost,* ed. Scott Elledge (New York: Norton, 1975), p. 151.
6. Wallace Stevens, *The Necessary Angel* (New York: Knopf, 1951), p. 35.
7. Robert Frost, *The Poetry of Robert Frost* (New York: Henry Holt, 1975), p. 331.
8. Charles Darwin, *The Darwin Reader,* ed. Mark Ridley (New York: Norton, 1996), p. 298.

6. Enigmatical Reserve: Robert Frost as Teacher and Preacher (136–149)

1. Lawrance Thompson, *Robert Frost: The Years of Triumph, 1915–1938* (New York: Holt, Rinehart and Winston, 1970).
2. Robert Frost, *Selected Prose of Robert Frost,* ed. Hyde Cox (New York: Collier Books, 1966), p. 460.
3. William Wordsworth, *The Prelude* (Boston: Houghton Mifflin, 1965).
4. Lawrance Thompson, *Robert Frost: The Years of Triumph, 1915–1938* (New York: Holt, Rinehart and Winston, 1978), p. 673.
5. Robert Frost, *Selected Prose of Robert Frost,* ed. Hyde Cox (New York: Collier Books, 1966), p. 107.

7. Robert Frost's "As If" Belief (pp. 150–168)

1. Robert Frost, *The Poetry of Robert Frost* (New York: Henry Holt, 1951).
2. Lawrance Thompson, *Robert Frost: The Years of Triumph, 1915–1938* (New York: Holt, Rinehart and Winston, 1978), p. 704.
3. William Shakespeare, *The Tragedy of Hamlet Prince of Denmark* (New Haven: Yale University Press, 1949), p. 81.
4. Thompson, *Robert Frost: The Years of Triumph,* p. 580.

8. Self-Deception, Lying, and Fictive Truthfulness (pp. 169–192)

1. Richard Dawkins, *The Selfish Gene* (New York: Oxford University Press, 1976), p. vi.
2. Ibid., p. 152.
3. Janet Malcolm, *Psychoanalysis: The Impossible Profession* (Northvale, N.J.: Jason Aronson, 1944), p. 6.
4. Daniel C. Dennett, *Kinds of Minds* (New York: Basic Books, 1996), p. 122.
5. Jared Diamond, *Why Is Sex Fun?* (New York: Basic Books, 1997), p. 67.

6. Franz de Waal, *Good Natured* (Cambridge: Harvard University Press, 1996), pp. 75, 77.

7. Robin Dunbar, *The Trouble with Science* (Cambridge: Harvard University Press, 1995), p. 130.

8. Sigmund Freud, *Collected Papers*, vol. 4 (New York: Basic Books, 1959), p. 293.

9. Ibid., p. 304.

10. Ibid., p. 316.

11. Richard Wrangham and Dale Peterson, *Demonic Males* (Boston: Houghton Mifflin, 1996), p. 63.

12. Jared Diamond, *The Third Chimpanzee* (New York: Harper Perennial, 1992), p. 297.

13. Sigmund Freud, *Three Essays on theTheory of Sexuality* (New York: Basic Books, 1962), pp. 58–59.

14. George Orwell, *A Collection of Essays* (San Diego: Harcourt, 1981), p. 166.

15. Ibid., p. 167.

16. Ibid., p. 170.

17. Charles Darwin, *The Descent of Man* (Princeton, N.J.: Princeton University Press, 1981), pp. 71, 82.

18. Robert Wright, *The Moral Animal* (New York, Pantheon, 1994), p. 201.

19. William Shakespeare, *The Tragedy of Hamlet* (New Haven: Yale University Press, 1949).

20. William Shakespeare, *The Tragedy of King Lear* (New Haven: Yale University Press, 1947).

21. William Shakespeare, *As You Like It* (New Haven: Yale University Press, 1951).

22. Plato, *The Dialogues of Plato*, vol. 1 (New York: Random House, 1937), p. 865.

23. Shankar Vedantam, "The Polygraph Test Meets Its Match," *The Washington Post*, November 12, 2001, p. A 02.

24. Lewis Thomas, *Late Night Thoughts on Listening to Mahler's 9th Symphony* (New York, Viking Press, 1983), p. 128.

25. Steven Pinker, *How the Mind Works* (New York: Norton, 1997), p. 193.

26. *U.S. News and World Report*, August 13, 2001, p. 41.

27. Alan Sokol and Jean Bricmont, *Fashionable Nonsense* (New York: Picador USA, 1998), p. 2.

28. Ibid., p. 269.

29. Lyall Watson, *Dark Nature* (New York: Harper Perennial, 1995), p. 253.

30. Sigmund Freud, *The Future of an Illusion* (New York: Norton, 1961), p. 63.

31. Lewis Carroll, *Alice's Adventures in Wonderland* (New York: The Modern Library, 2002), p. 78.

32. Wallace Stevens, *Opus Posthumous* (New York: Knopf, 1957), p. 238.

33. Philip Rieff, *Freud: The Mind of the Moralist* (New York: Viking, 1959), p. 123.

34. Richard Dawkins, *The Selfish Gene* (New York: Oxford University Press, 1976), p. 215.

35. Francis Bacon, *A Selection of His Works* (Indianapolis: Bobbs-Merrill, 1965), pp. 47–48.

36. Robert Frost, *Selected Prose,* ed. Hyde Cox (New York: Collier Books, 1956), p. 45.

37. Robert Frost, *The Poetry of Robert Frost* (New York: Henry Holt, 1975).

38. John Keats, *Selected Poems and Letters,* ed. Douglas Bush (Boston: Houghton Mifflin, 1959), p. 198.

39. Robert Browning, *Selected Poetry,* ed. Daniel Karlin (London: The Penguin Poetry Library, 1990), p. 188.

9. Reading the Landscape: Place and Nothingness (pp. 193–204)

1. Elizabeth Shepley Sergeant, *Robert Frost: The Trial by Existence* (New York: Holt, Rinehart and Winston, 1960), p. 312.

2. Heinz Pagels, *The Cosmic Code* (New York: Bantam, 1982), p. 283.

3. Quoted in Marcia Bartusiac, *Thursday's Universe: A Report from the Frontier on the Origin, Nature, and Destiny of the Universe* (Redmond, Washington: Tempus Books, 1988), pp. 257 and 256.

4. Brad Lemley, "Guth's Grand Guess," *Discover Magazine* 23:44 (April, 2002): 34 and 36.

5. Wallace Stevens, *The Collected Poems* (New York: Knopf, 1954), p. 411.

6. William Shakespeare, *The Tragedy of King Lear* (New Haven: Yale University Press, 1947).

7. William Shakespeare, *The Winter's Tale* (New Haven: Yale University Press, 1947).

8. Charles Darwin, "The Descent of Man," in *Darwin,* sel. Philip Appleman (New York: Norton, 1979), p. 200.

10. Parenthood and Perspective (205–227)

1. Theodore Roethke, *The Collected Poems* (New York: Doubleday, 1966).

2. Sigmund Freud, "Humor," *Collected Papers,* vol. 5, ed. James Strachey (New York: Basic Books, 1959), p. 220.

3. William Wordsworth, *Selected Poems and Prefaces* (Boston: Houghton Mifflin, 1965).

4. Dylan Thomas, *Collected Poems* (New York: New Directions, 1957).

5. Robert Frost, *The Poetry of Robert Frost* (New York: Henry Holt, 1975).

6. *Genesis,* trans. Robert Alter (New York: Norton, 1996).

7. John Keats, *The Selected Letters,* ed. Lionel Trilling (New York: Farrar, Straus and Young, 1951), p. 92.

Selected Bibliography of Critical and Biographical Works

Joseph Brodsky, Seamus Heaney, Derek Walcott. *Homage to Robert Frost*. Farrar, Strauss and Giroux, New York, 1996.

Reuben Brower. *The Poetry of Robert Frost: Constellations of Intention*. Holt, Rinehart and Winston, New York, 1965.

John Elder. *Reading the Mountains of Home* (on "Directive"). Harvard University Press, Cambridge, 1998.

Robert Faggen. *Robert Frost and the Challenge of Darwin*. University of Michigan Press, Ann Arbor, 1997.

Robert Frost. *Robert Frost: An Introduction, Poems, Reviews, Criticism*, edited by Robert Greenberg. Holt, Rinehart and Winston, New York, 1961.

Randall Jarrell. "The Other Robert Frost" and "To the Laodiceans." From *Poetry and the Age*. Alfred A. Knopf, New York, 1953.

Katherine Kearns. *Robert Frost and a Poetics of Appetite*. Cambridge University Press, Cambridge, 1994.

John C. Kemp. *Robert Frost and New England: The Poet as Regionalist*. Princeton University Press, Princeton, 1979.

John F. Lynen. *The Pastoral Art of Robert Frost*. Yale University Press, New Haven, 1964.

George W. Nitchie. *Human Values in the Poetry of Robert Frost*. Duke University Press, Durham, 1960.

Jay Parini. *Robert Frost: A Life*. Henry Holt, New York, 1999.

Richard Poirier. *Robert Frost: The Work of Knowing*. Oxford University Press, New York, 1984.

William H. Pritchard. *Robert Frost: A Literary Life Reconsidered*. Oxford University Press, New York, 1984.

Elizabeth Shepley Sergeant. *The Trial by Existence*. Holt, Rinehart and Winston, New York, 1960.

Donald G. Sheehy. "(Re) Figuring Love: Robert Frost in Crisis, 1938–1942. *New England Quarterly*, June 1998.

Radcliffe Squires. *The Major Themes of Robert Frost*. The University of Michigan Press, Ann Arbor, 1963.

Lawrance Thompson. *Fire and Ice: The Art and Thought of Robert Frost*. Russell and Russell, New York, 1942.

———. *Robert Frost: The Early Years, 1874-1915*. Holt Rinehart and Winston, New York, 1966.

———. *Robert Frost: The Years of Triumph, 1915-1938*. Holt, Rinehart and Winston, New York, 1970.

———. and R. H. Winnick. *Robert Frost: The Later Years 1938-1963*. Holt, Rinehart and Winston, New York, 1976.

Richard Thornton. *Recognition of Robert Frost: Twenty-fifth Anniversary*. Henry Holt, New York, 1937.

Index of Major Themes

Index of Authors, Works, and Literary Characters

CPSIA information can be obtained at www.ICGtesting.com
Printed in the USA
BVOW08s1621130114

341582BV00001B/28/A